T0330873

TRADE NEGOTIATIONS IN THE OECD

A PUBLICATION OF THE GRADUATE
INSTITUTE OF INTERNATIONAL STUDIES,
GENEVA

Also published in this series:

The United States and the Politicization of the World Bank
Bartram S. Brown

TRADE NEGOTIATIONS IN THE OECD

Structures, Institutions and States

David J. Blair

Routledge
Taylor & Francis Group

LONDON AND NEW YORK

First published in 1993 by
Kegan Paul International

This edition first published in 2010 by
Routledge
2 Park Square, Milton Park, Abingdon, Oxon, OX14 4RN

Simultaneously published in the USA and Canada
by Routledge
711 Third Avenue, New York, NY 10017

Routledge is an imprint of the Taylor & Francis Group, an informa business

British Library Cataloguing in Publication Data
A catalogue record for this book is available from the British Library

ISBN 10: 0-7103-0432-3 (hbk)
ISBN 13: 978-0-7103-0432-2 (hbk)

Publisher's Note
The publisher has gone to great lengths to ensure the quality of this reprint
but points out that some imperfections in the original copies may be
apparent. The publisher has made every effort to contact original copyright
holders and would welcome correspondence from those they have been
unable to trace.

TO MY PARENTS

CONTENTS

PREFACE

This book is situated at the intersection of three main areas of international relations research. The first of these areas is the study of international organisations. My initial objective in writing this volume was to contribute to a better understanding of how international organisations function, why they do what they do, and how they influence the behaviour of nation-states. In the search for answers to these questions I turned to the second area of inquiry, international relations theory.

Because the decisions reached within international organisations are generally the result of some form of bargaining among their members, an examination of the negotiations that go on among member countries is necessary in order to understand the functioning of these organisations. Even though I ended up examining some relatively explicit cases of negotiations, most important decisions made within any international organisation involve an element of bargaining, whether the decision concerns the publication of a report, what issues should be put on the agenda, or even who should fill certain posts in the Secretariat. I was interested in seeing how well some of the most familiar theories of international relations could help explain the outcomes of these negotiations, as well as the impact that those outcomes had on member countries.

My choice of the OECD as a subject of investigation stemmed from an interest in a third area of study, international political economy, in particular the relations among countries in the field of international trade. Upon reviewing the literature on the work of international organisations in this field, I noticed that there was an almost total absence of research on the organisation that grouped together the major trading nations of the world, and that had dealt with international trade matters for a considerable length of time. The trade-related activities of this organisation intrigued me not simply because they were so little known, but also because a number of trends seemed to favour a much more active role for the OECD in the international trading system in the future.

Among these recent trends are the growing importance of domestic policies as a source of friction in international trade, and the increasing linkages between trade and other issues that were not previously considered directly related to trade, such as the environment, culture and regional development. Because the OECD has had a "comparative advantage" in dealing with domestic policies and in examining the linkages between diverse issues, it seemed that the Organisation had the potential to become a more relevant forum for the negotiation of trade issues, particularly in view of the difficulties being experienced in the GATT.

As I embarked upon my study, I soon realised why this topic had been avoided by others. The OECD is a highly discreet organisation, and documentation on its internal operations is generally closed to the public. Hence, I had to begin my search by going through press clippings from over two decades in order to track down information that had been leaked to the media or presented in press conferences. In many cases, this was the only publicly-available account of the negotiations. Another important source of information was the Congressional Record of the United States, as the American system of government tends to favour a relatively extensive disclosure of the activities of government officials, a characteristic which has been criticised by some, but which is a definite boon to the academic researcher. I also drew upon a number of secondary sources for information about the general environment in which these negotiations took place, and used OECD publications for an official record of the various agreements that had been reached there.

I sent copies of a first draft of each empirical chapter, written on the basis of this information, to members of the OECD Secretariat and to government officials that were involved in the negotiations to verify the facts of the cases. Through an extensive series of interviews with these officials, I was able to correct any inaccuracies that my first round of research had yielded, and to close a number of gaps in information through the personal recollections of these officials and through the access that they often granted me to restricted documents. I then circulated revised drafts of my chapters for further verification. It took some time before I was satisfied that my portrayal of events was accurate and that at least the facts, if not my interpretation of them, were confirmed by the interviewees.

Because of the valuable role they played in my research, my first word of thanks goes out to those officials of several national governments and to members of the OECD Secretariat who generously took the time to read, correct and make extensive comments on my various drafts, as well as to answer my many interview questions. As much as I would like to give them personal credit for their contributions, these interviews were conducted on the understanding that the names of the interviewees would remain confidential. On the same basis, the restricted documents which they allowed me to read are not cited in this study. While these officials helped me set the factual record straight, the interpretation of those facts is mine alone, and although they never sought to impose their views on me, I know that some of them at least would disagree with certain of my conclusions.

On the academic side, I would like to thank by name some of the individuals who read and commented on various versions and parts of this book, including Philippe Braillard, Harish Kapur, Robert Keohane, Rob Paarlberg, Saadia Touval, I. William Zartman, and Jean Zwahlen. I also gratefully acknowledge the funding support I received from the Social Sciences and Humanities Research Council of Canada. I benefited greatly from an Albert Gallatin fellowship awarded to me by the Foundation for Education and Research in International Studies (FERIS), which permitted me to spend a year conducting research in the United States. My thanks also go to a number of institutions that provided me with office space, research facilities, and access to their in-house experts. They include, the Center for International Affairs at Harvard University, the Graduate Institute of International Studies in Geneva, the Royal Institute of International Affairs in London, the School for Advanced International Studies at Johns Hopkins University, and the United Nations and GATT libraries in Geneva.

Finally, as I wrote this book before taking up my current

position at the OECD, it was not submitted to the Organisation for approval. Nevertheless, in order to avoid any misunderstanding, I wish to underline the fact that this study does not reflect the views of the OECD.

David J. Blair

Paris
April 1991

Chapter One

INTRODUCTION

The international trading system is at a crossroads. States are opening up their markets to foreign goods and services, and dismantling trade distorting measures, at the same time as they erect new barriers to trade and introduce new policies which interfere with normal trading patterns. Regional trade arrangements are being concluded which appear to challenge the traditional multilateral approach to trade liberalisation based on the principle of non-discrimination, even as efforts continue to liberalise trade on a global basis. Trade disputes, some of which develop into trade wars, erupt with seemingly greater regularity even as nations work together to establish a more lasting basis for co-operation in trade matters.

International negotiations have been the principal means of managing this growing complexity and disarray in the trading system. Through international negotiations, states have attempted to resolve trade disputes, to promote the growth of international trade, and to cushion the impact of sudden shifts in international trade flows on their national economies. Whether such negotiations have always produced the most efficient or equitable outcomes is a question of no small controversy, but it does seem clear that the significance of international trade negotiations has grown steadily. While some producers are discovering the vast potential for growth in the global marketplace, others feel increasingly threatened by foreign competitors. Both groups realise that they stand to gain or lose a great deal from international trade negotiations and have gone to considerable lengths to influence them through their national governments. At the same time governments themselves have come to view the expansion of international trade as one possible way out of domestic economic problems. As a result, an increasing share of the attention and resources of both foreign and domestic policy decision makers has been directed towards the negotiation of trade issues. The results of these negotiations will to a large extent determine the future path that the international trading system takes.

Although many of these trade negotiations have been conducted on a bilateral basis in recent years, the most influential and wide-ranging negotiations are still those conducted in multilateral forums. The importance of multilateral negotiations in the management of international trade relations is reflected in the attention devoted to such negotiations in the literature on international political economy over the past two decades. A number of extensive studies have been carried out on negotiations conducted in the context of the General Agreement on Tariffs and Trade (GATT) and the United Nations Conference on Trade and Development (UNCTAD); however, the Organisation for Economic Co-operation and Development (OECD) has been almost entirely ignored by students of the international political economy of trade.[1] The OECD is among the major international economic organisations established since the Second World War, and is a place where numerous agreements have been reached on a variety of international trade issues. An analysis of negotiations leading to some of those agreements would help fill a considerable gap in the existing body of literature on multilateral trade negotiations.

It is the purpose of this study, then, to examine negotiations conducted in the framework of the OECD on international trade issues, and to evaluate the impact of OECD agreements on state behaviour. The analytical approach adopted here differs, however, from that of a theoretical school which typically treats topics such as this. That school focuses on the question of how co-operation can be achieved in the context of contemporary international relations. International negotiation is regarded as one of the common processes by which such co-operation is attained.[2]

The implicit assumptions of much of this literature are that co-operation is a necessarily desirable end, that states generally enter into co-operative arrangements uncoerced, and that all participants view these arrangements as mutually beneficial.[3] Many researchers reach out to economic analysis for help in

2

understanding why co-operation is sometimes achieved while at other times it is not. The failure to achieve co-operation is compared to market failure, which can inhibit the attainment of an optimal level of economic welfare.

The assumption that international co-operation is voluntary, mutually beneficial, or represents some form of general welfare has been called into question by a number of authors.[4] Indeed, what is seen by some as 'co-operation' is often viewed by others as co-optation or capitulation. Rather than reflecting collective self-interest, it is argued, co-operative arrangements such as international regimes may be the means by which some states attempt to exercise control over others. According to these authors, the question that should be posed is not how co-operation is achieved, but what *kind* of co-operation is achieved. This study avoids making assumptions one way or the other about the desirability of co-operative arrangements. Any failure to reach agreement will not be treated as a defect of the international political market, nor as breakdown in rationality or perception, but rather as one of the natural outcomes of a political process in which state interests collide and shift, with some states yielding and others prevailing.[5]

In short, rather than ask how co-operation is achieved, this study asks, who prevails in negotiations and why? The focus on this question may be criticised as an excessively zero-sum perspective by those who consider negotiations to be essentially co-operative exercises providing opportunities for joint gain. While it is true that such opportunities often exist, it is equally true that mutually beneficial agreements usually entail greater gains for some parties than for others. The point of agreement is rarely half-way between the proposals of each party, but tends to be closer to the preferences of certain parties.[6] Even when negotiations are aimed at creating a bigger pie for all, the question inevitably arises as to how much of the bigger pie each side will get, and how much each side should pay to increase the size of the pie. Negotiated agreements rarely leave one party with all its demands satisfied, or another with no satisfaction, as there is always some element of compromise involved. Consequently, the question of 'who prevails?' is used here as a short-form for 'who gains the most (or gives up the least) in a negotiation?'

A second question to be examined in this study is why states

3

comply or fail to comply with negotiated agreements. This is a logical extension of the question of who gains the most in negotiations, since the inevitable reaction to 'who wins?' is to ask, what difference does winning make? A victory in negotiations would be a hollow one if no one respected the agreement that was reached. The question of compliance is also central in the debate between realists and students of international institutions. The former tend to regard internationally negotiated agreements which establish rules and principles as of marginal importance, arguing that states pursue their self-interest (generally defined in terms of maximising power or at least maintaining their relative position in the international system) regardless of any international commitments they may have entered into, while the latter hold that international rules and principles can act as important constraints on state behaviour. In order to shed light on this issue, then, this study will examine the record of state compliance with agreements reached in the OECD, and attempt to explain why states comply or fail to comply.[7]

It is argued here that the parsimonious theories currently being developed by political scientists are inadequate to explain or predict outcomes in international negotiations. In particular, this study demonstrates that attempts to explain negotiations and the impact of agreements at the level of the international system alone are incomplete at best, and can be misleading or even fallacious at worst. Certainly systemic factors provide constraints and opportunities, but within the boundaries set by such factors there is a wide range of possible outcomes. Moreover, constraints can often be overcome, just as opportunities can be wasted. It is not enough to turn to domestic factors only when systemic variables fail to provide satisfactory explanations or accurate predictions.[8] Correlations between systemic factors and predicted outcomes can be coincidental, and inferring causality when expectations of systemic theories are upheld may contribute more to misunderstanding than to greater insight.

A central conclusion of this study is that the strongest party, whether defined in aggregate or in contextual terms, does not always prevail over weaker parties in negotiations over international rules and norms. Often the outcome of negotiations is closer to the preferences of weaker states, and even when stronger states get their way it is not always due to their superior

4

material capabilities. Intangible, or qualitative, factors that operate at the level of the state play an important role in the translation of capabilities into power over outcomes, by either facilitating or hindering the mobilisation of those capabilities. Consideration of these variables is essential in explaining both the outcome of international negotiations and the impact of negotiated agreements on state behaviour.

International Trade Relations and the Organisation for Economic Co-operation and Development

The OECD has generally been neglected by international relations scholars, despite the Organisation's considerable resources.[9] Its staff of 1, 800 and annual budget of over 180 million dollars make it the largest intergovernmental organisation outside the UN system and the European Community.[10] One of the three basic aims of the OECD set forth in its charter is to contribute to the expansion of world trade on a multilateral basis, and over a dozen committees and working groups are regularly engaged in the discussion of trade issues. The Organisation has also published scores of reports dealing with a wide variety of trade matters, and produces many more unpublished reports for the use of its member governments.

The neglect of the OECD in studies of international trade relations, therefore, is not attributable to the insignificant size or limited scope of the Organisation, but neither can this lack of attention be justified by claiming that the OECD's work is trivial. Member governments representing the world's major trading powers frequently send high-level officials to OECD meetings. Ministers of those governments gather together at least once a year to issue well-publicised joint statements which, despite their outwardly bland appearance, often represent highly significant agreements on norms and principles of international trade resulting from long drawn-out and sometimes intense bargaining sessions.

The main obstacle to the study of these sessions is the fact that one of the primary rules of procedure of the Organisation is confidentiality. Meetings are conducted in strict privacy, and participants are often reluctant to discuss publicly the nature of their discussions. Minutes of these meetings (if they are kept at all) are carefully shielded from public scrutiny. The chief

5

reason for all of this discretion is to encourage frank and open debate, as well as to foster a free exchange of information among government officials, which makes the nature of these discussions all the more enticing for the interested researcher.

Thus, the research task is daunting and yet, given the significance of the OECD's work, it is much needed. Because of the difficulty in studying the Organisation, the subtle nature of its operations, and because of the more visible role of the GATT in trade negotiations, many observers seem to have concluded that it is unimportant in international economic relations. Hopefully, this study will reveal something about how seriously member governments take the discussions which go on within the OECD, and about the impact that the outcome of those discussions can have on government policies and practices.

One common misconception about the OECD is that it does not engage in the *negotiation* of trade issues. Fred Iklé has defined negotiation as "a process in which explicit proposals are put forward ostensibly for the purpose of reaching an agreement on an exchange or on the realisation of a common interest where conflicting interests are present".[11] On a number of important trade issues over the years, OECD members have made explicit proposals in the Organisation for agreements of various sorts. Opinions on what the content of such agreements should be (and sometimes whether there should be any agreement at all) are often conflicting, and several sessions may be required before a text acceptable to all parties can be hammered out. Discussion of the merits and drawbacks of various proposals usually ensues, threats, warnings and promises may be made, and either an agreement is reached or else a stalemate occurs and discussion moves on to other matters.

According to Iklé's definition, then, what goes on inside the OECD often qualifies as negotiation. The nature of OECD trade negotiations does vary, however. Some negotiations may simply be over whether or not a certain report should be published, or whether it should be modified in some way. Other negotiations involve the adoption of general principles or norms of international trade.[12] Sometimes the negotiating process will end at this stage, with governments expected unilaterally to adopt policies which are consistent with these principles and norms. Often, though, an agreement on principles is seen as a prelude to further negotiations where more specific rules will

6

be agreed upon.[13] Bargaining over details may be transferred to the GATT framework, but at times the OECD will be chosen as the appropriate forum when for one reason or another it is felt that an issue cannot be negotiated effectively in the GATT.

Certainly not all of the OECD's activities in the trade field involve negotiating. Discussion of many issues is often ephemeral, with complaints or concerns expressed once or twice and then forgotten. Much of what goes on in OECD committees is a simple exchange of information or views, where market trends are analysed or policies are reviewed, without any serious effort made to alter the behaviour of member states. It would not be possible to examine in detail all of the trade matters discussed in the OECD, but a greater insight into the negotiating activities of the Organisation and a greater appreciation of its contribution to the management of international trade relations can be gained by focusing on those trade issues which have been the subject of the most intensive and prolonged negotiations.

This study examines four such cases, covering negotiations on export credits, agricultural trade, steel trade, and trade in ships. Apart from being among the main trade issues dealt with by the OECD over the past twenty years, these cases also involve some of the key sectors in world trade. Official support for export credits is an important tool of national trade policy, and is extensively used to promote the export of the biggest ticket items in world trade today, including capital goods ranging from passenger aircraft to nuclear power plants. Agricultural products accounted for 18 per cent of the total value of world exports during the 1970s and 14 per cent in the 1980s. Steel and shipbuilding are two major heavy industries experiencing extensive and rapid structural change in the world market, and which are often regarded as having special symbolic and strategic significance for the traditional producing countries.

The four cases presented here have also involved some of the longest-standing conflicts in world trade. The export credits and agricultural trade disputes are essentially about competition for export markets, in which subsidies are the major irritant, while disagreements on steel and shipbuilding concern the protection of older industries from low-cost imports. The export credits question was a source of tension between the US and the EC for over a decade, eventually leading to a subsidies war between the two parties. Agriculture was one of the most divisive issues in the Kennedy, Tokyo and Uruguay Rounds, and has been a constant source of bilateral trade disputes involving the United States, the EC, Japan and other OECD countries. The dispute over steel trade was one of the major causes of the deterioration of US-EC relations during the early 1980s, just as shipbuilding contributed to an atmosphere of hostility between Japan and the EC. Hence, OECD trade negotiations were not always purely co-operative exercises in which countries sought joint gains, but were often conducted in a conflictual climate where participants sought to impose their will on one another. In such a context, a zero-sum perspective is not entirely inappropriate.

Besides the theoretical interest of this study, an in-depth analysis of negotiations in the OECD seems warranted on policy grounds as well. Following the Second World War the major barriers to trade were quantitative restrictions, exchange controls and tariffs. With the gradual dismantling of the first two of these barriers by European countries, the most prominent barriers to trade were tariffs. A consequence of the successive rounds of multilateral trade negotiations conducted in the 1950s, 1960s and 1970s was that tariffs became less of an obstacle to trade and non-tariff measures (NTMs) became more prominent. As the 1970s and 1980s wore on, NTMs became a concern of those interested in trade liberalisation not simply because they were becoming more visible with the rollback of tariff barriers, but because they were actually growing in number and in importance.[14]

Non-tariff measures included health and sanitary regulations, safety and quality standards, government procurement policies, and a range of government subsidy programmes aimed at assisting national producers. NTMs differed from tariffs in that they were quite often not intended to interfere with international trade flows, but were introduced in response to purely domestic demands and problems. In most cases, NTMs have emanated from and been administered by ministries other than those responsible for foreign trade. As a result, curtailing NTMs and managing disputes over their use have been formidable tasks, and many have questioned whether the traditional forum for trade negotiations, the GATT, is the most suitable place to manage them. Because many of these 'new' barriers to international trade are not trade policies at all, but domestic policies, it has been suggested that the most practical place for dealing with them would be in an organisation such as the OECD, which has already had a long experience in fostering the harmonisation of domestic policies.[15]

The OECD may be appealing as a forum for trade liberalisation efforts for a number of reasons. First of all, agreement may be achieved more easily due to the greater homogeneity of OECD nations in terms of level of economic development, level of industrialisation, ideology, values and concerns. Secondly, co-operation could be facilitated in an organisation with a relatively small number of members, an argument which is supported by certain collective goods theorists.[16] Thirdly, the OECD may be attractive because the types of agreements arrived at in that organisation offer greater flexibility to negotiating parties. The non-binding agreements which are typical of the OECD may be reached more easily than the more formal codes and agreements negotiated under the GATT. The OECD provides a forum where at least some measure of constraint on state behaviour can be produced whenever countries are reluctant to bind themselves legally, as is often the case when domestic policies and practices are involved.

The next chapter of this book sets out the framework to be used in analysing OECD trade negotiations. A separate chapter is devoted to each of the four case studies. Each chapter begins by briefly sketching the context of the issue area in which the negotiations were situated, and then looks at the background of those negotiations within the OECD since the Organisation's creation. Next, a detailed description of the agreements reached in the OECD in that sector is given, and the impact of those agreements on the policies and practices of participating countries is evaluated. This is followed by an account of the bargaining positions of the main participants or groups of participants, and the outcomes of the negotiations which took place during the 1970s and 1980s. These fairly descriptive sections are necessary to give coherence to the analytical section which follows, but also provide an account of this set of negotiations which is not available in this degree of detail in any published works. In the following section of Chapters Three to Six, the analytical framework set out in Chapter Two is applied and the value of each independent variable in explaining the outcomes of bargaining and the impact of agreements is weighed.

In the conclusion to this study the findings of the four empirical chapters will be reviewed and an assessment made of the explanatory power of each of the independent variables presented. Based on the findings of this study, an effort will be made to suggest some conditions under which each variable might be expected to influence the outcomes of international negotiations and the impact of international agreements. This will be followed by a more general evaluation of systemic and unit-level variables. Finally, on the basis of this examination of negotiations in four sectors, some observations about the role of the OECD in international trade relations will be put forward, along with a discussion of the Organisation's future prospects in the trade field.

Notes

1 See, for example, Gilbert R. Winham, *International Trade and The Tokyo Round Negotiation* (Princeton, N.J.: Princeton University Press, 1986); Vinod K. Aggarwal, *Liberal Protectionism: The International Politics of Organized Textile Trade* (Berkeley, Los Angeles, London: University of California Press, 1985); Robert L. Rothstein, *Global Bargaining: UNCTAD and the Quest for a New International Economic Order* (Princeton, N.J.: Princeton University Press, 1979); Ernest H. Preeg, *Traders and Diplomats: An Analysis of the Kennedy Round under the General Agreement on Tariffs and Trade* (Washington: Brookings Institution, 1970).

2 Examples include Robert O. Keohane, *After Hegemony: Cooperation and Discord in the World Political Economy* (Princeton, N.J.: Princeton University Press, 1984); Robert Axelrod, *The Evolution of Cooperation* (New York: Basic Books, 1984); Kenneth A. Oye, ed., *Cooperation under Anarchy* (Princeton, N.J.: Princeton University Press, 1986); and much of the literature on international regimes. While analysts of co-operation regard international regimes as mechanisms for facilitating international co-operation, the *formation* and *maintenance* of these regimes themselves are also considered to be the product of co-operation in most cases.

3 For further discussion of this point, see James F. Keeley, "Toward a Foucauldian Analysis of Regimes", *International Organization* 44 (Winter 1990), pp. 83–105. While the possibility of imposed regimes is acknowledged by some students of co-operation, the general assumption still appears to be that regimes are generally voluntary and mutually beneficial.

4 Ibid.; Susan Strange, "Cave! Hic Dragones: A Critique of Regime Analysis", in *International Regimes*, ed. Stephen D. Krasner (Ithaca and London: Cornell University Press, 1982), pp. 344–346, 351–354.

5 Keeley argues that, 'Order, thus regimes, are foci and loci of struggle; these are two sides of the same coin. We may therefore ask

not simply how order can be created and maintained but also how 'disorder' and resistance can persist in the face of ordering efforts or even be created by them.' "Toward a Foucauldian Analysis", p. 93.

6 Within the literature on international negotiations, a distinction is often made between integrative and distributive bargaining, the former referring to situations in which parties with common interests seek to reach a mutually beneficial agreement, while the latter refers to bargaining over the division of a good that is mutually desired. However, it is generally acknowledged that in practice this distinction is never clear, and that negotiations are seldom entirely integrative. Glenn H. Snyder and Paul Diesing, *Conflict among Nations: Bargaining, Decision Making, and System Structure in International Crises* (Princeton, N.J.: Princeton University Press, 1977), pp. 23–24. See also, R.E. Walton and R.B. McKersie, *A Behavioral Theory of Labor Negotiations* (New York: McGraw-Hill, 1965).

7 Keohane and Nye point out that while many studies have been conducted on international regimes over the past decade, there have been relatively few evaluations of the impact these regimes have had on the policies and practices of states. Robert O. Keohane and Joseph S. Nye, Jr., *"Power and Interdependence Revisited"*, *International Organization* 41 (Autumn 1987), pp. 742–743.

8 This is the approach suggested in Robert O. Keohane and Joseph S. Nye, *Power and Interdependence: World Politics in Transition* (Boston, Toronto: Little, Brown, 1977), pp. 58, 152, 224. See also, Robert Keohane in "The Demand for International Regimes", in *International Regimes*, ed. Stephen D. Krasner, p. 144; and Aggarwal, *Liberal Protectionism*, pp. 4, 37–38, 187–188.

9 Only two monographs in the English or French languages have been published on the general topic of the OECD to date, but neither provides a systematic analysis of the decisions and agreements reached within the Organisation. Henry G. Aubrey, *Atlantic Economic Cooperation: The Case of OECD* (New York: Praeger, 1967); Miriam Camps, *'First World' Relationships: The Role of the OECD* (Paris, New York: Atlantic Institute for International Affairs, Council on Foreign Relations, 1975). The work of the Development Assistance Committee of the OECD has been examined in two other works. Milton J. Esman and Daniel S. Cheever, *Common Aid Effort: The Development Assistance Activities of the Organisation for Economic Co-operation and Development* (Columbus: Ohio State University, 1967), and Seymour J. Rubin, *The Conscience of the Rich Nations: The Development Assistance Committee and the Common Aid Effort* (New York: Harper and Row, 1966).

10 United States, Department of State, *United States Contributions to International Organizations: Report to the Congress*, various years.

11 Fred Charles Iklé, *How Nations Negotiate* (New York: Harper and Row, 1964), pp. 3–4. An even broader definition of negotiation is offered by Roger Fisher, who includes "all cases in which two or

more parties are communicating, each for the purpose of influencing the other's decision." Roger Fisher, "Negotiating Power: Getting and Using Influence", *American Behavioral Scientist* 27 (November/December 1983), p. 150.

12 This resembles what I. William Zartman and Maureen R. Berman refer to as the 'diagnostic' and the 'formula' phases of negotiation, in *The Practical Negotiator* (New Haven and London: Yale University Press, 1982). Vinod Aggarwal uses the term 'meta-regimes' to describe agreements on principles and norms resulting from these two phases. *Liberal Protectionism*, p. 18.

13 This role was in fact recommended for the OECD in a report published in the early 1970s. OECD, *Policy Perspectives for International Trade and Economic Relations*, Report by the High Level Group on Trade and Related Problems to the Secretary General of the OECD (Paris: OECD, 1972), pp. 105–106.

14 Joan Edelman Spero, *The Politics of International Economic Relations*, 3rd ed., (London: George Allen and Unwin, 1985), pp. 101, 114; Gary Clyde Hufbauer and Joanna Shelton Erb, *Subsidies in International Trade* (Washington: Institute for International Economics, 1984), pp. 2–5.

15 Emile van Lennep, "Protectionism vs. Economic Policy". *OECD Observer* 115 (March 1982); John Zysman and Stephen S. Cohen, "Double or Nothing: Open Trade and Competitive Industry", *Foreign Affairs* 61 (Summer 1983).

16 Mancur Olson, Jr., *The Logic of Collective Action: Public Goods and the Theory of Groups* (Cambridge, Mass.: Harvard University Press, 1965).

Chapter Two

THE ANALYTICAL FRAMEWORK

In the search for answers to the questions posed at the outset of this study, namely who prevails in OECD trade negotiations and what impact do OECD trade agreements have on state behaviour, I turn first of all to some of the more or less established theories of international relations. The analysis begins by presenting a series of propositions inferred from these general theoretical frameworks. While it may be argued that these frameworks were not intended to be used to explain specific events or situations, but rather aim at uncovering certain regularities or tendencies in international relations, it can nonetheless be instructive to apply these theories to particular cases. In operationalising some of the apparent or explicit assumptions of these theoretical formulations we can put to the test a few of the connections between variables that are contained in those assumptions. Also, as has been pointed out elsewhere, it may be as important to be able to explain exceptions to trends as it is to explain the trends themselves.[1] If the cases presented here do not confirm the expectations of various theories, perhaps they can indicate the limits of each theory and suggest the conditions under which the outcomes they predict will materialise.

The first group of propositions to be tested is drawn from the structural realist (or neo-realist) paradigm, in particular that aspect of the paradigm dealing with the relationship between the distribution of capabilities and outcomes. The general expectation of neo-realists is that the strong will tend to prevail over the weak, strength being measured in terms of either overall capabilities or issue-specific (contextual) resources. Another group of theorists, which are often referred to as pluralists (or

13

neo-liberals), has argued that this expectation of neo-realists may not always occur. They contend that a number of factors, including international organisations, transnational and trans-governmental contacts, and the existence of international rules and norms may constrain the power of the strong, preventing them from prevailing over weaker countries.[2]

These two theoretical schools tend to share at least one common trait; they both attempt to explain outcomes in inter-national relations at the level of the international system. This systemic approach has been adopted by a number of scholars who are seeking to develop parsimonious theories of inter-national negotiations, co-operation, and other forms of international interaction. Yet, these scholars frequently find themselves turning to certain domestic (unit-level) factors when more tangible systemic variables do not provide an adequate explanation of outcomes.[3] While these domestic variables are considered to be influential, neo-realists and neo-liberals have not always been clear on *how* influential they are, or *when* they can be expected to be influential. In this study, I have selected three such unit-level variables, and rather than consider them only when systemic factors fail to produce the anticipated results, I test them systematically through each case study alongside the systemic variables.

This study does not present an exhaustive list of possible unit-level variables, but rather focuses on a few factors that appear to be the most frequently mentioned unit-level sup-plements to systemic explanations. Other unit-level variables have also been cited by "systemic theorists", but are not tested here. For example, it has been suggested that the perceptions that states or leaders have of the capabilities and interests of other states may affect the outcome of negotiations, although the extent of this influence has been called into question by some students of international negotiations, who argue that any such errors in perception tend to be corrected during the bargaining process.[4]

Another commonly cited unit-level variable is bargaining skill.[5] This factor has not been considered here because judging the level of skill in bargaining is a highly subjective matter, and settling on an operational definition of bargaining skill alone would involve a substantial treatise. Even if there were a widely accepted standard of bargaining skill, reliably assessing the degree of skill manifested in these negotiations would require an intimate knowledge of each move in the bargaining process, information which is not presently available for the cases examined in this study.

While the existing theoretical international relations literature may be used to seek a better understanding of OECD trade negotiations, a study of these negotiations may at the same time provide a good test of the neo-realist and neo-liberal approaches. This study fits the conditions under which certain of the variables to be examined here are expected to have the greatest influence over outcomes. In particular, it has been argued by neo-liberals that issue-specific power resources, international organisations, and transgovernmental and transnational contacts will be more influential under conditions of "complex interdependence".[6] This model of interdependence is considered most applicable to economic/ecological issue areas and in relations among advanced industrialised countries.[7] Moreover, a number of neo-liberals feel that developments in the modern world are challenging many of the traditional realist assumptions, and that the conditions of complex interdependence are most likely to appear in the latter part of the twentieth century. Trade negotiations among OECD countries during the 1970s and 1980s certainly meet all of these conditions.[8] Hence, this study may to a certain extent be considered a "crucial" test of neo-realist and neo-liberal theories.[9] If those variables proposed by neo-liberals are not found to be influential in trade negotiations among OECD countries, it could be argued that they are not likely to be important anywhere else. If neo-realist theory provides a satisfactory explanation of outcomes in this set of relations, then this would tend to verify the contention of certain neo-realists that their approach is valid in most contexts.

The methodological approach adopted here is similar to what Alexander George calls "structured, focused comparison".[10] This approach basically involves examining a small number of cases in considerable detail, but focusing on a common set of variables in each of the cases in order to determine whether the predicted relationships between independent and dependent variables, as set out in a particular theoretical model, actually exist. This approach has an advantage over single case studies, in that it allows the observer to determine immediately whether the findings of one case are upheld in other cases, thus giving greater authority to conclusions drawn from the test results. Furthermore, the structured, focused comparison approach has certain advantages over statistical-correlative studies since it permits the evaluation of a greater number of variables, and provides more a more in-depth examination of each test case than larger samples can offer, thereby helping to avoid drawing potentially spurious conclusions about the causal links between variables.

In this comparative study, a number of factors are held constant, including the time period (1970s and 1980s), and the general issue area (trade). The participants in the negotiations are also basically the same across the four sectors, and they all generally share a certain number of characteristics, such as their level of development and type of political system (advanced industrialised democracies).[11] The rest of this chapter discusses the independent variables to be tested in each of the four case studies.

1. *Overall Capabilities*

The first proposition to be tested in this study is that the strongest state, measured in terms of overall capabilities, will prevail over weaker states in negotiations aimed at setting international rules and norms, and will enforce those rules and norms once they have been set. This proposition is inspired by the structural realist literature which, as Krasner has pointed out, assumes that "outcomes are a function of the distribution of power in the system".[12] While few neo-realists would argue that the distribution of power determines all outcomes, it is important to understand how much of a constraint this structure constitutes, as well as when and how it is likely to constrain state behaviour. The first step in uncovering these conditions is to identify cases where the strongest do not prevail, and to identify the reasons why their superior capabilities did not bring about a satisfactory outcome for them.

Exceptions to the tendency of the strong to prevail over the weak (sometimes referred to as "the paradox of power") are generally explained by neo-realists, and by certain neo-Marxists, as cases in which the dominant power, or hegemon, co-opts smaller powers by permitting them to "win" relatively minor conflicts.[13] The problem with this explanation is that it provides no guide as to when the hegemon can be expected to concede to its relatively weaker allies, and hence can only be offered on a *post hoc* basis. A further problem, particularly in the cases examined here, is that one would most expect the hegemon to insist on having its way when it comes to such important matters as setting international norms of behaviour and rules of action. Hence, neo-realist and neo-Marxist theorists might reasonably expect that in OECD trade negotiations, the hegemon would prevail over other parties.[14]

The structural realist paradigm can be applied at a number of different levels. The first of these is the level of aggregate power resources, where the sum of *all* of a country's capabilities must be taken into consideration in measuring its ability to prevail over other states.[15] Even if a state is relatively weak in a particular issue area, it will be able to get its way by linking its demands in that area with unrelated issues where it is in a stronger position.[16]

According to this model, then, one would expect that in OECD trade negotiations, the United States would impose its will on other participants due to its clear superiority over other OECD members in economic, military and other capabilities, and that any agreement reached would be enforced by the mobilisation of these capabilities. While there was some erosion in relative US economic capabilities during the two decades examined here, in overall terms it remained the predominant member of the OECD. In this study, the European Community (EC) is treated as a single bargaining unit, since on trade issues it normally presents a unified bargaining position. On military matters, however, the EC does not function as a unit, and any attempt to calculate overall power capabilities (including military capabilities) of EC member countries must be made at the national level. Comparing the military power resources of EC member countries and Japan is not necessarily helpful because they are relatively isolated from one another in the military sphere. Hence, apart from the clear superiority of overall American power capabilities, establishing a hierarchy of overall power for the largest Western European countries and Japan outside of their respective regions is both difficult and of questionable value.

In order to avoid drawing spurious conclusions about causality in those cases where the strongest state does get its way in negotiations, it is necessary to look for evidence that the superior capabilities of the hegemon were in fact responsible for its objectives being obtained. If any linkage of unrelated issues were made, this could only have been carried out with the approval of top-level decision makers at the Cabinet level, since linkages between unrelated fields usually involve decisions in two or more government departments, and normally would require the support of the head of government. The decision-making process within the most powerful state should be examined to see if there is evidence of any involvement of the top leadership in the negotiation in question. Also, since it is unlikely that any such linkages would be made without first issuing a threat or warning, high-level international meetings such as economic summits or OECD Ministerials should be examined to determine whether the issue under negotiation was in fact discussed at that level.

2. *Issue Area Structure (International Trade Structure)*

A more refined structural model focuses on the distribution of power resources in the general issue area within which negotiations on a particular issue are conducted. According to some neo-liberal theorists, in economic relations among OECD countries in particular, where force is not considered an effective instrument of policy and military security concerns do not predominate, one might expect the distribution of capabilities within the relevant general issue area to explain the outcomes of international negotiations and the impact of agreements.[17] Hence, the most powerful state in international trade relations, for example, would be able to prevail in negotiations over specific trade issues and enforce agreements by mobilising its trade power resources. This model shares a similarity with the overall capabilities model in that linkages are expected, except that these linkages would be restricted to other *trade* issues. In fact, such linkages are sanctioned under international rules, since the GATT allows retaliatory action in other trade products as a remedy of last resort in trade disputes.[18]

There are a number of factors which should be taken into account when evaluating the distribution of trade power in the international system. The most common indicators of trade power have traditionally been the degree to which a country

18

Chart 2.1
Exports as a Share of GDP

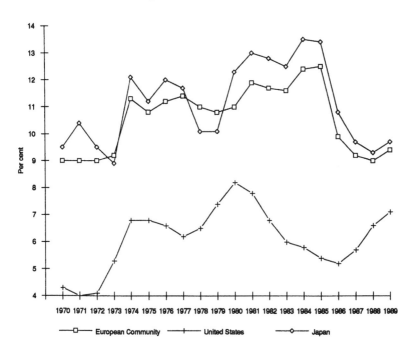

Excluding intra-EC trade. Only includes countries that were EC members during year listed.

Source: IMF, *International Financial Statistics: Supplement on Trade Statistics*, 1982, 1988; IMF, *Direction of Trade Statistics*, various issues; OECD, *National Accounts*, various issues.

relies on exports for its economic well-being, measured in terms of exports as percentage of GNP, and its share of total world exports. During the 1970s and 1980s, the United States remained the least dependent OECD member on international trade, with exports of goods and services accounting for an average 6 per cent of GDP during this period. For both the EC and Japan, an average 11 per cent of GDP came from exports. On the other hand, the EC was the largest exporter in the OECD during these two decades, accounting for over 16 per cent of world exports (excluding intra-EC trade). US exports were an average 12 per cent of the world total during this period, and Japan accounted for about 8 per cent of world exports.[18]

However, another power resource, asymmetrical depen-

Chart 2.2
Market Shares
(Exports as a Percentage of World Imports)

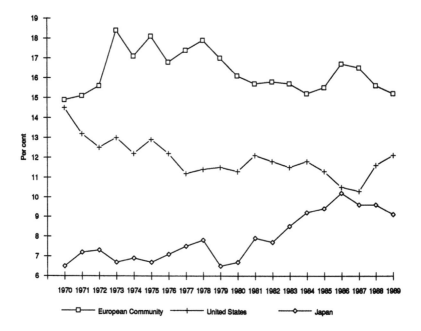

Excluding intra-EC trade. Only includes countries that were EC members during year listed.

Source: IMF, *International Financial Statistics: Supplement on Trade Statistics*, 1982, 1988; IMF, *Direction of Trade Statistics*, various issues.

dence, may be more relevant to bargaining situations. For example, if country A is relatively more dependent on access to markets in country B than B is on A, then B may be in a position to use its relatively lower dependence to exact concessions from A in trade negotiations or to enforce trade agreements, since it would suffer relatively lower costs by reducing or cutting off trade between the two.[19]

The degree of dependence of these three parties on one another in international trade may be a better indication of their ability to exercise trade power in international negotiations. During the 1970s and 1980s, exports to the EC accounted for an average 22 per cent of total US exports, while only 13 per

Chart 2.3
United States-European Community Trade
As a Share of Each Actor's Total Exports

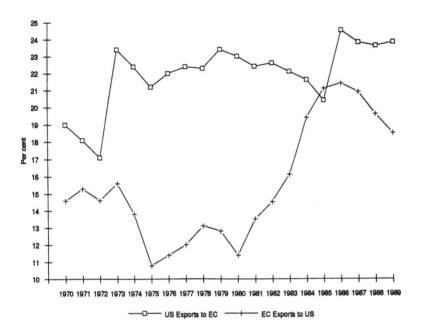

Excluding intra-EC trade. Only includes countries that were EC members during year listed.

Source: IMF, *Direction of Trade Statistics*, various issues.

cent of EC exports went to the US during the 1970s and 17 per cent in the 1980s. The US depended on the Japanese market for around 10 per cent of its exports, while over 30 per cent of Japanese exports went to the United States during the 1970s and 1980s. The EC accounted for an average 12 per cent of Japanese exports during these two decades, while the EC sent less than 3 per cent of its exports to Japan.

Because of the differences among these three actors in their degree of dependence on international trade, however, a better indicator of relative trade dependence seems to be the share of GDP accounted for by the markets of each actor's trading partners. Using this measure, the percentage of US GDP accounted for by exports to the EC during the 1970s was 1.1 per cent, rising

21

Chart 2.4
United States-Japanese Trade
As a Share of Each State's Total Exports

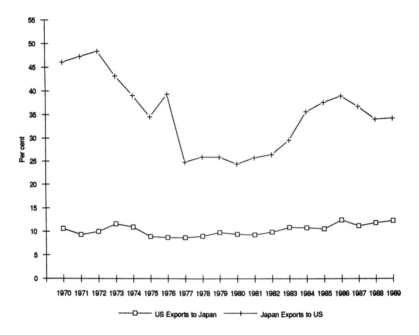

Source: IMF, *Direction of Trade Statistics,* various issues.

to 1.4 per cent in the 1980s, while the share of the collective GDP of EC countries accounted for by exports to the US averaged 1.4 per cent in the 1970s and around 2 per cent in the 1980s. Trade interdependence between the US and Japan was somewhat more asymmetrical, on the other hand. During most of the 1970s and 1980s American exports to Japan were less than one per cent of US GNP, while Japanese exports to the United States made up an average of almost 4 per cent of Japan's GNP during this period. Thus, while the EC was only slightly more dependent on the American market than the US was on the EC market during the 1970s and 1980s, Japan was roughly six times more dependent on the American market than vice versa during this period. The relationship between Japan and the EC was similar to that between the EC and the US, in that Japan was

22

Chart 2.5
European Community-Japanese Trade
As a Share of Each Actor's Total Exports

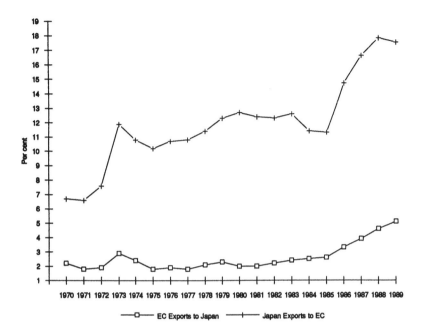

Excluding intra-EC trade. Only includes countries that were EC members during year listed.

Source: IMF, *Direction of Trade Statistics,* various issues.

around five times more dependent on access to the EC market than vice versa during the 1970s and 1980s.

These figures suggest, then, that the most powerful OECD countries in the trade field over the 1970s and 1980s were the United States and the EC, followed by Japan, since presumably the US and EC economies would be harmed less by a curtailment of trade with Japan than Japan would be damaged by reduction of exports to the United States and the European Community. While trade interdependence between the US and the Community appeared to be roughly symmetrical on average during the two decades, as Chart 2.6 indicates, for certain parts of this period the EC was up to twice more dependent on the US market than the US was on the EC market.[21] It could be

23

Chart 2.6
United States-European Community Trade
As a Share of Each Actor's GDP

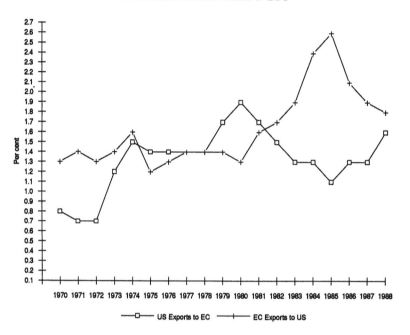

Excluding intra-EC trade. Only includes countries that were EC members during year listed.

Source: IMF, *Direction of Trade Statistics*, various issues; OECD, *National Accounts*, various issues.

argued that during these periods, roughly from 1970 to 1972 and from 1983 to 1988, the United States possessed greater international trade power capabilities than the Community, and consequently was in a position to prevail over the EC in trade negotiations and to ensure that the EC complied with trade rules and norms.

Due to the generally greater contribution that trade makes to their gross domestic product and the relatively greater degree of dependence on their larger trading partners, the other OECD countries are expected to be dominated in OECD trade negotiations by the US, EC and Japan. The trade structure model would predict that these countries could not exercise much power individually in negotiations, and it seems unlikely that

Chart 2.7
United States-Japanese Trade
As a Share of Each State's GDP

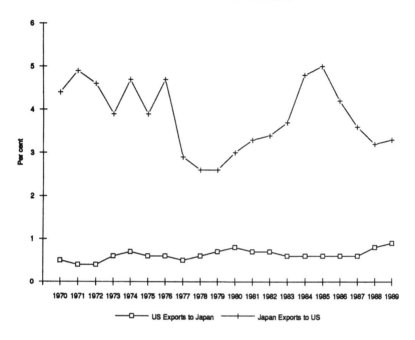

Source: IMF, *Direction of Trade Statistics*, various issues; OECD, *National Accounts*, various
issues.

they would be able to take concerted trade measures against
larger states in order to enhance their trade power.

3. *Issue Structure*

A third structural model focuses on the distribution of capabilities in the context of the specific issue under negotiation. It has
been suggested by some neo-liberals that this model is most
likely to apply to economic relations among advanced industrialised countries.[22] Their reasoning is that it may become difficult
to link various trade issues because of the rising influence of
domestic groups and governmental sub-units in the foreign
policy processes of these countries (both of which resist
attempts to link issues of importance to them with unrelated

25

Chart 2.8
European Community-Japanese Trade
As a Share of Each Actor's GDP

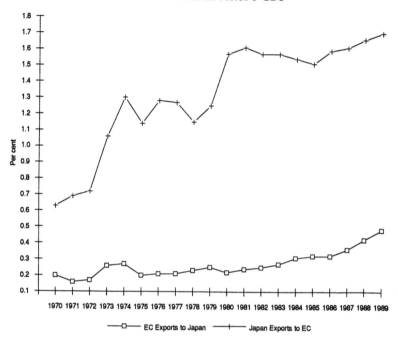

Excluding intra-EC trade. Only includes countries that were EC members during year listed.

Source: IMF, *Direction of Trade Statistics*, various issues; OECD, *National Accounts*, various issues.

issues), and due to the increase in transnational contacts and transgovernmental coalitions which reinforce the influence of these domestic groups and governmental sub-units. The increasing relevance of issue-specific capabilities may enhance the influence of weaker states over bargaining outcomes and over patterns of compliance with agreements because weaker states in overall terms may have greater power resources with regard to a particular issue than do larger states.[23]

A distinction is made here between the competitiveness of a country's products and the country's bargaining power. The competitiveness of a national industry in world markets is determined by such factors as relative cost and quality. Bargaining

26

power in international trade negotiations, on the other hand, derives from the policy instruments at the disposal of government officials which can be used to put pressure on other governments to alter their behaviour. It is possible for a country to be relatively weak in bargaining power on a particular trade sector or product (as Japan tends to be), while being relatively strong in terms of the competitiveness of its industries with respect to the same sector or product (as Japanese industries tend to be).

Thus, in measuring the distribution of issue-specific power in a set of negotiations, the competitiveness of the industries under negotiation would not necessarily be considered. Bargaining power would be determined by such factors as relative dependence on the markets of opponents and the ability to offer subsidies to exporters and domestic suppliers. If country A is a major export market for a product from country B, while country A exports relatively little of the product to country B, then country A would be in a position to threaten or carry out a restriction on the import of that product without suffering any significant costs from country B, assuming that the latter does not link trade in that product to other products. This would be particularly true in sectors with considerable world surplus production capacity, where lost markets are not easily replaced. In the case of subsidy disputes, the country which has the fewest budgetary constraints in the issue area in question and the greatest absolute amount of funding allocated to that area would be in a position to prevail in a subsidies competition with less well-endowed countries. For each of the four cases, the power structure in the relevant issue-area will be determined, and attempts to mobilise issue-specific power resources will be examined.

4. Influence of Institutions

A common assumption of neo-liberal scholars is that international institutions can be an important influence on the processes and outcomes of bargaining.[24] Institutional influences may first of all include characteristics of the international organisation within which negotiations are conducted. These characteristics may include the particular grouping of states, the

27

influence of the Secretariat, and even the mere existence of a permanent negotiating forum.

The membership of a particular organisation can influence bargaining in a number of ways. It may help determine whether or not a state is likely to get its way, or whether any agreement is possible on an issue. States may prefer to bargain in one particular organisation rather than in another if they feel that they are more likely to prevail there, because the composition of the membership increases their chances of forming a winning coalition or developing a consensus. States may also prefer to negotiate within a relatively small organisation because they feel agreement will be easier to reach among fewer parties.

Another feature of negotiations conducted in international organisations is the presence of Secretariat officials, who may exert subtle influence on the process.[25] By providing a neutral source of information about the issues under negotiation, they can lower suspicions about the facts and figures on the table, providing greater certainty about what is being negotiated and perhaps what the likely consequences of an agreement will be. Also, if the Secretariat is able to monitor state compliance, this may make the parties more (or sometimes less) inclined to enter into an agreement.[26] Moreover, to the degree that their impartiality is trusted, Secretariat officials may be able to play a mediatory role in the negotiations.[27] Finally, the Secretariats of international organisations may help set the international agenda, bringing certain issues to the attention of high-level officials and thus influencing the setting of governmental priorities.

The role that an international organisation plays simply as a permanent negotiating forum can also be influential. International organisations typically hold continuous, regularly-scheduled meetings which in a sense force parties to talk to one another. This makes it easier both to initiate negotiations on a particular subject and to keep those negotiations going.[28] In addition, these meetings may ensure that compliance with international agreements is regularly monitored, thereby permitting moral pressure to be applied against any violators. Regular meetings can also facilitate the development of transgovernmental contacts, in which government officials can exchange information informally, and thereby reduce uncertainty among states over each other's intentions.[29] These contacts may have been built up prior to the actual negotiations (for example, during previous meetings of the organisation intended solely for the exchange of information), so that when a decision is made to initiate negotiations, time need not be spent getting to know the quirks and styles of other negotiators. The socialisation process that these contacts facilitate may result in altered perceptions of national interest by delegates, which could ultimately result in changes in policy.[30]

These transgovernmental contacts may also permit coalitions to be built between negotiators aimed at influencing public opinion or other subunits of their governments at home.[31] For example, one official may transmit information to another about problems his department or government may be having in gaining acceptance for a particular proposal either from other departments or from public opinion. The recipient of this inside information may encourage his own government to take some strategically targeted action aimed at strengthening the hand of the department or government in the other state, thereby facilitating an agreement or compliance with an agreement which might not otherwise have been politically possible.[32] While socialisation and coalition-building are also possible in bilateral negotiations, they can be expected to occur more frequently and more easily in negotiations taking place in international organisations because of the regularised nature of transgovernmental contacts. Moreover, Secretariat officials may also play a role in directly socialising delegates and in fostering transgovernmental coalitions.[33]

International institutions also include international regimes, defined as networks of rules, norms and procedures that affect and to some extent govern international bargaining.[34] Thus, knowledge about the nature of regimes may contribute to a greater understanding of international negotiations and of the impact of negotiated agreements.[35] It has been noted that international regimes on specific issues can be "nested" within broader international regimes, and that these broader regimes can influence negotiations and state behaviour within the specific regime.[36] In the case of the OECD trade negotiations, the broader regime that one would expect to have the most direct impact is the international trade regime (sometimes equated with the GATT regime), some of whose principles and norms include liberalisation, multilateralism, and non-discrimination.[37]

29

5. *Unit-level Variables*

While some neo-realists have acknowledged that unit-level variables can be potentially important in explaining outcomes in international relations, it is the neo-liberal theorists who have devoted the greatest attention to the influence of these variables. For many of these neo-liberals, however, these domestic factors are considered only as a supplement to systemic explanations. In this study, a number of unit-level variables are evaluated for each of the four cases, even when it might appear that the expectations of systemic theories are supported by the pattern of outcomes. Three of the unit-level forces that have been referred to most frequently in the neo-liberal literature are examined here, and an attempt is made in the following paragraphs to clarify the nature of each variable and to present some of the propositions that have been made about their potential influence. This group of variables is included more to compare the relative influence of systemic and unit-level variables, and have not been selected from any particular model of domestic determinants of international politics or theory of the state.

Domestic Group Opposition The first unit-level variable to be evaluated here is the degree of opposition to a country's bargaining position in international negotiations from major domestic groups. One proposition put forward by Keohane and Nye is that domestic interest groups, sometimes reinforced by transnational ties, can constrain the freedom of manoeuvre of more powerful states in international negotiations and prevent them from linking issues together, or from manipulating their advantage in relative dependence.[38] This proposition can be carried further to explain the impact of international agreements, since domestic group pressure may at certain times prevent a government from complying with internationally-agreed norms or principles.

Governmental Cohesion The second unit-level variable is that of governmental cohesion, or the coherence of the foreign policy-making process, which may be hampered by the size of government, by the decentralised nature of authority in certain

30

governments, or by a relative lack of concentration on a particular issue.[39] A stronger state may have difficulty mobilising its capabilities if there are divisions among decision-makers or between the various branches of government, particularly in an American-style separation of powers system. A small state may find it easier to coordinate its policies simply due to the smaller number of government actors involved, and may also be able to concentrate its attention on an issue more easily than a larger state because of the relatively fewer foreign policy issues and interests with which it has to cope. Consequently, fewer opportunities may arise for conflicts among these issues and interests in a small state.

An alternative view of the effect of cohesion on international negotiations has been presented by Robert Putnam. Instead of weakening the bargaining position of a state, Putnam argues that internal divisions in a government may actually strengthen the hand of delegates, who can claim that any modification of their country's position is impossible due to such divisions.[40] More research is needed to determine the conditions under which each of these interpretations operate, but it seems plausible that either way the coherence of the internal decision-making process can have a strong effect on international negotiations and on the impact of international agreements.

Preference Intensity   Finally, the bargaining process may be influenced by the strength of a state's preferences for certain objectives or bargaining positions. The assumption here is that the mere existence of superior power resources is no guarantee that they will be used or that the knowledge of their existence will be sufficient to influence the behaviour of others, since others may anticipate that those resources cannot or probably will not be utilised. Preference intensity (also referred to here as will, resolve, determination or commitment) is one of the most difficult factors to identify, let alone measure.[41] Moreover, use of this concept has been criticised by some as a convenient means of explaining away what appears to be inexplicable.[42] Still, preference intensity may in certain cases be a powerful explanation of state behaviour and bargaining outcomes. Certainly no one can deny that an important determinant of whether a party wins a negotiation or not is how badly it wants or needs to win; that is, the extent to which a state is willing to pay the opportunity costs involved in the mobilisation of resources, as well as that state's willingness to suffer whatever punitive action other countries may impose in response to its resistance to their demands.[43] Preference intensity may also help to explain the strength or weakness of a country's own efforts to comply with an international agreement, or of its attempts to get other states to comply.

Rather than simply ignore this important factor, a means should be designed to demonstrate the level and influence of preference intensity, so that it is not simply used as an after the fact rationalisation of outcomes. Evidence of commitment to an objective or line of action can be found first of all by examining whether issue linkage was attempted, and secondly, the degree to which issue-specific resources were mobilised. Thirdly, the level to which the issue is taken in the decision-making hierarchy is often a sign of the importance that states attach to their objectives.[44]

Once it has been established whether preferences were intense or weak in a bargaining situation, the reasons for the intensity of preference should be investigated. A number of possible determinants of preference intensity are proposed here, which might eventually be used to build predictions about the influence of this variable on outcomes in international nego-tiations. Commitment to an objective in international nego-tiations may first of all be the product of domestic political imperatives. If a government feels it can profit politically from pursuing a certain line in negotiations (particularly if its con-tinued existence is threatened by an upcoming election or possi-ble coup) then its pursuit of that line will tend to be vigorous. Similarly, widespread and intense popular protest against a particular line may weaken the commitment of even a relatively secure government. For example, in the United States, the anti-war movement may have contributed to uncertainty about the objectives of the campaign in Vietnam and affected the willing-ness to utilise the country's resources to their fullest.

A second source of commitment in negotiations may be the ideological character of a particular government. If issues tend to be viewed through a highly ideological lens by a government, then compromise on the issues under negotiation will be more difficult.[45] Thirdly, the broader foreign policy objectives and concerns of a particular government will often determine its commitment to specific bargaining objectives. Such broader objectives may include military security concerns (such as the desire to weaken a military adversary), the desire to preserve a certain international economic order or to exert and demonstrate leadership in the international system, and concern about a possible decline in the country's relative economic strength or international competitiveness.

One source of concern about a country's economic strength can be a significant and growing bilateral trade deficit with a major trade partner, particularly at a time when the country's overall trade balance is deteriorating badly. The deficit country may consequently strengthen its resolve to prevail in negotiations with those trading partners that are making a major contribution to the trade deficit. Chart 2.9 indicates the extent of the bilateral trade imbalances between the US and Japan (which was particularly dramatic after 1983) and between the EC and Japan (which deteriorated rapidly after 1985). The US actually ran a trade surplus with the EC until 1983, and the subsequent deficit was much less severe than it was with Japan. Hence, it might be expected that US resolve in trade negotiations with Japan would be increasingly strong after 1975, and would intensify even further after 1983. The growing deficit with the EC in the mid-1980s would also lead one to anticipate a stronger US commitment in trade negotiations with the EC in the second half of the 1980s. The Community would also be expected to be increasingly assertive with Japan after 1985.

Finally, evaluating the level of commitment should also take into account factors which might offset those listed above. The existence of competing domestic political imperatives, or competing foreign policy objectives (such as alliance solidarity) may act to weaken a government's commitment to a particular position in negotiations.

6. Changes in Interest Definition

One important consideration which is often overlooked in structural analyses, but which has been seen to play an important role in certain studies of negotiations, is the definition of self-interest by states, and in particular, changes in that definition.[46] It is vital that any such changes be identified in studies of

Chart 2.9
Bilateral Trade Balances

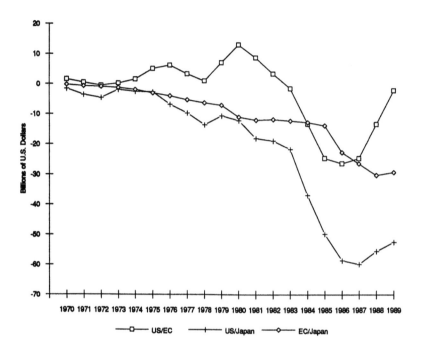

Only includes countries that were EC members during year listed.
Source: IMF, *Direction of Trade Statistics*, various issues.

negotiations and regime impact, because a failure to do so could produce erroneous conclusions about the relationship between independent and dependent variables. For example, a positive relationship between superior capabilities and the success of the dominant actor in obtaining its goals may lead one to conclude that the distribution of capabilities was responsible for that outcome. However, this conclusion would be invalidated if it were found that weaker states changed their bargaining positions or began complying with an agreement as a result of purely internal developments or due to changes in international conditions over which the dominant state had no control. This variable is set apart from unit-level factors because while changes in interest definition can result from domestic conditions, they could also be the product of international forces, whether political or economic.

The interests of a state can shift for several reasons. One could speak of a change of interest in cases where a stronger state threatens to take some action which would impose significant costs on another state. In such cases the interest in the issue being negotiated could be overridden by the interest in avoiding the threatened action. However, this example is probably better characterised as *coercion*, and so would best fit into the structural models outlined above. The kinds of interest change referred to in this section are those brought about by various conditions exogenous to the specific bargaining process. These conditions may fall into two broad categories, each of which can be further divided into two subcategories.

The first category of causes of interest change roughly corresponds with the "economic process" model set out by Keohane and Nye.[47] This category includes movements in international market conditions, such as price levels, exchange rates, supply and demand, and shifts in comparative advantage. Other international economic forces in this category include technological developments and changes in the intensity and direction of trade and investment flows. In addition to these international economic conditions, certain *domestic* economic developments can alter a state's definition of self-interest. Shifts in the level of economic growth, unemployment, and inflation, as well as growing budget and trade deficits are examples of such developments.[48]

The second category of causes of interest change are political, rather than economic. This category can include changes in the international political context, such as a general movement in the direction of either detente or cold war. It also includes changes in domestic political conditions, such as changes in governments through elections, coups d'état, revolutions, and national or regional political unrest. An analysis of the relative importance of various factors in explaining interest change is beyond the scope of this study, but it is worthwhile outlining some of these factors in order to illustrate what is meant by the phrase "change in interest definition" as it is use here, as well as to provide suggestions for the direction that further research could take.

Changes in interest definition do not always answer the question of who prevails in international negotiations because it often renders this question irrelevant. When one party changes its interests to match those of parties, one can no longer speak of prevailing. The value of this variable in the context of the present study is that it can in some cases disprove arguments that other variables were responsible for a particular outcome. An initial situation of conflicting interests can transform into an situation where interests become more compatible due to exogenous factors. Hence, it is always important to seek evidence of any changes in interest definition, in order to determine whether agreements are the result of coercion or the product of convergent interests.

Notes

1 Zeev Maoz, "Power, Capabilities, and Paradoxical Conflict Outcomes", *World Politics* 61 (January 1989), p. 265.
2 For a further discussion of these two schools, see Joseph S. Nye, Jr., "Neorealism and Neoliberalism", *World Politics* 40 (January 1988), pp. 235–251. Neo-liberalism has also been at various times referred to as the interdependence approach or the international organisation school.
3 See for example, Robert O. Keohane and Joseph S. Nye, *Power and Interdependence: World Politics in Transition* (Boston, Toronto: Little, Brown, 1977), pp. 15, 18–19, 30–36, 44, 53, 57–58, 203–208, 224–226, 237; Robert O. Keohane, *After Hegemony: Cooperation and Discord in the World Political Economy* (Princeton, N.J.: Princeton University Press, 1986), pp. 34–35, 141, 177–179, 211–213; Vinod K. Aggarwal, *Liberal Protectionism: The International Politics of Organized Textile Trade* (Berkeley, Los Angeles, London: University of California Press, 1985), pp. 4, 37, 185–6, 193–194. For a discussion of the debate between structural and unit-level approaches, see Alexander E. Wendt, "The Agent-Structure Problem in International Relations Theory", *International Organization* 41 (Summer 1987).
4 Glenn H. Snyder and Paul Diesing, *Conflict among Nations: Bargaining, Decision Making, and System Structure in International Crises* (Princeton, N.J.: Princeton University Press, 1977), pp. 191, 280–339.
5 Ibid., pp. 190, 194, 498; Aggarwal, *Liberal Protectionism*, pp. 36–38, 189.
6 Keohane and Nye, *Power and Interdependence*, pp. 23–60. See also Keohane and Nye's reappraisal of this concept in *"Power and Interdependence* Revisited".
7 Keohane and Nye, *Power and Interdependence*, p. 226.
8 Joseph M. Grieco similarly argues that a study of economic relations among advanced democracies would provide the best test of the

validity of neo-liberal and realist theories. "Anarchy and the Limits of Cooperation: A Realist Critique of the Newest Liberal Institutionalism", *International Organization* 42 (Summer 1988), p. 504.

9 For a discussion of crucial case studies, see Harry Eckstein, "Case Study and Theory in Political Science", in *Handbook of Political Science*, Vol. VII, ed. F.I. Greenstein and N.W. Polsby, (Reading, Mass.: Addison-Wesley, 1975), pp. 113–123.

10 Alexander L. George, "Case Studies and Theory Development: The Method of Structured, Focused Comparison", in *Diplomacy: New Approaches in History, Theory, and Policy*, Ed. Paul Gordon Lauren (New York: Free Press, 1979), pp. 43–68.

11 Only in the case of shipbuilding is there any significant variation in actors, since the United States did not participate in OECD negotiations on shipbuilding during the 1970s and most of the 1980s.

12 Stephen D. Krasner, "Regimes and the Limits of Realism: Regimes as Autonomous Variables", in *International Regimes*, ed. Stephen D. Krasner (Ithaca and London: Cornell University Press, 1982), pp. 355–356.

13 For examples of this explanation, see Keohane and Nye, *Power and Interdependence*, p. 47, 179; Keohane, *After Hegemony*, p. 146; Robert W. Cox, "Social Forces, States and World Orders: Beyond International Relations Theory", *Millennium: Journal of International Studies* 10 (Summer 1981), pp. 126–155; and Robert W. Cox, "Gramsci, Hegemony and International Relations: An Essay in Method", *Millennium: Journal of International Studies* 12 (Summer 1983), pp. 162–175.

14 Keohane and Nye, *Power and Interdependence*, pp. 43–44. Krasner argues that "powerful states create regimes that enhance their interests". "Regimes and the Limits of Realism", p. 357. Keohane points out the central proposition of the theory of hegemonic stability that "order in world politics is typically created by a single dominant power", and consequently, "the formation of international regimes normally depends on hegemony". *After Hegemony*, p. 31.

15 Kenneth N. Waltz, *Theory of International Politics* (Reading, Mass.: Addison-Wesley, 1979), pp. 131, 192; Keohane and Nye, *Power and Interdependence* pp. 42–44. James G. March refers to models which use overall tangible power resources as "basic force models". "The Power of Power", in *Varieties of Political Theory*, ed. David Easton (Englewood Cliffs, N.J.: Prentice-Hall, 1966), pp. 39–70, cited in Keohane, *After Hegemony*, p. 20.

16 Arthur Stein, "Research Note: The Politics of Linkage", *World Politics* 33 (October 1980), p. 81.

17 Keohane and Nye, *Power and Interdependence*, p. 31.

18 Kenneth W. Dam, *The GATT: Law and the International Economic Organization* (Chicago and London: University of Chicago Press, 1970), pp. 356–364.

19 International Monetary Fund, *Direction of Trade Statistics*, various years.
20 Albert Hirschman, *National Power and the Structure of Foreign Trade* (Berkeley: University of California Press, 1945), pp. 26, 41–52; Keohane and Nye, *Power and Interdependence*, pp. 10–19; Waltz, *Theory of International Politics*, p. 159; Snyder and Diesing, *Conflict among Nations*, p. 477.
21 This finding contrasts with that of Keohane, who concluded that the EC was less dependent on the US market than vice versa. *After Hegemony*, pp. 201–202. Keohane reached this conclusion on the basis of data for a single year (1980), which, as Chart 2.6 indicates, was not typical of the pattern of trade relations during the overall period of the 1970s and 1980s.
22 Keohane and Nye, *Power and Interdependence*, p. 60. Other analysts, who would not necessarily consider themselves neo-liberals, have also argued that the context in which power is exercised must always be taken into consideration. See, for example, David A. Baldwin, "Power Analysis and World Politics: New Trends versus Old Tendencies", *World Politics* 31 (January 1979); Stephen D. Krasner, *Structural Conflict: The Third World Against Global Liberalism* (Berkeley: University of California Press, 1985), pp. 33, 36.
23 While linkages among trade issues might be expected in multilateral trade negotiations under the auspices of the GATT, one GATT official has observed that in fact this practice is becoming more difficult as the focus of negotiations moves from tariffs to non-tariff measures. Bernard M. Hoekman, "Determining the Need for Issue Linkages in Multilateral Trade Negotiations", *International Organization* 43 (Autumn 1989), pp. 695–698.
24 See, for example, Robert O. Keohane, "International Institutions: Two Approaches", *International Studies Quarterly* 32 (December 1988).
25 Chadwick F. Alger, "Personal Contacts in Intergovernmental Organizations", in *International Behavior*, ed. Herbert C. Kelman (New York: Holt, Rinehart and Winston, 1965), pp. 536–540.
26 Keohane, *After Hegemony*, pp. 90, 94, 102.
27 For a discussion of this role, see Gilbert R. Winham, "The Mediation of Multilateral Negotiations," *Journal of World Trade Law* 13 (May:June 1979).
28 If one prefers to use the language of economics, this is one of the ways in which international organisations can lower transaction costs. Keohane, *After Hegemony*, pp. 89–90.
29 Alger, "Personal Contacts", pp. 527–532.
30 Ibid., pp. 532–536, 540–543.
31 For a case study illustrating this process, see Ronald I. Meltzer, "The Politics of Policy Reversal: The US Response to Granting Trade Preferences to Developing Countries and Linkages Between International Organizations and National Policy Making", *International Organization* 30 (Autumn 1976), pp. 649–668.
32 Keohane, *After Hegemony*, p. 102; Robert O. Keohane and Joseph

S. Nye, "Transgovernmental Relations and International Organisations," *World Politics* 27 (October 1974). Also, see the discussion of the socialisation process in Peter Wolf, "International Organization and Attitude Change: A Re-examination of the Functionalist Approach", *International Organization* 27 (Summer 1973), pp. 347–371.

33 Keohane and Nye, "Transgovernmental Relations and International Organisations", pp. 45–53; Keohane and Nye, *Power and Interdependence*, pp. 35–36, 118–119.

34 This definition is derived from Keohane and Nye, *Power and Interdependence*, pp. 19, 21. For an alternative definition, see Stephen D. Krasner, "Structural Causes and Regime Consequences: Regimes as Intervening Variables", in *International Regimes*, ed. Stephen D. Krasner, pp. 1–5.

35 Keohane argues that "one of the key features of international regimes is that they limit the ability of countries in a particularly strong bargaining position . . . to take advantage of that situation". *After Hegemony*, p. 116.

36 Aggarwal, *Liberal Protectionism*, p. 27.

37 Jock A. Finlayson and Mark W. Zacher, "The GATT and the Regulation of Trade Barriers: Regime Dynamics and Functions", in *International Regimes*, ed. Stephen D. Krasner, pp. 278–305. For a discussion of how institutional factors influence the pattern of compliance with regimes, see Keohane, *After Hegemony*, pp. 98–106.

38 Keohane and Nye, *Power and Interdependence*, pp. 31, 34.

39 Ibid., pp. 207–208.

40 Robert D. Putnam, "Diplomacy and Domestic Politics: The Logic of Two-level Games", *International Organization* 42 (Summer 1988).

41 See, for example, the discussion of "level of aspiration" in Dean G. Pruitt, *Negotiation Behavior* (New York: Academic Press, 1981), pp. 25–30; and the concept of "resolve" in Snyder and Diesing, *Conflict among Nations*, pp. 185–195, and in Zeev Maoz, "Resolve, Capabilities, and the Outcome of Interstate Disputes, 1816–1976", *Journal of Conflict Resolution* 27 (June 1983), pp. 195–229. The importance of "motivation" for effective coercive diplomacy is also discussed in Alexander L. George, David K. Hall, and William R. Simons, *The Limits of Coercive Diplomacy: Laos, Cuba, Vietnam* (Boston: Little, Brown and Co., 1971), pp. 216–220. Hans Morgenthau briefly mentions the significance of "will" in explaining the lack of US leadership in international relations between the First and Second World Wars. *Politics Among Nations: the Struggle for Power and Peace*, 5th ed. (New York: Alfred A. Knopf, 1978), p. 141. Keohane and Nye also refer to "will" and "commitment" throughout *Power and Interdependence*, pp. 15, 18, 53, 57–58, 203–208, 225. Arthur Lall points out that a "persistent attitude of a preponderant interest in an issue may have the result of gaining, even for the relatively weak, a considerable degree of acceptance of its point of view in international negotiation", in *Modern International Negotiation* (New York and London: Columbia University Press, 1966), p. 317. R.

Harrison Wagner implicitly acknowledges the importance of preference intensity, when he criticises structural approaches and argues
that the value to parties of the concession being demanded in
negotiations can override any apparent weakness stemming from
asymmetrical interdependence. "Economic Interdependence, Bargaining Power, and Political Influence", *International Organization*
42 (Summer 1988).

42 Keohane's main criticism is that it precludes any *a priori* predictions,
and is therefore inimical to theorising about international relations.
After Hegemony, pp. 20, 34–35, 38–39. David Baldwin criticises references to insufficient will to explain the "paradox of unrealised
power" as "sloppy power analysis". "Power Analysis and World
Politics", pp. 169–170.

43 Two other ideas or concepts that have been discussed in various
works would seem to fit into this category. One is the concept of
"issue salience", which basically means the importance of an issue
to a particular party. The expectation is that the more vital outcomes
over a certain issue under negotiation are to a state, the more
vigorously it will seek to obtain those outcomes. The other point
that has been raised is that the degree to which a party needs an
agreement with others will influence international bargaining. This
is essentially a variation on the first point, except that in the case
of issue salience, the desired outcome may be *no* agreement. In
both cases, the value of an issue or an outcome will determine the
level of preference intensity. See Keohane and Nye, *Power and
Interdependence*, pp. 203–205; Keohane, *After Hegemony*, p. 71; and
John Harsanyi, "Measurement of Social Power, Opportunity Costs
and the Theory of Two-Person Bargaining Games", *Behavioral
Science* 7, no.1 (1962).

44 One measure of preference intensity that has been used is the
frequency of mention of a position by a delegation in negotiations.
While this indicator may be useful in ranking the relative commitment to several demands, it does not necessarily tell us much about
the absolute value attached to a single position or package. Rhetoric
is generally low in cost, while the actual mobilisation of resources
which involves more significant costs would appear to be a much
more reliable indicator of commitment.

45 The claim that certain issues are matters of principle or ideology is
one tactic that can be used to demonstrate a state's commitment to
its position, since it is generally recognised that compromise on
matters of principle is very difficult. Thomas C. Schelling, *The Strategy of Conflict* (Cambridge, Mass.: Harvard University Press, 1960),
p. 34. However, a state that truly does view issues as matters of
principle or casts them in ideological terms will be at least as
strongly committed to its position as a state that uses this claim as
a bargaining tactic to resist the effort of others to make it change
its position.

46 Robert O. Keohane and Joseph S. Nye, Jr., *"Power and Interdepen-*

dence Revisited", *International Organization* 41 (Autumn 1987), pp. 739–742.

47 *Power and Interdependence*, pp. 39–42.

48 Demographic change is another possible cause of interest change, and could fit into either economic or political categories. However, demographic changes tend to occur over a relatively long period of time, and so would not likely alter the course of a particular international negotiation.

Chapter Three

EXPORT CREDITS

1. *Trends in Officially Supported Export Credit*

Perhaps the most concise definition of export credits available is set forth by the OECD in its review of the export credit financing systems of member countries:

> Broadly defined, an export credit arises whenever a foreign buyer of exported goods or services is allowed to defer payment. Export credits . . . may take the form of "supplier credits", extended by the exporter, or of "buyer credits", where the exporter's bank or other financial institution lends to the buyer (or his bank). Export credit agencies may give official support to both types of credit.[1]

There are a number of ways in which governments can give support to export financing. Official support may include insurance against commercial and political risk, guarantees of repayment, and insurance against cost-inflation and foreign exchange risk. Governments may also give financial support in the form of direct credits, refinancing and the subsidisation of interest rates.

Until the 1950s, the main role of governments in the export credit field was to provide short-term insurance for political credit risks. This role was later expanded to include coverage of commercial risk and the provision of unconditional bank guarantees. Between 1960 and 1970, the contract value of officially supported long-term export credits rose from under SDR 1 billion to around SDR 8 billion.

In the wake of the major world oil price increases in 1973–74 and 1979–80, many governments attempted to deal with the resultant balance of payments deficits and rising unemployment

42

Chart 3.1
Officially Supported Long-Term Export Credits

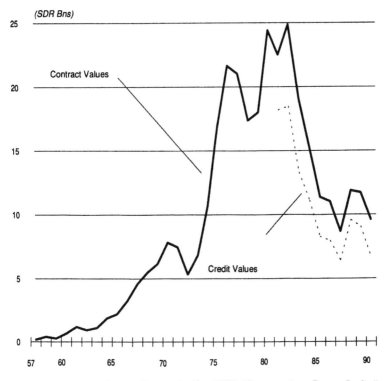

Source: John E. Ray, "Recent Changes in The OECD 'Consensus' on Export Credits",
Mimeograph.

by boosting their financial support for exporters. One of the
mechanisms they used was the extending of export credits with
favourable terms, such as subsidised interest rates or longer-
than-usual repayment periods. Although most governments
recognised the economic costs of such practices, they found
them irresistible in the face of mounting domestic economic,
social and political pressures.

The value of exports financed by officially-supported long-
term export credits soared in the 1970s and early 1980s, as is
indicated in Chart 3.1. Export credit subsidies in OECD countries increased from an estimated $2 billion in 1978 to $5.5 billion
in 1979. The total subsidy figure rose to $6 billion in 1980 and
peaked at around $7 billion in 1981. The figure dropped signifi-

Chart 3.2

Officially Supported Medium and Long Term Export Credits

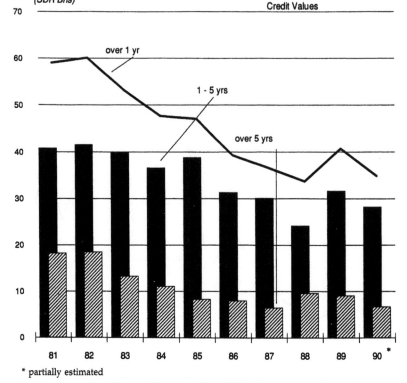

(SDR Bns)   Credit Values

over 1 yr

1 - 5 yrs

over 5 yrs

* partially estimated

Source: John E. Ray, "Recent Changes in The OECD 'Consensus' on Exports Credits",
    Mimeograph.

cantly thereafter, to $4.5 billion in 1982 and to $3.5 billion in
1983.[2] According to the International Monetary Fund, in the
early 1980s, the share of all exports receiving official financial
support was 18 per cent for the US, 34 per cent for France, 35
per cent for the UK, and 39 per cent for Japan.[3] The value
of medium- and long-term officially supported export credits
steadily declined after 1983 for the rest of the 1980s, except for
a modest increase in 1988 in long-term credits.[4]

2. Background to OECD Export Credit Negotiations

Export credits were first dealt with by the Organisation for
European Economic Co-operation (OEEC) in the context of rules

set out in 1955 which committed member countries to abstain from artificial aid to exporters. Among the prohibited measures was the charging of premiums for government export credit guarantees "at rates which are manifestly inadequate to cover the long-term operating costs and losses of the credit insurance institutions". In 1958, further prohibitions were placed on the granting of export credits by government agencies "at rates below those which they have to pay in order to obtain the funds so employed" and on governments bearing "all or part of the costs incurred by exporters in obtaining credits".[5] When the OEEC was transformed into the OECD, the list of prohibited export credit practices was transferred to the GATT. At that time a GATT working group noted in a report that these practices were generally to be considered subsidies in the sense of Article XVI(4).[6]

In November 1963 the OECD Trade Committee set up a permanent high-level Group on Export Credits and Credit Guarantees (ECG) to discuss regularly government policies in these two fields.[7] The objective of these discussions was to identify and resolve, or at least mitigate, problems arising from such policies. In addition, members were urged to work out common guiding principles with a view to minimising competition in the provision of government assistance for export credits.[8] The Group concentrated on conditions for granting credits and credit guarantees with maturities of over five years, and discussed procedures for prior notification and consultation for individual transactions.[9] However, no substantial actions were taken during the 1960s either in the areas of information gathering or in the establishment of common guidelines.[10]

After the seven summit countries reached an agreement on export credits in 1976, the Participants in this agreement began meeting at the OECD in April 1977. The Participants Group (PG) was not technically an OECD body, and thus was not bound by OECD rules, such as having certain actions approved by the OECD Council. Although the Participants sat separately from the ECG, the membership of the two bodies was basically the same, the same delegates generally attended the meetings of both groups, and both shared the same chairman and OECD Secretariat support staff.[11]

One major procedural issue dealt with by the Participants during the 1970s and 1980s was whether the PG's membership should be expanded to include non-OECD nations, particularly certain newly-industrialising countries (NICs). According to the president of the Export-Import Bank of the United States (Exim-bank), John L. Moore, Jr., a number of NICs like India, Mexico and Brazil wanted to join the Participants Group in the late 1970s. The US position was to admit these countries to the PG, in order to obtain their adherence to the rules being developed there, but European countries were reportedly in favour of keeping participation in Group's meeting limited to OECD countries.[12] By the mid-1980s, the US opposed expanding the Participants Group while the issue of mixed credits was being discussed.[13] The only other significant procedural issue affecting the Participants Group was the question of whether export credits should be introduced at the multilateral trade nego-tiations being conducted in the GATT framework, both in the 1970s and in the 1980s. The general feeling that emerged, how-ever, was that export credits were better dealt with in the OECD context.[14]

3. *Agreements in the Export Credits Field*

The first general agreement on export credits reached in the OECD was of an informational nature.[15] In June 1972, the OECD Council endorsed an agreement worked out in the ECG setting up an Exchange of Information System (EIS), which was to include all of the 20 countries represented in the ECG. Under this system, any member country which received an application for official support of export credits over 5 years in duration could request information from any other member on the terms of credit they were prepared to support for that transaction. After the exchange of information took place, countries taking part in it could support credit terms as favourable as any which the exchange revealed. If one of the participants in the EIS ultimately decided to match the credit offer of another, it was required to notify all other participants.[16] The objective of this system was to prevent competition among participants in the offering of export credit by making transparent the offers made by each. It was hoped that buyers would be prevented from playing one bidder off against another by making exaggerated claims of the credit terms they were being offered, and that comparable export credit terms among ECG members could be encouraged.

Agreement was also reached in the OECD in June 1972 to establish a Prior Consultation Procedure. Only 16 member countries were parties to this agreement, which excluded most notably the United States and Japan, and which was confined to credits extended to industrialised countries.[17] When planning to guarantee a commercial credit of over five years duration, each participating country undertook to inform other participants of the terms it was contemplating and to take no final decisions before its partners had had the opportunity to make comments on the planned bid within prescribed time limits.[18]

In May 1975, the Understanding on Local Cost was concluded, requiring that the financing of local costs (ie. costs for the supply of goods and services arising in buyer countries) not exceed the amount of the downpayment received for the exported goods or services.[19] Information on interest rates was included in the EIS after a decision reached in the ECG in October 1975, and coverage was further extended to data on the cost of credit to export credit agencies the following year.[20] In 1976, the ECG undertook a comprehensive study of the export credit financing systems of member countries, permitting the Group to keep track of major changes in the export credit policies and practices of these countries.

Gentlemen's Agreement The year 1976 was marked by the conclusion of the first comprehensive agreement on export credits, which was formally called the "Consensus on Converging Export Credits Policies of July 1976", but which later came to be known as the "Gentlemen's Agreement".[21] Most of the negotiations for this agreement in fact took place outside the OECD framework, although the final agreement was more or less concluded in the OECD in March 1976, and country delegations registered their adherence to the Agreement by sending letters to the OECD Secretariat.[22] There was no formal text of an agreement signed, but the seven major industrialised countries verbally agreed to implement its terms by means of unilateral declarations of policy changes, effective from 1 July 1976 for a one-year trial period.[23] The Secretariat convinced the United

47

States to have its declaration, the first made by a summit country, printed up as an OECD document.[24]

The main feature of the Gentlemen's Agreement was the setting of minimum interest rates which varied depending on the wealth of the buyer country and the length of the credit.[25] The interest rate matrix set out in the Agreement was as follows:

	2–5 years	over 5 years
I. Relatively rich countries	7.75%	8%
II. Intermediate countries	7.25%	7.75%
III. Relatively poor countries	7.25%	7.5%

The maximum repayment period for credits extended to relatively poor countries was set at ten years. For relatively rich and intermediate countries, the maximum term was set at 8.5 years. When the repayment period for credits extended to relatively rich countries exceeded five years in a particular deal, the granting country was required to give relevant information 7 days in advance to the export financing agencies of other Participating countries. The reason for this prior notification procedure on interest rates, and on other aspects of the Gentlemen's Agreement, was to permit other participants to make matching credit offers. The objective was to discourage certain practices by reducing the competitive advantage exporters would have in offering credit terms which were considered undesirable by the participants.

The Gentlemen's Agreement also contained a set of procedures concerning mixed credits, which arise when a country mixes export credit with development assistance in a single package. If the grant element of a financial package was less than 15 per cent, participants were required to give "prior notification" (ie. seven days notice before making a commitment to the recipient) to other participants. Where the grant element was between 15 and 25 per cent, "prompt information" (ie. notice given upon making a commitment) was required. If the grant element exceeded 25 per cent, the package was to be regarded as official government aid and consequently would not be subject to the notification procedures of the Gentlemen's Agreement.

Under the Gentlemen's Agreement, if a country entered into a credit commitment before July 1976, it could extend terms which exceeded those contained in the Agreement without the need for advance notice. If a country derogated from the guidelines after this date, it was required to inform other participants seven days in advance, with an additional nine days allowed for discussion if requested by another participant. In such a case, other participants were permitted to match the terms of the offer. When matching another participant's offer, a country was to give prompt information to the credit agencies of all participants. Finally, minimum cash payments of 15 per cent of the export contract value were required by the Gentlemen's Agreement.

The 1976 Agreement did not apply to agricultural commodities or to military equipment. The guidelines also did not apply to the two sectors covered by standstill agreements (aircraft and nuclear power plants), or to new ocean-going ships, which were covered by the Understanding on Export Credits for Ships. Downpayment and maturities guidelines did not apply to satellite ground stations. As well, conventional power plants and steel plants were exempt from the maturity guidelines up to the maximum current practices, which basically amounted to a standstill on maturities in these sectors. However, when repayment periods exceeded 5 years for rich countries, 8.5 years for intermediate countries and 10 years for poor countries, seven days advance information to other participants was required.[26] In May 1977, the 20 OECD members who had by that time announced their adherence to the Gentlemen's Agreement agreed to extend it until the end of 1977 in its existing form.[27]

Consensus On 22 February 1978, the 20 participants in the Gentlemen's Agreement adopted the "Arrangement on Guidelines for Officially Supported Export Credits", which came to be known simply as the Consensus.[28] The Consensus is not formally an OECD agreement, but all the negotiations affecting the agreement have been carried out in the OECD and the OECD Secretariat is responsible for the servicing of the agreement, so for all intents and purposes the Consensus must be considered *de facto* an OECD agreement.

The terms of the Consensus were generally the same as those of the Gentlemen's Agreement, with the major exception of the notification procedures. When planning to derogate from the

49

terms of the Consensus (for example, by exceeding maturities or going below matrix interest rates), a participant was required to notify other participants 10 days prior to making any commitment. In addition, any participant could request a discussion with the derogating country, which would result in a further 10-day delay. Any changes resulting from these discussions were to be communicated to all other participants. Another major change from the Gentlemen's Agreement was that terms of export credits for steel plants were to be fully consistent with the Consensus.

The Consensus also included a provision for local costs, which were not mentioned in the Gentlemen's Agreement. Official support for local costs in relatively rich countries was to be confined to insurance or guarantees. As well, the requirement that the amount of local costs supported not exceed the amount of downpayment, as set out in the Understanding on Local Cost, was incorporated into the Consensus.[29]

The Consensus continued to be the main instrument for regulating export credit policies for the next decade. Although the general form of the Consensus remained relatively unchanged, a number of specific features were altered over this period. First, in the area of interest rate limits, the matrix rates were adjusted each year between 1980 until 1983 as the result of negotiated agreements in the Participants Group. In 1981, currencies of countries with market interest rates below the lowest minimum rate in the matrix were subject to a special minimum rate of 9.25 per cent, and in July 1982 the definition of this special rate was changed to no less than 0.3 per cent above the market rate of the currency.[30] At the same time, participants agreed not to derogate from the Consensus on interest rates or maturities after October 1982, although they were permitted to derogate in order to match offers. At the July 1982 meeting of the Participants, new definitions were also set for each category of country in the matrix. Category I countries were those with an annual per capita GNP of over $4,000 in 1979, Category II countries had an annual per capita GNP between $625 and $4,000 in 1979, and Category III countries were those eligible for International Development Association loans, that is, with an annual per capita GNP less than $624 in 1978.

In October 1983, agreement was reached to begin adjusting the matrix interest rates automatically every six months, starting in January 1984, in line with changes in a representative international weighted average interest rate over the preceding six months.[31] The matrix rates were to be changed only if such average rate movements were at least 0.5 percentiles.[32] The matrix rate reductions of 0.5 to 0.65 per cent agreed to in October 1983 were to be erased between July 1985 and July 1986, unless the matrix rates were adjusted downward in the meantime, when the October 1983 reductions would be reversed earlier.[33]

Another major change introduced in October 1983 was that for currencies whose commercial lending rates were below the matrix ceiling of 12.4 per cent, commercial interest reference rates (CIRRs) were to be established. For those currencies, export credits could be extended at the CIRR plus 0.2 per cent.[34] A common formula for calculating CIRRs was agreed upon in 1986, based upon the interest rate for government bonds plus a one per cent premium.[35] In March 1987, participants in the Consensus agreed to abolish interest rate subsidies on export credits for rich countries listed in Category I. At the same time, CIRRs were adopted for *all* currencies, including the ECU, and these were to be charged to Category I countries in place of the old matrix rates.[36] Finally, matrix rates for Categories II and III were to be increased by 0.3 per cent across the board as of 15 July 1988.[37]

The second feature of the Consensus which underwent major alteration was the treatment of mixed credits. In 1978 the Consensus merely repeated the notification requirements set out in the Gentlemen's Agreement. But in August 1981, credits with a grant element of less than 15 per cent were subject to 10 days prior notification with an additional 10–day delay if any other participant requested a discussion of the intended offer. Credits with a grant element between 15 and 20 per cent were to be submitted to prior notification at least 10 calendar days before making a commitment, although there was no requirement for discussion. For credits with more than 25 per cent grant element, "prompt notification" (ie. notification of other participants as soon as a commitment was made) was required.[38]

In July 1982, agreement was reached not to use mixed credits when the grant element of a financial package was less than 20 per cent.[39] For mixed credits with between a 20 and 25 per cent grant element, ten days prior notification was required.[40] The

Table 3.1
Consensus Matrix of Interest Rate Minimums
(Per cent)

	Relatively rich countries (Category I)	Intermediate countries (Category II)	Relatively poor countries (Category III)
Credits for 2 - 5 years			
July 1976 - July 1980	7.75	7.25	7.25
July 1980 - Nov 1981	8.50	8.00	7.50
Nov 1981 - July 1982	11.00	10.50	10.00
July 1982 - Oct 1983	12.15	10.85	10.00
Oct 1983 - July 1984	12.15	10.35	9.50
July 1984 - Jan 1985	13.35	11.55	10.70
Jan 1985 - Jan 1986	12.00	10.70	9.85
Jan 1986 - July 1986	10.95	9.65	8.80
July 1986 - Jan 1988	9.55	8.25	7.40
Jan 1988 - July 1988	10.15	8.85	8.00
July 1988 - July 1990	--	9.15	8.30
Credits for 5 - 8.5 years			
July 1976 - July 1980	8.00	7.75	7.50
July 1980 - Nov 1981	8.75	8.50	7.75
Nov 1981 - July 1982	11.25	11.00	10.00
July 1982 - Oct 1983	12.40	11.35	10.00
Oct 1983 - July 1984	12.40	10.70	9.50
July 1984 - Jan 1985	13.60	11.90	10.70
Jan 1985 - Jan 1986	12.25	11.20	9.85
Jan 1986 - July 1986	11.20	10.15	8.80
July 1986 - Jan 1988	9.80	8.75	7.40
Jan 1988 - July 1988	10.40	9.35	8.00
July 1988 - July 1990	--	9.65	8.30
Credits for 8.5 - 10 years			
July 1976 - July 1980	--	--	7.50
July 1980 - Nov 1981	--	--	7.75
Nov 1981 - July 1982	--	--	10.00
July 1982 - Oct 1983	--	11.35*	10.00
Oct 1983 - July 1984	--	10.70*	9.50
July 1984 - Jan 1985	--	11.90*	10.70
Jan 1985 - Jan 1986	--	11.20*	9.85
Jan 1986 - July 1986	--	10.15*	8.80
July 1986 - Jan 1988	--	8.75*	7.40
Jan 1988 - July 1988	--	9.35*	8.00
July 1988 - July 1990	--	9.65*	8.30

* Available only for countries that were classified in Category III
before 6 July 1982.

Source: OECD, *The Export Credit Financing Systems in OECD Member Countries*, 3rd Ed.
(Paris: OECD 1987), p.8; *OECD Press Release*, various issues.

minimum grant component of mixed credits was raised to 25 per cent in April 1985, and if a country offered a financial package with a grant element between 25 and 50 per cent, it was required to give 20 *working* days prior notification. This was a considerable increase since the limits set on previous notification requirements had been measured in *calendar* days.[41]

Participants agreed in July 1985 to broaden the definition of "tied aid" to include concessional loans with a low grant element (less than 50 per cent) and "parallel financing" which *de facto* ties together concessional financing and export credits, even if the link is not set out explicitly in a loan agreement. This group of practices, along with mixed credits, came to be known as tied aid credits, or tied aid financing. The agreement also brought into the Consensus "partially untied" aid financing, in which concessional financing is tied to the procurement of goods and services from a restricted number of countries, instead of only from the donor country.[42] Henceforth, all of these practices came under the same rules as mixed credits on minimum grant element and notification.

In March 1987, agreement was reached to increase the minimum allowable grant component in tied aid credits to 30 per cent from 15 July 1987 and to 35 per cent from 15 July 1988. The minimum grant element for least developed countries was increased to 50 per cent.[43] A further change introduced to reduce the subsidy element in tied aid packages was a new method for calculating the grant portion of these packages. Instead of using a standard 10 per cent interest rate to discount the "concessionality level", or subsidy element, a "differentiated discount rate" (DDR) was introduced. As an interim measure, from July 1987, this rate was set at the CIRR of a particular currency plus one-half the difference between the CIRR and 10 per cent. After July 1988, the differentiated rate equaled the CIRR plus one-quarter the difference between the CIRR and 10 per cent.[44]

Sectoral Agreements   The first sectoral agreement negotiated in the ECG was the Understanding on Export Credits for Ground Satellite Communications Stations, approved by the OECD Council in July 1974. In this Understanding, thirteen countries agreed to limit the duration of export credits to a maximum 8 years and to fix the minimum downpayment at 10 per cent.[45]

Table 3.2
Changes in Terms of Gentlemen's Agreement and Consensus
(excluding matrix rates)

	1976	1978	1981	1982	1983	1985	1987	1988
Notification Procedures	7 days prior notification on 5 to 8.5 year credits for Category I, and on mixed credits with under 15% grant element. Prompt notification when matching, and on mixed credits with between 15% and 25% grant element.		10 days prior notification plus 10-day delay when grant element of mixed credits less than 15%. 10 days prior notification when grant element between 15% and 20%. Prompt notification when grant element under 25%.	10 days prior notification when grant element of mixed credits between 20% and 25%.		20 working days prior notification for mixed credits with grant element between 25% and 50%.		
Mixed Credits	No restrictions when grant element over 25%.			Grant element under 20% prohibited.		Grant element under 25% prohibited. Partially untied credits brought into Consensus.	Grant element under 30% prohibited for Category II countries. Grant element under 50% prohibited for LLDCs. DDR established to calculate grant element.	Grant element under 35% prohibited for Category II countries.
Derogations	7 days prior notification plus 9-day delay for discussion.	10 days prior notification plus 10-day delay for discussion.		No derogation in interest rates or maturities.				
Other	15% minimum downpayment.	Steel plants fully integrated. Local cost covered.	Special minimum interest rate of 9.25% for currencies whose interest rate falls below floor of matrix.	Special minimum interest rate set at market rate plus 0.3% when national rate falls below floor of matrix. New definition of Categories I, II and III.	CIRRs established for currencies whose interest rate falls below ceiling of matrix. CIRR set at market rate plus 0.2%.		Interest rate subsidies for Category I countries prohibited. CIRRs established for all currencies. Common formula for calculating CIRRs.	Ground satellite stations brought into Consensus.

The Understanding, which entered into force on 1 July 1974, permitted the granting of credits on more favourable terms for the purposes of foreign aid under certain conditions.[46] In 1988, ground satellite communication stations were brought fully into the Consensus, and the Understanding lapsed.

In May 1975, two "standstill" arrangements were adopted covering aircraft and nuclear power plants. Under these arrangements ECG participants declared that they would not grant softer export credit terms in the two sectors than their current practices. The aircraft standstill covered only the duration of export credit. The ECG noted that the most generous terms then offered for aircraft leasing contracts was generally 10 years for large commercial jets, and 5 to 7 years for smaller aircraft. An exception of 12 years was made for Airbus deals.

In August 1981, the United States, the United Kingdom, France and Germany (then the only exporters of large commercial aircraft) concluded the Agreement on Export Credit Terms for Aircraft. Under this "commonline" agreement, the participants accepted to charge a 12 per cent minimum interest on export credits denominated in US dollars for wide-bodied jet aircraft.[47] In addition, the United States was to charge a one-time "front-end" 2 per cent loan commitment fee.[48] The minimum interest rate for financing in French francs was 11.5 per cent, and the rate for Deutschmarks was to reflect the market rate (9.5 per cent at the time). The maximum amount of the price of aircraft which could be financed by officially-supported export credits at the fixed minimum interest rates was 62.5 per cent when repayment of the loan was spread over the full 10 year repayment period, and 42.5 per cent when repayment of the loan was spread over the last 5 years of the financing period. The maximum repayment period for this type of aircraft was to be 10 years. The maximum official support for spare parts was 15 per cent of the aircraft price for the first five aircraft of a particular type in a fleet, and 10 per cent for any additional aircraft.[49]

In 1985, the 22 Participants agreed to set the interest rate for 10-year credits at 1.2 per cent above the prevailing rate for 10-year Treasury bonds. For 12-year credits, interest rates were to be 1.65 per cent over the reference rate. The agreement, which came into effect on 1 July 1985, also prohibited the use of mixed credits for aircraft.[50] Participants reached agreement later that year on a Sector Understanding on Export Credits for Civil Aircraft, which incorporated the commonline agreement and added guidelines for three other categories of aircraft besides large commercial jet aircraft. These were turbine-powered aircraft with between 30 and 70 seats (Category A), other turbine-powered aircraft (Category B), and other aircraft (Category C). Maximum maturities were 10 years for Category A, 7 years for Category B, and 5 years for Category C.[51]

The standstill agreement for nuclear power plants covered both maturities and downpayments, and the ECG pointed out that the most generous terms being offered at the time were 15–year credits with a minimum 10 per cent down payment.[52] In 1984, the participants concluded the Sector Understanding on Export Credits for Nuclear Power Plants. Under this agreement, interest rates for nuclear plants were to be 1 per cent above the normal Consensus rates. The maximum maturity was set at 15 years, to take into account the lengthy construction periods required for nuclear plants, and the use of mixed credits was prohibited in this sector.[53]

Monitoring of compliance with the various export credit agreements listed above was effectively provided by the Exchange of Information system, under which countries reported the terms being offered on individual transactions whenever this information was requested by other members of the system. The information was sent to the party which made the request, with a copy going to the OECD Secretariat and other interested parties (ie. those who were known to be bidding on that particular deal). The reports of the Export-Import Bank of the United States to the Congress also acted to a certain extent as a check on compliance with OECD agreements, since they included information on the export credit programmes of other countries which were compared with American programmes. The EIS was often used to verify Eximbank estimates of the terms of offers extended by other export credit agencies.[54] Exporters would also provide information about alleged violations of OECD guidelines, and this information would often result in complaints registered during regular meetings of the ECG which, if confirmed, normally resulted in a discontinuation of the offending practice. As well, the Secretariat would write to Participants to ask for explanations or clarification if it saw anything unusual in a particular deal.[55]

Table 3.3
Export Credit Agreements

1972	-Exchange of Information System -Prior Consultation Procedure
1974	-Understanding on Export Credits for Ground Satellite Communications Stations
1975	-Understanding on Local Cost -Standstills on Aircraft and Nuclear Power Plants
1976	-Consensus on Converging Export Credits Policies (Gentlemen's Agreement)
1978	-Arrangement on Guidelines for Officially Supported Export Credits (Consensus)
1981	-Agreement on Export Credit Terms for Aircraft (Commonline)
1984	-Sector Understanding on Export Credits for Nuclear Power Plants
1985	-Sector Understanding on Export Credits for Civil Aircraft

4. *Impact of OECD Agreements*

The general view of government officials and independent observers has been that the OECD guidelines in the field of export credit were respected by participating governments.[56] Complaints of violations were often based on rumour, as exporters would rationalise their loss of contracts to foreign competitors by overstating the credit terms offered by these competitors. Moreover, importers would sometimes try to obtain more favourable credit terms from one exporter by exaggerating the terms it claimed another exporter was offering.[57] Some practices denounced as violations in the end turned out to be consistent with OECD rules, and often the complainants either did not understand how the export credit agreements operated, or else they were simply dissatisfied with those rules,

57

arguing that if the letter of the agreements had not been broken then at least the spirit had.[58]

A particular source of concern was the credit terms offered by European countries to the Soviet Union, which appeared to exceed the interest rate limits of the Gentlemen's Agreement. However, the credits in question were part of credit lines extended to the USSR prior to the signing of the Agreement, and so were permitted. In any case, after the Soviet invasion of Afghanistan, the European Community decided that the terms of all officially-supported credit for the Soviet Union, even if arranged before the Agreement was concluded, should be in strict accordance with the OECD guidelines.[59]

One celebrated case where both the standstill on aircraft and the understanding on local costs appear clearly to have been violated, was the support given by the British government to finance the sale of Rolls-Royce engines for the Lockheed Tri-Star airliner. The British offer included a 15 year maturity and local cost support, even though no cash downpayment was made. After vigorously protesting, the American government, was assured "at the highest levels" that the British government would not violate these agreements again, and at the time it was admitted by American officials that this violation was an exception to the generally good record of compliance with the OECD guidelines.[60]

Another case arose when Canada offered repayment periods which exceeded the Consensus limits. The offer was labelled an "aberration" by Canadian officials, who assured that it "certainly would not happen again".[61] In late 1981 and early 1982, Canada's Export Development Corporation (EDC) exceeded OECD guidelines on maturities and interest rates in a deal to supply subway cars to the city of New York. Despite Canadian claims that it was matching a French offer, a practice permitted under the Consensus, the US government concluded that in fact the EDC had been the first to derogate from the Consensus terms.[62]

A repeated complaint of the United States was that other participants were not properly following the notification procedures. The US argued that at times information was incomplete, given too late, or not at all. Prior notification was to be given as soon as an export credit agency "intended" to derogate from the guidelines, but one American official noted that in practice notification was often not given until a firm commitment had been made in connection with the signing of a contract or letter of intent. This problem in some cases appeared to stem from the differences in interpretation of what was supposed to be notified.[63] The United States itself began to derogate from the Consensus when, in November 1980, it announced that the Eximbank would extend maturities on export credits to between 15 and 20 years, and even longer in some cases. The US was consciously exceeding the guidelines as a bargaining tactic to pressure other participants to agree to a revision of the Consensus rules.[64]

Despite these apparent lapses in compliance with the OECD guidelines, as was mentioned earlier, the overall sentiment was that participants were for the most part conforming with the rules, and that this had contributed to preventing an export credit race.[65] Indeed, there are examples of cases where participants turned down requests from highly valued clients for softer credit terms on the grounds that they did not wish to exceed the OECD guidelines. In 1978, Japan refused such a request from China, and in 1977 Britain was willing to refuse similar requests from the Soviet Union, until it discovered that the requests regarded credit extended before the signing of the Gentlemen's Agreement.[66]

5. Bargaining Positions and Outcomes

Bargaining over export credits in the OECD was an extremely complex and protracted affair. In contrast with the other three trade sectors examined in this study, where bargaining tended to be intense for a period of time and then was transformed into a simple exchange of views, throughout the period between 1974 and 1987 the Export Credits Group and the Participants Group were constantly engaged in intensive negotiations on one topic or another. Countries went into negotiating sessions with long-range goals in mind, but also usually had more immediate objectives which fell considerably short of these ideal aims. In order to facilitate the task of evaluating the outcome of bargaining on the Gentlemen's Agreement and on the Consensus, it is useful to divide the long period under consideration into a number of "rounds" which take into consideration the immediate objectives of the participants. The starting point of each of the rounds presented here is the issuing of a set of demands (usually by the United States) and the end of each round is marked by the reaching of a major decision. Negotiations for sectoral agreements can be more easily examined as a whole.

An examination of each of the six main rounds of negotiation in the general export credit field reveals that while the United States took the lead in setting the agenda, it did not consistently attain all of its objectives. In some rounds the US obtained most of what it was demanding, in others it gained only some concessions from the other parties, and in still others most of its demands were rejected. When the stated long-range objectives of the United States are examined, however, it appears that the US did obtain most of what it wanted, although it had a very difficult time doing so.[67]

Prior to 1974, the United States was decidedly opposed to setting restrictions on export credit practices, or even to bringing greater transparency to transactions. During the 1960s, European governments were particularly interested in banning export credits with repayment periods over 5 years, or at least requiring prior consultation before such long periods could be extended.[68] The US, supported by Canada, was able to prevent any OECD measures which would restrict their activities in the export credit field. While the Americans finally accepted the Exchange of Information system in 1972, they remained opposed to prior notification and refused to participate in the Prior Consultation Procedure which was set up the same year. In 1974, however, the US negotiating position changed dramatically, with the passage by Congress of amendments to the Export-Import Bank Act, which directed the Bank to "seek to minimise competition in government-supported export financing" and to "reach international agreements to reduce government-subsidised export financing".[69]

Round One of the export credit negotiations began in 1974, and ended with the Gentlemen's Agreement of June 1976. In this round the United States obtained most of its objectives.[70] The initial American proposal was for a minimum interest rate of 8 per cent, and maximum maturities of 8.5 years for relatively rich countries and 10 years for developing countries. The US later modified its proposal, calling for a 10 per cent minimum rate for relatively rich countries, and an 8 per cent rate for all other countries. The US also wanted adequate provisions to prevent subsidisation of local costs, the granting of exceptions to maturity limits for large-scale projects, and restrictions on the use of mixed credits and cost-escalation insurance.[71]

In the Gentlemen's Agreement, the US settled for an 8 per cent interest rate minimum for relatively rich countries, and somewhat lower rates for the other categories of countries. The US did obtain maximum maturities of 8.5 years for relatively rich countries and 10 years for developing countries, and it gained acceptance for the principle of higher interest rates on export credits with longer maturities. American proposals for restrictions on mixed credits and cost-escalation insurance had to be dropped, and the Agreement did not permit extensions beyond the maximum 10–year maturity limit. Finally, the US was able to get some measure of restriction on local cost financing through the May 1975 Understanding on Local Cost.

The European Community clearly yielded on maturities, since it had sought lower repayment periods for relatively rich countries and longer maturities for developing countries. The EC and Japan also appeared to give in slightly more than the US on interest rates during this round, as they had not wanted to accept any minimums above 7.5 per cent. However, the EC did succeed in blocking agreement on mixed credits and cost escalation insurance, as well as resisting American requests for longer maturities for the more developed countries.[72]

The second round of the negotiations resulted in the 1978 Consensus. The United States wanted to tighten the terms of the Gentlemen's Agreement, with a 0.5 per cent interest rate increase for intermediate countries and the ability to grant longer maturities which would carry higher interest rates. A ban on local cost financing and a restriction on the offering of cost escalation insurance and exchange risk guarantees were also sought. As well, the US wanted the use of mixed credits curtailed, and asked for a clearer definition of mixed credits as well as a means of bringing greater transparency to their use. Greater transparency was also proposed on deals which derogated from the OECD guidelines. Few of these demands were accepted by the other participants, and the Consensus only included greater transparency for mixed credits and for derogations, while local costs were eliminated for relatively rich countries alone. Thus, in the second round the EC, which had not wanted to make any major changes to the terms of the Gentlemen's Agreement, appeared to have prevailed.[73]

Round Three of the negotiations involved further American attempts to strengthen the Consensus and resulted in a number of changes adopted in October 1981. The US proposed that certain sectors left out of the Consensus, such as aircraft, nuclear power plants and ships, be brought into the agreement, with longer maturity periods permitted for the latter two. It also proposed that agricultural commodities with maturities over 3 years be included. A 0.25 to 0.75 per cent increase in matrix rates was sought, and the US proposed the adoption of different interest rate limits for different currencies, reflecting the interest rates in the home country of each currency. By May 1980 the US changed its demand to a 2 per cent across-the-board interest rate increase, as a result of soaring market rates, and in October 1981 this demand was again increased to 4 per cent. The request for a clearer definition of mixed credits was repeated, as was the call for a ban on export credit coverage for local costs. The US sought even greater transparency for mixed credits, and proposed that they be permitted only for the least developed countries. Finally, the US asked that the minimum interest rate charged on exchange risk insurance and normal guarantees on commercial and political risk be fixed by the Consensus.[74]

The changes to the Consensus finally adopted in October 1981 represented a partial success for the United States, excluding many of its proposals but including a number of compromises which were to open the way for future reforms. Matrix rates were only increased 2.25 per cent for credits over 5 years for relatively poor countries and 2.5 per cent for all other categories, changes which were closer to European proposals. The US failed to win acceptance for a differentiated, self-adjusting interest rate system, and had to settle for the annual review of interest rates proposed by the EC. However, in supporting Japan's successful request for a special rate for the yen and other low-interest rate currencies against EC opposition, the US did obtain acceptance of the *principle* of a differentiated system. The major success for the US in the October revision of the Consensus was the new procedure for notification of mixed credits, which met American demands for greater transparency and which the EC had not wanted to include.

In the fourth round of the negotiations, the United States

sought to move the Soviet Union into the matrix category for relatively rich countries, and to increase interest rates for this category by 2.25 per cent. This proposal was later changed to 1.5 per cent for relatively rich countries, 0.7 per cent for intermediate countries and no change for relatively poor countries. The US also called for a commitment by participants not to derogate from the Consensus on interest rate limits, and asked that negotiations be opened on aircraft and nuclear power plants. The US proposed that mixed credits be prohibited when the grant element of a package was less than 20 per cent.

In the changes to the Consensus adopted in July 1982, the US saw all of its proposals accepted, except for those on interest rates. The Soviet Union was classified as a relatively rich country, through a new system for defining the three categories of countries proposed by the EC. A no-derogations clause was written into the Consensus for interest rates, although as a trade-off the US had to accept a commitment not to derogate on maturity limits. Negotiations were opened on aircraft and nuclear plants, and a prohibition was placed on mixed credits with a grant element under 20 per cent. The interest rate increases for relatively rich and intermediate countries were closer to the EC proposal, but the US was able to keep interest rates for relatively poor countries unchanged, despite EC efforts to reduce it. Japan managed to get the 0.75 per cent surcharge on its market interest rates lowered to 0.3 per cent, which the US supported over EC demands for a surcharge of no lower than 0.5 per cent. However, Japan had to drop its request for a total elimination of the surcharge.[75]

Round Five involved still further efforts by the United States to revise the Consensus, and resulted in an agreement which was finalised in October 1983. The US proposed increasing downpayments by developed countries from 15 to 40 per cent, and opposed any decrease in matrix rates, despite the decline of market interest rates. The EC opposed raising the minimum downpayments and demanded a 2 per cent matrix rate reduction. Finally, the Americans requested that the minimum allowable grant element in mixed credits be raised to 40 or 50 per cent.

By 1983 most participants had come to accept the need for an automatic adjustment mechanism for interest rates, known as the Uniform Moving Matrix (UMM), so the American proposal for such a system was no longer really a bargaining position at that point.[76] Japan succeeded in getting the surcharge on low interest rate currencies reduced to 0.2 per cent. The major result of this round of negotiations was the adoption of the automatic system, but also a reduction in the matrix rates of 0.5 per cent for relatively poor countries and for 2- to 5-year credits for intermediate countries, and a reduction of 0.65 per cent for credits over 5 years for intermediate countries, which were relatively minor concessions to the EC. These reductions were to be erased within a maximum of two and a half years, however. The American proposals on minimum downpayments and on mixed credits were rejected. In sum, the fifth round was by and large a source of satisfaction for the US primarily due to the adoption of the automatic adjustment mechanism, which it had been advocating since at least 1980.

The sixth round of negotiations proved to be the longest and most arduous, and dealt primarily with the question of mixed credits. The United States pushed for greater discipline in the practice of offering mixed credits and a stronger exchange of information system for these credits. It suggested setting a deadline of 2 years for the phasing out of all mixed credits, and proposed in the meantime a ban on mixed credits containing less than a 25 per cent grant element, prohibiting mixed credits offered in the form of lines of credit, and requiring 60 days prior notification for mixed credit offers with up to a 50 per cent grant element. As well, the US called for the elimination of mixed credits for steel mills and for other sectors of oversupply. Later, the US set its sights on obtaining a ban on mixed credits with a grant element less than 50 per cent. Canada, the United Kingdom, Germany and Spain supported the idea of raising the minimum grant element, while France proposed that parallel financing and tied aid with a low grant element be placed under the Consensus rules on mixed credits.[77]

An interim agreement was reached in April 1985 which went some way towards meeting the American demands. The EC finally agreed to increase prior notification requirements to 20 working days in mixed credit offers with a grant element under 50 per cent, and to prohibit mixed credits with less than a 25 per cent grant element. Mixed credits for nuclear power plants and aircraft were prohibited altogether, although US attempts to eliminate mixed credits for steel mills were rejected by the

EC, joined by Australia. In July of the same year the agreement to include parallel financing, low-grant-element tied aid and partially-untied tied aid credits in the Consensus represented a victory for France and a concession by Japan, which had opposed the change since it brought in a number of formerly unrestricted Japanese practices.[78]

In April 1986, the EC made a further concession, proposing that the minimum allowable grant element in mixed credits be raised to 30 per cent for a one-year period and thereafter to 35 per cent, and that for the least developed countries it be raised to 50 per cent. The EC also proposed a ban on tied aid financing for the richest developing countries. A condition of this proposal package was that a new system for calculating the grant element in mixed credits be adopted to replace the standard 10 per cent discount rate. This proposal was generally acceptable to the US and Canada, although they believed that the minimum grant element should be increased to at least 40 per cent. However, the US became more supportive of the proposal when it realised that in many cases the cost of mixed credit packages would be the same using the new discount rate as would a 50 per cent minimum grant element using the old 10 per cent discount factor.[79]

Agreement was blocked by Japan, however, since the proposed differential discount rate (DDR) would cost the Japanese more to offer the same level of mixed credits. A compromise formula was worked out between the commercial DDR and the 10 per cent rate, and the European proposal was accepted in March 1987.[80] In addition, the European proposal to end interest rate subsidies for relatively rich countries was accepted by the US. The United States emerged from round six generally satisfied with the new rules on mixed credit practices, while the EC appeared to have moved the farthest from its original position on this issue.

In the aircraft sector, the United States attained most of its objectives, although it took about ten years of negotiations to get an agreement with which it was satisfied. The US tried without success to get other ECG participants to negotiate an agreement during the early 1970s. In May 1975 it proposed a "standstill" agreement which was accepted by the other participants as an alternative to a stricter set of guidelines. US attempts to obtain greater discipline were rebuffed in 1978 and 1979, and it was not until the EC compromised in August 1981 that it finally saw the adoption of the "commonline" agreement on wide-bodied jet aircraft. In order to obtain this agreement, however, the US had to drop its demands for maturities over 10 years.

In November 1981 the Americans again attempted to lengthen maturities in the commonline, as well as to increase interest rates by 3 to 4 per cent for US dollar financing, and to bring general aviation aircraft into the agreement. In the 1982 discussions, the US further proposed that government support for commercial aircraft export financing be limited to guarantees of private credits rather than direct loans. It also suggested a classification of aircraft according to propulsion type, empty weight and seat capacity. The US continued to be dissatisfied with the commonline and proposed a system of self-adjusting interest rates (ie: CIRRs) reflecting changes in market rates.[81] The EC successfully resisted US demands, countering with a proposal to adopt a single interest rate for wide-bodied aircraft and differentiated interest rates, depending on the wealth of the recipient countries, for all other types of aircraft.[82] The Europeans were reluctant to accept longer maximum maturities because of their more limited access to long-term funds with maturities of over ten years.[83]

In 1985 the US proposed the raising of interest rates for French franc financing, and repeated its demands for making the interest rate floor vary with market rate changes, and for broader coverage of the commonline to include commuter and other smaller commercial aircraft. The US preferred to see an end to all officially-supported export credits on these smaller aircraft, but was willing to settle for a prohibition on subsidised export credits.[84] In the 1985 revision of the commonline agreement, maturities were lengthened to 12 years with correspondingly higher interest rates, and an automatic interest rate adjustment system was set up. Finally, in 1986 the US succeeded in getting the Sector Understanding adopted, bringing in smaller aircraft and helicopters which the French had been opposed to including. Interest rate minimums for these aircraft were to be adjusted automatically in line with fluctuations in market interest rates. However, US attempts to limit aircraft export financing to guarantees and to eliminate export credits on smaller aircraft were not successful.

The United States also enjoyed a fair measure of success in negotiations on nuclear power plants. In 1979 the US proposed a minimum interest rate limit of 8.5 per cent, a 15 per cent minimum downpayment, and maturities of 10 years for relatively rich countries, 12 years for intermediate countries and 15 years for relatively poor countries. The US was trying to bring interest rates as close as possible to market rates. The EC responded by proposing shorter maturities and lower interest rates than the US proposals. In July 1984 the US succeeded in getting 15 year maturities for all categories of countries, and in raising interest rates by one per cent above the matrix rates in the Consensus. In February 1985, the US sought to eliminate local cost financing for nuclear power plants, but was not able to get this proposal adopted.[85]

In terms of its general long-range negotiating objectives, the United States also appears to have been largely successful. The mandate given to the Administration by Congress in 1974 called on the President to negotiate a reduction of government-subsidised export financing and of export credit competition. The US most certainly did obtain a reduction of subsidies, although competition among export credit agencies continued for more than a decade.[86] The long-range objective set by the Carter Administration in 1979, and then adopted by the Reagan Administration, was the *elimination* of subsidies for export credits, a goal which by the end of the 1980s had not been realised, and which many feel may never be fully attained.[87] Under the Reagan Administration, the long range goal of eliminating mixed credits was abandoned in 1984 and replaced with the more immediate objective of bringing "discipline" to the use of mixed credits which, as has been seen, was attained to a large degree.[88]

In summary, the United States did succeed in reducing the subsidisation of export credits and in bringing Consensus rates closer to market interest rates. It was much less successful in getting longer maximum repayment terms, and although it did get much of what it wanted in the mixed credits field, it took a very long time to do so. What is clear is that the US did not easily impose its will on other countries. It failed to obtain a number of its short-run goals, had to compromise on many others, sometimes altered its objectives, and even where certain objectives were attained, this was only after long and difficult negotiations. The questions to be asked, then, are why the United States experienced so much difficulty in the export credit negotiations, and when it got its way, how it did so.

6. *Explaining OECD Agreements and their Impact*

(a) Overall Capabilities

The export credits issue was discussed at five of the economic summit meetings between 1975 and 1981, although it did not figure prominently in these meetings. During negotiations for the Gentlemen's Agreement and for the Consensus, summit communiqués contained brief statements of support for a prompt conclusion of the talks. There is no record of the United States linking progress in the export credits field with military or economic issues outside the trade area in summits prior to 1982. In 1981, the US mounted a diplomatic offensive, using bilateral contacts and other multilateral forums in an attempt to reach a breakthrough in the OECD negotiations. The issue was brought up in numerous bilateral meetings at the Ministerial level, as well as at the Ottawa summit. However, the US was not satisfied with the outcome of this effort.[89]

At the Versailles summit of June 1982 export credits became a major point of contention between the US and the four European participants. The Reagan Administration had adopted a hard-line policy in its relations with the Soviet Union in the wake of the imposition of martial law in Poland, and was trying to convince its major trading partners to act accordingly. In particular, the US was critical of what it considered to be excessively favourable credit terms offered to the Soviets by Western European governments.[90]

The US was not particularly successful in pressuring the EC on export credits at the June summit, despite the high priority it gave to the issue. The Reagan Administration proposed that the Soviet bloc countries be required to pay market rates for export credits and that a ceiling be placed on the total volume of credits extended to these countries, but failed to persuade the other summit participants to accept these measures.[91] The United States did not even obtain an agreement on precise increases of interest rates for credits extended to the Soviet

Union, and the best that it could obtain was a rather vaguely worded undertaking to,

> . . . handle cautiously financial relations with the USSR and other Eastern European countries in such a way as to ensure that they are conducted on a sound economic basis, including also the need for commercial prudence in limiting export credits.[92]

There were reports that Secretary of State Alexander Haig had urged the President to link US flexibility on other East-West issues (perhaps even a lifting of the American pipeline sanctions) and on global negotiations over North-South issues, to the acceptance by summit participants of US proposals on export credits and high-technology transfer. It was also suggested by American officials that US concessions on intervention in foreign exchange markets, which was a major concern of France, might be possible if progress were made on the export credits issue. At the end of the meeting only the proposal to hold "global negotiations" on North-South issues, which was strongly supported by France and Canada, and the export credits issue remained on the table. President Mitterand finally accepted the watered down text on export credits and the US agreed to include a statement of support for global negotiations.[93]

US Treasury Secretary Donald Regan said at the end of the summit that the United States was "more than satisfied", and that it had "accomplished what we set out to do" on export credits. However, American officials were disappointed when French President Mitterand later announced that the summit agreement left each country "sovereignly responsible for deciding what is prudent" in trade with the Soviet Union.[94]

The Reagan Administration demonstrated its displeasure with what it perceived as the lack of co-operation from the Europeans by extending the pipeline embargo to American subsidiaries in other countries two weeks after the summit.[95] However, this move did not appear to have influenced significantly the export credit negotiations going on in the OECD. The movement of the USSR into Category I had been agreed on within the EC in early February 1982, primarily for economic reasons, and had been accepted by Japan in May of the same year, well before the summit meeting and the embargo extension.[96] On the matrix rates, the United States had originally wanted a 2.25 per cent increase on Category I credits, and in May lowered this demand to 1.5 per cent. A few days before the US announced the extension of the pipeline embargo the EC made a counterproposal of a one per cent increase for Category I countries. On June 30, the EC accepted a compromise proposal put forward by the Swedish chairman of the Participants Group, increasing the matrix rate for Category I to 1.15 per cent, some-what closer to the EC position.[97]

It was not until November 1982 that the pipeline sanctions were lifted, indicating that the Reagan Administration did not consider the July 1982 agreement to be adequate and/or had not really extended the embargo primarily because of the export credits issue.[98] In fact, it appears that the sanctions were lifted largely because they were seen as divisive and ineffective, in view of the strong and unified European resistance to them. Pressure from Congress and the affected US business interests to lift the embargo were also important factors.[99] After this brief interlude, the East-West issue ceased to figure prominently in export credit negotiations, and the central issue became once more the competitive subsidisation of trade.

The possibility of linkage was again raised in 1985, when a member of Congress suggested that the United States use American military equipment contracts as leverage in export credit negotiations with the EC. The Director of the Office of Trade Finance in the Treasury Department, John D. Lange, replied that he was not sure the US wanted to use all the options at its disposal.[100] The distribution of overall capabilities, then, did not appear to have determined either the outcome of export credit negotiations or the impact of export credit agree-ments, since there was no discernable attempt to enforce those agreements using non-trade power resources.

(b) International Trade Structure

An interesting aspect of the export credit negotiations con-ducted in the OECD was that the United States was reluctant to link the issue of export credits to other trade issues in order to attain its bargaining objectives or to enforce compliance with OECD agreements. A vague warning was issued by Robert A. Cornell, the American Deputy Assistant Secretary of the

Treasury, in July 1981, when he said that countries resisting changes to the Consensus, "must come to realise that the costs of continuing not to agree with the U.S. position on subsidies becomes very great, because they slop over into other issues of trade policy that are of great concern to all".[101] However, specific cases of such linkage were not evident, and as has been seen, the US failed to attain most of its objectives in the October 1981 agreement. Cornell had been simultaneously responsible for the export credit negotiations and the Tokyo Round negotiations during the 1970s, and although he was in a position to propose linkages between the two sets of talks, he apparently avoided doing so.[102]

The US and the EC raised the issue of Japan's trade and current account surpluses to put pressure on Japanese negotiators in 1986, although issue specific pressure was also exerted by the US. This implicit linkage seems to have been at least partly responsible for the eventual concession made by Japan on the new system of calculating the discount rate in mixed credit packages, since Japan was quite sensitive to complaints about these growing surpluses.[103]

(c) Issue Structure

Within the export credits field, there were two principal ways in which power resources were mobilised in negotiations: the offering of longer repayment periods, and the subsidisation of interest rates and of mixed credit packages. In one of these categories the United States proved to be in an advantageous position, while in the other its issue-specific capabilities were more constrained.

Because of the greater availability of long-term financing in North American capital markets compared with European markets, the United States and Canada had the ability to extend long-term credits beyond the ten-year limit imposed by the Consensus. The US used this capability in an attempt to pressure countries to revise the agreement. Initially, Eximbank chairman John Moore was sceptical about the effectiveness of such a strategy, telling a House committee that competitors would probably match those longer maturities and continue to subsidise interest rates.[104] Nevertheless, in May 1980, Assistant Secretary for International Affairs in the Treasury Department,

C. Fred Bergsten, said that the US was considering extending maturities on export credits, matching mixed credit offers, and enlarging the financial guarantees programme of Eximbank.[105]

Chairman Moore changed his opinion about the potential effectiveness of extending maturities in the spring of 1980, and claimed that the threat of doing so would be a strong one because it would hurt European exporters.[106] The following month, Bergsten again warned France and other Consensus Participants that if progress was not made in the OECD to deal with credit subsidisation, then the US would "take unilateral action", including derogating from the Consensus on maturities.[107] In November Bergsten said that repayment periods on Eximbank loans could be extended to 15 to 20 years or even longer in some cases on a selective basis, particularly in competition with French offers, since the US had identified France as the main culprit in holding up an agreement to revise the Consensus, although he admitted that the impact of this measure would be reduced by the need to charge higher interest rates on these loans.[108]

After the failure of Participants to meet US demands in the December 1980 meeting, the measures outlined by Bergsten were implemented, and Canada joined the US in derogating from the Consensus on maturities. American negotiators seemed to think that this action was an effective one, and John Lange of the Treasury Department later told a Congressional panel that while matching interest rate subsidies did not appear to advance US negotiating efforts, extending repayment terms "has caused our competitors more anguish than anything else we do . . ."[109] It appears, however, that the effectiveness of this strategy was overplayed by American officials. The US gave up this bargaining chip when it agreed in July 1982 not to derogate from the Consensus on maturities. Yet, the two agreements reached between the initiation and the termination of the extended maturities programme did not go very far in meeting American demands. The only significant achievements for the United States in 1982 were greater transparency for mixed credits and a minimum 20 per cent grant component in mixed credit packages.

A much more important agreement for the US, on an automatic interest rate adjustment system and on CIRRs for low interest rate currencies, was reached more than a year after the

United States had abandoned its extended maturities option, and a much higher grant minimum in mixed credits was not achieved until five years later. The exaggerated credit given to the practice of offering very long maturities helped the Reagan Administration relieve pressure from the Congress at a time when the Administration was trying to cut back the Export-Import Bank's budget. It gave the appearance of providing an effective countermeasure to the subsidy practices of other countries at a fairly low cost.

The threat to lengthen maturities was also used by the United States in negotiations on export credits for aircraft. In May 1979, Eximbank vice-chairman, H.K. Allen, announced that the US was preparing to extend its usual 10–year maximum repayment period on Boeing deals in order to match the 12–year periods being offered by France and West Germany for potential buyers of the Airbus A-300.[110] In mid-1982 the US threatened to unilaterally extend repayment terms on aircraft to 15 years if the Airbus countries refused to revise the commonline agreement.[111] These threats did not appear to be immediately effective, since eventual changes to the existing guidelines were not accepted until two to three years after the threats were made.

The ability of countries to subsidise export credits is partly determined by the flexibility and mandate of national export credit agencies, but also reflects the fiscal situation in each country, and the government's attitude towards state intervention in the economy in general.[112] Since this latter factor is a function of values and definition of self-interest, it will be considered below in another section of this chapter. The subsidisation of export credits in Europe and Japan took the form of entitlement programmes, where sufficient resources were provided to support all applicants fitting certain broad standards. In the United States applicants had to demonstrate that they needed government support in order to win a contract on a case-by-case basis. Hence, European and Japanese export credit systems were much more flexible, and subsidisation a much more acceptable practice, than was the case of their North American counterparts. These differences prompted one Eximbank president to observe:

In this area, countries such as France and Japan are playing in a totally different league than the United States . . .

73

True competitiveness of the U.S. export credit system with that of France and/or Japan would require a substantive change in U.S. political/economic thinking.[113]

Precise comparative figures of export credit subsidies are not available due to the confidentiality of such data in many countries, but also because of national differences in reporting procedures and in export credit systems. However, fairly reliable estimates have been made by the OECD and other sources which give an indication of the extent of subsidisation in the major exporting nations. According to an OECD report, of the $5.5 billion in export credit subsidies provided by OECD countries in 1979, $2.3 billion was accounted for by France, $1 billion by the United Kingdom, $566 million by Japan, $425 million by Italy, $315 million by the United States, and $215 by Germany.[114] France continued to dominate other countries in export credit subsidisation throughout the 1980s, while the officially-supported export credit programmes of the United States were much more limited than most of its major trading partners. Nevertheless, at various times the US attempted to increase its ability to subsidise interest rates and mixed credits over the course of the export credit negotiations.

In 1978, in order to convince other Participants to tighten the Consensus, the United States warned that it could take retaliatory action, in particular the matching of interest rate subsidies offered by foreign competitors. The Congress passed legislation in 1978 enabling Eximbank to undertake this matching, but the resources at its disposal were still inferior to those of other Participants.[115] By late 1978 the US was matching competing financial packages on a case-by-case basis, offering interest rates as low as 4 or 5 per cent. After six months of this new matching practice, Eximbank was offering fifty per cent of its loans below its standard scale of interest rates, which were above the minimum rates set by the Consensus. However, the US did not move beyond the case-by-case matching approach, because of the fear of Treasury officials that an all-out attack on foreign competitors would result in a major drain on revenues, and their belief that a selective approach could be effective.[116]

In 1979 the Carter Administration raised the ceiling on Eximbank's total loans and guarantees from $25 billion to $40 billion over the next five years. The Administration also increased the direct lending authority for Eximbank from \$3.6 billion to \$4.1 billion. However, the ability of Eximbank to subsidise interest rates remained limited, since these subsidies had to be paid out of the Bank's own capital and reserves.[117] When the Reagan Administration took up office in 1981, a reduction of the Eximbank loan authority was announced, from \$5.5 billion in fiscal year 1981 to \$4.4 billion in 1982, with further annual reductions planned for the following three years. The Congress later cut back the 1982 budget even further, to \$3.5 billion.[118] As well, a moratorium was imposed on all new loan commitments by Eximbank, although this was lifted several months later.[119] The US Trade Representative William Brock commented at the time that,

> . . . the first step is in the negotiating area, and I think that perhaps we have limited tools with which to deal. We frankly do not have much leverage, because we have put a ceiling on Eximbank, and that would be one very nice negotiating tool if we were not under such severe budgetary constraints.[120]

In 1981, a bill was introduced in Congress which would establish a \$1 billion fund giving interest rate support for exports up to a total value of \$7 billion. While the Reagan Administration welcomed the bill as a useful bargaining tool, it felt that its immediate passage would set a dangerous precedent for other sectors seeking subsidies, and that the cost involved would end Eximbank's policy of financial self-sufficiency.[121] Nevertheless, in October 1982, Eximbank introduced a new matching programme providing financing for medium-term export sales up to \$5 million that were facing subsidised foreign competition.[122] However, given the relatively limited financial resources of Eximbank, the threat and use of interest rate subsidies were not very credible.[123]

The US began threatening to offer its own mixed credit packages in mid-1980, in order to pressure other OECD countries to curtail this practice.[124] In 1982, the Agency for International Development (AID) decided to finance mixed credits on a selective basis in order to match foreign mixed credit offers for priority development projects. In November 1983, the Trade and Development Enhancement Act created a mixed credit matching programme, co-ordinated by AID and Eximbank, to assist negotiations for a restriction on the use of mixed credits. However, this programme was constrained by its cost to Eximbank, which wanted to maintain its commercial standing, and by the reluctance of AID to see a diversion of development assistance funding to promote US exports. As well, the need for co-ordination between these two agencies slowed down the American response to foreign mixed credit offers.[125]

In November 1984, the Deputy-Secretary of the Treasury, Tim McNamar warned, "I would hope we would not get into a mixed credits war. If that happens, the U.S. has the deepest pocket in the world. We'll match everybody". He mentioned in particular the possibility of the use of agricultural mixed credits by the US.[126] At the same time, Eximbank vice-president John Bohn said that if no progress were made at the December OECD meeting, Congress would establish a $300 million mixed credit "war chest", intended to be aggressive and pre-emptive, not simply for matching.[127] In March 1985, Assistant Treasury Secretary for International Affairs, David Mulford, warned that Congress was in the process of creating a warchest and that if the mixed credits issue were not resolved there would be an escalation of the issue to the ministerial level.[128] Eximbank chairman William Draper was less optimistic about the effectiveness of an American mixed credits programme, when he told a Senate subcommittee,

> Even if we had a big barrel of money for mixed credits, I don't think it would change the attitude of the various countries a bit because I think right now France, England, Germany and Japan are all competing in this area of mixed credit. When there's a mixed credit, they can all match and they do . . . I think there are so many in that particular game that our muscle won't go that far.[129]

By the autumn of 1985, however, the Reagan Administration reversed its opposition to the creation of a mixed credits war chest. Up to this point the US was only matching mixed credit offers of other countries, and of the eleven matching offers that Eximbank had made, only three had been accepted. This matching of mixed credits was judged by John Lange to be insufficient in strengthening the American negotiating position.[130] In October 1985, Eximbank announced plans to initiate $280 million in mixed credit offers for six deals in the fields of transport, power and computers, and two further offers were made in early 1986. These offers were targeted against countries which were resisting US attempts in the OECD to raise the minimum aid component in mixed credits to 50 per cent, namely France, Italy and Belgium. In November 1985, Eximbank chairman William Draper said that the US would drop its aggressive bidding if France and other Participants agreed to US proposals. He also said that the US did not expect to win all the contracts for which it had made bids, but that even if it did not win the contracts, the US had made it more expensive for the French to win.[131] In October 1986, the $300 million warchest was authorised by Congress, and by the following May, the US had made 13 mixed credit offers, winning 5 of them.

It has been argued that the war chest was responsible for the shift in the European bargaining position, a conclusion based largely on the temporal sequence of events. This conclusion has been cited as evidence supporting the hegemonic stability theory in explaining bargaining outcomes:

> Only the extension of long-term credits, and later a special congressional allocation for a "war chest", created a credible U.S. threat. At this point, France capitulated.[132]

However, a closer examination of the events suggests that this conclusion is incorrect. The initial French reaction to the American offensive was to declare that it would match any new concessionary finance offered by the US if this was necessary to win contracts in developing countries. While admitting that the French government would find it difficult to match all of the grant element in US offers, given its own budgetary problems, the French Minister of Industry and External Trade, Edith Cresson, noted that there were other means of promoting exports besides mixed credits.[133] She dismissed the US move as "gesticulatory rather than operational".[134]

The Assistant Director of the Direction des Relations Economiques Extérieures (DREE), Jacques Joutard, expressed a similar lack of concern about the aggressive stance of the United States, saying that "If the Americans want to use such means, we think it is a good idea".[135] After the Eximbank announcement, France continued to block attempts to give the EC Commission a negotiating mandate, and the OECD meetings in November 1985, January 1986 and March 1986 failed to make any progress on the mixed credits issue.[136] Moreover, the size of the war chest was much smaller than the one billion dollar fund originally requested by Congress, and a number of American exporters complained that it was too small to be effective.[137] Rather than simply yielding to American power, the shift in the EC position seemed to be more the result of a change in the interest structure of France, a point which will be pursued later in this chapter.

The target of the warchest shifted from France to Japan in late 1986 in response to the Japanese blocking of a mixed credit agreement, after the EC had finally made a proposal acceptable to the US. Eximbank began negotiating a $100 million concessionary line of credit with Indonesia, and planned to work out a similar credit line for Thailand, two traditional recipients of Japanese export financing. There were also suggestions that Eximbank would make offers to India and China if no agreement were reached within the OECD.[138] Against Japan, the war chest may have been more effective, although as noted earlier US and EC grumbling over Japan's trade surplus and the assurance made to Japan that the differentiated discount rate would not be used in the DAC were probably also important influences.

The US also raised the export credits issue in the GATT Committee on Subsidies and Countervailing Measures in order to put pressure on those countries opposing American proposals in the OECD. It suggested that the standstills on aircraft and nuclear power plants were not exempted by the Subsidies Code as was the Consensus, and that the US could consequently use its trade laws to retaliate against practices which were covered by the standstills.[139] However, this interpretation of the Subsidies Code was not shared by a number of other participants in the Subsidies Committee, and the matter was dropped after 1982.[140]

Issue-specific power resources *were* significant in ensuring compliance with the OECD guidelines. The effectiveness of these guidelines was ensured in part through the process of self-help, since in the event of any derogation, other participants were entitled to match the terms offered by the offending party, thus eliminating any competitive advantage from such departures from the rules.[141] Yet the *distribution* of resources was not always important in this process, since the marginal

cost of matching an offer was rarely prohibitive for most participants, and so the ability to match was more or less evenly
distributed. Matching was conducted on a fairly regular basis,
not always due to derogations by Consensus participants but
because of terms offered by non-participating countries which
exceeded the OECD guidelines, in which case matching by
participants was permitted.

(d) Influence of Institutions

The OECD itself appeared to play a fairly modest role in exert-
ing influence over bargaining outcomes and over state
compliance with export credit agreements. The Organisation
provided a convenient forum for export credit negotiations,
since it included the major extenders of export credits while
excluding the major recipients. It was primarily for this reason
that the issue was negotiated in the OECD instead of the GATT,
where developing countries and centrally-planned economies
could have been expected to resist attempts to limit export credit
subsidisation.

The decision-making procedure of the OECD based on the
unanimity rule appeared to have had an important influence
on at least one bargaining outcome. The ability of the largest
parties to veto agreements they opposed made reaching an
agreement much more difficult than blocking one. The United
States had failed to get an agreement on an automatic system for
setting matrix interest rates between 1978 and 1983, primarily
because of the ability of the EC to veto the adoption of this
proposal. As long as market interest rates remained well above
the matrix rates, EC countries could continue to subsidise their
export credits without breaking the Consensus rules, so the EC
blocked American proposals for an automatic system and for
significantly higher matrix rates. The tables turned, however,
in 1982, when market interest rates fell through the matrix
ceiling. It was now the EC that was most interested in changing
the status quo, and the US used its veto power to block any
reduction in matrix rates until the automatic system was
adopted (See Chart 3.3).

While it was not uncommon for a single country to *block* an
agreement, it was of course vital for a country *proposing* an
agreement to have at least some initial support in order to have

Chart 3.3
SDR-Weighted Average Interest Rate and OECD Minimum Matrix
Rate

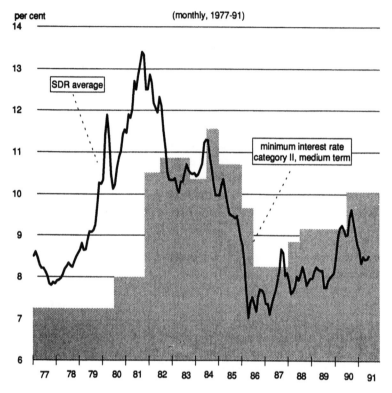

Source: John E. Ray, "Recent Changes in The OECD 'Consensus' on Export Credits",
Mimeograph.

any chance of keeping that proposal alive. The US could usually
count on support from Canada, the UK and often the Nordic
countries, and would then lobby other members who shared
similar interests on the issue at hand. However, when no such
support was forthcoming, even the US could not carry on alone.
For example, when it first demanded a 50 per cent minimum
grant limit on mixed credits, the US received virtually no support for the proposal, and American delegates soon retreated,
stating that the 50 per cent figure was negotiable and downplay-
ing the importance of mixed credits.[142]

The Secretariat proved influential at times, primarily by proposing compromise solutions when negotiations were dead-locked. In 1979 and 1980, during intensive negotiations on a system for regulating the interest rates offered in export credit bids, the Participants asked the Secretariat to carry out a study of the relationship between inflation rates, exchange rates and interest rates. These studies examined the possibility of chang-ing the existing system of fixed interest rates prescribed by the OECD, and finally set out three alternative systems: the Uni-form Moving Matrix, a Differentiated Rate System, and a combi-nation of the two.[143] Commenting on the Secretariat report directed by ECG chairman Axel Wallen, Eximbank chairman John Moore said: "A first-class technical paper was developed over the course of a year. It was never questioned, because of its excellent grouping and presentation of the issues. Accord-ingly, the Wallen report succeeded in framing the issues although not in resolving them".[144]

In 1985, the Secretariat was also instructed by the Participants to conduct a study on how to strengthen the transparency of mixed credit practices, with a view to establishing greater discipline in their use by member countries. This study contri-buted to the new rules on notification adopted that year.[145] Finally, the Secretariat played an important role in facilitating the 1987 agreement on mixed credits. By proposing an alterna-tive to the standard 10 per cent interest rate used to discount the subsidy element in mixed credit packages, the Secretariat was able to attract the French to the agreement, since the DDR would reduce the cost of mixed credits for France.[146]

The fact that the export credit negotiations were conducted in the permanent forums of the Participants Group and the ECG ensured that talks did not break down completely when conflicts were most intense. The assurance that there would always be another meeting in a few months time, helped keep the discussions going until conditions were right for an agree-ment. In an *ad hoc* forum, a stalemate could have brought dis-cussions to an end, and starting them up again, while not out of the question, would have entailed additional time and effort.

Elite socialisation on the export credits issue in the OECD was hindered by the fact that delegates were drawn from so many different government agencies, and in the case of the EC, different levels of government. For example, the US delegation usually included representatives from Eximbank, Treasury,

Commerce and sometimes from State and the Office of the United States Trade Representative (USTR).[147] Due to the sheer number of participants, the diversity of their backgrounds and the departments they represented, it was unlikely that all would be socialised in the same way and to the same extent. A similar situation existed for EC member states who were represented both by national delegations and by EC Commission officials. Also, as there were no major intra-governmental divisions on the issue of export credits in most participating countries, trans-governmental coalition building was not considered necessary by any of the delegates.

The influence of the broader international trade regime on the export credit negotiations does not seem to have been particularly strong. The norm of multilateralism was followed, but largely because there was no realistic alternative to a multilateral approach to the problem of competitive export subsidisation. The non-discrimination norm was not upheld when different subsidy limits were set for different groups of recipient countries, depending on their level of development, although this could be considered consistent with the "development" norm identified by some observers as constituting part of the GATT regime.[148] Finally, the liberalisation norm was not strongly supported by the majority of OECD member countries in the export credit discussions. The United States, Canada, Germany and Japan were the strongest and most consistent supporters of the effort to eliminate export credit subsidies. Support for liberalising export credit practices was not always shared by many within the Community, particularly not by France, and it was only budget pressure which somewhat weakened resistance to the liberalisation norm.

There did not appear to be any serious fear in the export credit negotiations that a failure to reach agreement would pose a threat to the broader international trade regime. The export credits issue was essentially one aspect of the larger subsidies issue, on which international rules and norms were relatively underdeveloped. Hence, any agreements reached on export credits, or any failure to reach such agreements, would not seriously weaken regime rules on subsidies, since such rules and norms were already weak as it was.

The export credits regime itself did appear to have played an instrumental role in ensuring state *compliance* with the guidelines. As mentioned in the previous section, issue-specific resources for matching derogations were an important factor behind the high degree of respect for the agreements, but this matching would have been extremely difficult without the notification procedures of the export credit regime. One common danger was that rumours (often intentionally spread by potential buyers) about the terms of offers could be incorrect, leading to the matching of offers which had never in fact been made, and thereby undermining confidence in other participants and ultimately, in the agreement itself. By providing a mechanism for verifying such rumours, the transparency provisions of the regime prevented the erosion of confidence and ensured that matching would be restricted to actual cases of derogation.[149]

As the export credits regime was strengthened over the period examined, the value placed on it by the participants appeared to increase. The United States suggested that it could not guarantee its continued adherence to the Gentlemen's Agreement unless its terms were tightened in December 1977, but thereafter made no further threats to fully abandon the regime.[150] It was recognised that the US would be harmed as much as anyone by the absence of constraint on export credit practices, and the threat to abandon the guidelines was not pursued. When President Carter broke off negotiations on export credits in 1979, he ruled out withdrawing from the Consensus. In a letter to the Congress, he said that "the United States will continue to adhere to the International Arrangement on Export Credits because it remains a useful, if limited, instrument of international discipline in the provision of officially supported export credits.[151] On another occasion, in mid-1984, John Bohn, then vice-chairman of Eximbank, said that unless Participants accepted American proposals to limit mixed credit practices the US was "ready to go it alone". US government officials were quick to label this threat an "exaggeration", and nothing more was said about the matter.[152]

Participants in the regime stopped placing deadlines on negotiations after a time, perhaps because of the fear that a party might withdraw from the agreement after its deadline had been exceeded in order to save face.[153] By the late 1980s, the general opinion was that no participant would be willing to risk the collapse of the Consensus or other export credit agreements.[154] As a result, the negotiations were not seriously influenced by any concerns about the erosion or termination of the export credits regime. At issue in most of these negotiations was whether and how much the rules should be strengthened, and those who had an interest in strengthening them certainly had no interest in jeopardising the rules that already existed. Comparing the relative value of the regime to various participants would be pointless, since none seriously contemplated abandoning it.

The regime never eroded over this period because, as has been seen, violations of rules were relatively minor and sporadic, while the restrictiveness of the regime continued to grow over the years. The major source of tension was over practices which were left out of the rules, rather than lack of respect for the rules themselves. There were fears expressed at various times about the possible outbreak of an export credits war if action were not taken to strengthen the regime. Such a war would involve competitive subsidisation of export credits in areas not covered by the regime, however, rather than a wholesale abandoning of the regime itself.[155]

(e) Unit-level Variables

Domestic Group Opposition Opposition from domestic groups did not appear to have played a role in weakening the bargaining position of the US, or of any other OECD member countries in export credit negotiations. American export industries were strong supporters of US negotiating objectives and, in fact, were often a source of the American delegation's proposals. For example, in 1975 the US government was under strong pressure from American industries to do something about the cost escalation insurance programmes being offered by foreign governments. Also, a survey conducted by the National Association of Manufacturers in 1977 indicated that US exporters wanted coverage of the Gentlemen's Agreement to be broadened to include restrictions on mixed credits, local costs, inflation and exchange rate insurance schemes, the financing of pre-shipment costs, and foreign content restrictions.[156] While some of these demands were not pursued by American negotiators, most of them did find their way onto the US negotiating agenda. The relationship became mutually reinforcing when the Reagan

Administration consciously worked to build domestic support for the American negotiating position in the OECD by convening meetings between several government departments and private industry.[157]

American trade unions were not always strong supporters of these attempts to assist the export of capital goods in the 1970s, since they feared that such exports would eventually threaten American jobs. However, by the 1980s US labour was working with industry to try to strengthen the Consensus. For example, in the early 1980s the Labor-Industry Coalition for International Trade (LICIT) actively sought a more aggressive US negotiating position, seeking to strengthen the Export-Import Bank and submitting a Section 301 complaint to the USTR, suggesting that the opposition of the French to reforming the Consensus constituted a restriction of US commerce.[158]

Governmental Cohesion   The American bargaining position did not seem to have been seriously weakened by any major divisions within the Executive branch or between the branches of government. After 1974 there was almost unanimous support for the objective of reducing export credit subsidisation from the two political parties both in Congress and in successive Administrations. The main differences that arose were over the amount of financial resources that should be devoted to government-supported export credits.

Under the Nixon and Ford Administrations, Eximbank tightened its financial practices by raising interest rates and reducing the scale of its lending. During the Carter Administration, Eximbank took on a more activist role, increasing credits and lending at interest rates below commercial rates. When the Reagan Administration came into office, it once again tightened Eximbank's budget, although it later requested additional funding from Congress for new programmes intended to target its main opponents in the OECD negotiations.[159] The financial restraint in export credits exercised by the Republican Administrations did seem to be inconsistent with their desire to compel other countries to alter their policies. However, this inconsistency stemmed from their own aversion to government involvement in export financing and from the desire of these Administrations to reduce government spending, rather than from any divisions between governmental bodies.

On the European side, despite the difficulty the EC Commission often experienced in obtaining a negotiating mandate, within the OECD export credits negotiations the EC acted with remarkable unity, sticking to proposals which were sometimes opposed by most EC members, with France usually leading the minority position. Indeed, it was this solidarity which made it difficult for the US to isolate France and other EC countries opposing American demands. In 1980, the US attempted to separate France from its EC partners by singling out the French as the main obstacle to progress in the negotiations and focusing its retaliatory measures on France rather than the EC as a whole, even though the latter was obliged to adopt the French bargaining position. Despite this American tactic, the EC remained united within the Participants Group and continued to defend the position insisted upon by France.[160]

Progress in negotiations was often delayed because the EC could not agree on a common position, a situation which tended to suit those countries opposed to any change in the OECD export credit rules.[161] In 1982, the EC was seen as engaging in diplomatic brinkmanship after the US said that it would not further negotiate the first Wallen compromise proposal. The EC made a counter proposal one day before the expiry of the Consensus, banking on the assumption that the US and Japan would not want to jeopardise the Consensus by rejecting the EC proposal. Even when the other parties had accepted the second Wallen compromise, the EC went over the newly extended deadline before it finally accepted the proposal, to which it attached two conditions. The US had ruled out any further extension of the Consensus deadline, but did not make an issue of the EC exceeding it, and even accepted one of the conditions.

The EC on this and on other occasions took advantage of its difficulties in establishing a common bargaining position in order to stretch out the decision-making process in the OECD, a practice which often appeared to exhaust other negotiators and to heighten their anxiety over the future of the Consensus.[162] However, this situation also caused a certain amount of strain within the EC, and one reason the EC finally accepted the US proposal for an automatic interest rate adjustment mechanism in 1983 was the desire to avoid further divisions within the EC over interest rate proposals.[163]

Preference Intensity The strength of the US government's commitment to its preferences on the export credits issue appeared to be rather uneven during the 1970s and 1980s. There was little inclination to link the issue even to other trade issues, and after the brief extension of maturities between 1980 and 1982, the only issue-specific resource to be mobilised was a "war chest" that was much smaller than what Congress and Eximbank had wanted and whose effectiveness was questionable.

On the other hand, the level of decision making involved in the export credits issue was quite high. American delegations to export credit negotiations usually included high-level officials, such as the Deputy Assistant Secretary of the Treasury, and the issue regularly came to the attention of the Cabinet and sometimes even the President. But the principal resource most consistently utilised by the United States remained diplomatic. The United States succeeded in keeping the issue on the agenda of most OECD Ministerial meetings between 1974 and 1989, and the issue was briefly discussed at the first three summit meetings. At the 1980 Venice summit, President Carter said that he viewed the improvement of the Consensus as a priority issue. Just before the summit meeting, Fred Bergsten told the Congress that,

> We view this area of export credits as a major if not the major piece of business left unresolved by the Tokyo round of trade negotiations last year . . . We therefore give it very high priority. It clearly will be the single trade issue given most of the attention at the economic summit.[164]

However, in the end, little attention was devoted to trade issues at this summit, which was instead pre-occupied with the issues of rising oil prices and the invasion of Afghanistan.

Most of the summit meetings that dealt with export credits merely endorsed progress already made and expressed support for upcoming negotiations. The only summit meeting where the issue became a major source of controversy was in 1982, but only because it was a part of the larger issue of East-West economic relations. The brief, but intense attention given to the issue by the President was not so much an attempt to get movement on the export credits issue *per se*, but rather represented the intrusion of an extraneous issue upon the ongoing OECD negotiations and which, as has been seen, had little or no impact on the outcome of those negotiations.

Both the Carter and Reagan Administrations made fairly vigorous rhetorical statements of support for US objectives throughout most of the export credit negotiations. Fred Bergsten was quoted in the autumn of 1978 as saying that the Carter Administration considered the tightening of the Consensus an important issue, and in July 1981, Robert Cornell of the US Treasury commented that "this is no longer a technical matter to be resolved by international financial experts. It is a matter of increased political concern . . . '[165]

However, the intensity of the US commitment to its objectives appeared to moderate a few years later. In early 1985, when US efforts to obtain greater restraint in the use of mixed credits were not making much progress, John Lange of the Treasury Department, suggested that mixed credits were not a major trade issue and said that it was "almost silly that it had got so much attention". He stated that there were only about 20 cases a year that caused a problem.[166] Also, beginning in 1985 the Export-Import Bank reports to the Congress included a paragraph which argued that "The mixed credit issue is not as large a problem as is commonly thought", and noted that mixed credit offers which actually secured purchases were a fairly small percentage of export credits for capital goods.[167]

Thus, the American commitment to the export credit issue was strong enough to produce a diplomatic offensive and some allocation of financial resources on a fairly selective basis. However, after the Carter Administration, the commitment was not strong enough to contribute to a more general strengthening of American export credit practices by giving more flexibility to the Export-Import Bank. This approach seemed to reflect the belief of the Treasury Department that selective measures could be effective, a belief that was probably also shaped by a desire to reduce government expenditure as much as possible.[168]

The mixed commitment of the US government resulted from a number of conflicting domestic and foreign policy interests and objectives. In both the Carter and Reagan Administrations the impetus for a hard line in export credit negotiations was the growing US trade deficit, as well as pressure from Congress and the export industries to take action against "unfair" trade practices, of which subsidised export credits were considered a fairly prominent example.[169] The main difference between the Carter and Reagan Administrations was that the latter's concern for asserting American leadership encouraged it to take a more aggressive stance verbally and substantively, for example, in its stand on credits for Eastern European countries and when it finally gave in to Congressional pressure to create a warchest. Yet the Reagan Administration's ideological opposition to government intervention in the economy constrained it from engaging in the more extensive commitment of resources that would have been necessary for it to wage an effective export credits subsidy war.

There also appeared to be differences in the level of commitment to eliminate mixed credits between agencies of the American government. Eximbank was the most strongly committed, with Eximbank presidents typically making the most aggressive statements on the issue, and requesting a greater allocation of resources to the Bank, while the Treasury was generally more guarded.[170] For example, as early as December 1984, John Lange conceded that the US proposal for a 50 per cent minimum grant element in the mixed credits agreement was negotiable, and he was apparently willing to accept a 40 per cent figure, while Eximbank was less willing to compromise on the official US position.[171]

The US Congress was also more strongly committed than the Administration on the export credits issue, and had been proposing a war chest of $1 billion since 1981. It was largely in order to ward off protectionist pressure from Congress, which had been mounting due to the worsening trade deficit, that the Administration reluctantly adopted a much smaller fund in 1985, even though mixed credit offers had actually been declining.[172] The fact that the "war chest" was continued after the May 1987 agreement on mixed credits is a further indication that the Administration may have been more interested in relieving Congressional pressure and in boosting exports through subsidisation in order to reduce the trade deficit, and that it was perhaps not fully committed to forcing its trade partners to abandon this practice.[173]

The commitment of other participants in the export credits negotiations was strong enough to block agreement on many of the demands put forward by the United States after 1974. The commitment of these countries is explained first by their greater reliance on exports, but also by the greater ideological acceptance of government assistance to exports, particularly in countries like France. In addition, certain countries saw export credits as a cheaper and politically more acceptable alternative to unemployment and welfare payments, and as a form of foreign aid to developing countries.[174] Japan, on the other hand, was generally opposed to interest rate subsidisation, since interest rates for the yen were generally well below the Consensus ceiling and Japan did not enjoy the same opportunity for interest rate subsidisation that high interest rate countries had.

The US dropped its goal of eliminating mixed credits after a Congressional staff study mission visited the OECD in early 1984 and concluded that several countries, France in particular, were strongly committed to their mixed credit programmes and would be unlikely to give them up.[175] Further evidence of the strength of this commitment is the fact that despite the adoption of mixed credit matching programmes in the late 1970s and early 1980s by Canada, Japan, Germany and others to counter the French practice, France did not agree to take steps to reduce its activity in this area until 1986, and even through to the end of the 1980s continued to offer between 40 and 50 per cent of all OECD mixed credits.[176]

(f) Changes in Interest Definition

The interests and objectives of the US on the export credits issue remained relatively constant after 1974, the only notable shift being the acceptance by the mid-1980s that subsidies could not be entirely eliminated from export credit practices, particularly in tied aid credits. Despite this realisation, the US government continued to hold that the elimination of all subsidy practices was a desirable, if unattainable, goal.

The main observable change of interest in the export credit negotiations was in Europe, where greater restrictions on export credit subsidies gradually gained acceptance. During 1980 and 1981 soaring interest rates increased the cost of subsidising interest rates down to the Consensus matrix rates at the same

Chart 3.4
OECD Matrix Rate Limits and Long-Term Government Bond Yields

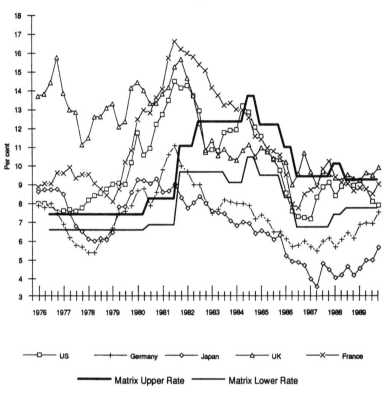

Source: IMF, *International Financial Statistics*, various issues; OECD, *The Export Credit Financing Systems in OECD Member Countries*, 4th ed. (Paris: OECD, 1990), p.9; OECD, *Press Release*, various issues.

time as many governments were experiencing serious budgetary problems and were trying to bring inflation under control (See Chart 3.4). By 1981 many export credit agencies were also suffering from the growing debt crisis and from events in Iran, Turkey and certain African countries which increased the volume of political risk insurance claims.[177] As a consequence most European governments began supporting an increase of the matrix minimums.[178]

Gary Hufbauer, of the US Treasury department, acknowledged this shifting interest when he reported to the Congress in the spring of 1980,

At the present time, there is an improved climate for negotiations resulting from the recognition that the extent of
subsidy in export credit financing has become much too
great and is highly wasteful for industrial exporting
nations taken as a group.[179]

This change in perception of self-interest was also partly
responsible for the record of compliance with the Consensus
guidelines, particularly after 1982 when the no-derogations
commitment was adopted and generally respected. Many
governments were willing to follow the guidelines because of
their growing interest in reducing expenditure on subsidies,
and indeed, after 1982 the volume of export credit subsidies
steadily declined in the OECD.

France was the most reluctant EC member to accept increases
in matrix rates, but did agree to the adjustments of May 1980,
October 1981 and July 1982. However, the French, while realis-
ing that leaving the matrix rates unchanged was unrealistic in
view of rapidly rising market rates, usually managed to keep
increases lower than what most other countries preferred. By
the autumn of 1980, most of the EC members were supporting
the EC Commission recommendation to adopt a uniform
moving matrix. France prevented the EC from endorsing the
UMM for three years, and it appears that the shift in its position
resulted primarily from developments in international financial
markets and in the domestic political and economic situation.[180]
Between May 1982 and the spring of 1983 world interest rates
had fallen an average 2 per cent, and interest rates in some
countries, most notably Japan, were well below the floor of
the Consensus rates. Because Japan and others were permitted
under the Consensus to offer their market rates plus a small
(0.3 per cent) charge, France found herself in a position of
vulnerability, since French export credits could not be offered
at rates lower than the Consensus rates.[181]

The French government was already distressed at the growing trade deficit which in 1982 had doubled to $13.5 billion
from the previous year, prompting the foreign trade minister to
resign.[182] The growing gap between Japanese market rates and
the Consensus rates, it was felt, jeopardised French capital
goods exports. So France demanded a reduction in the Consensus rates. However, as was mentioned earlier, while the United

States experienced difficulty in compelling the EC to accept increases in Consensus rates, because of its veto power in the OECD, it had a much easier time preventing any decrease in the matrix when market rates were falling.[183] As a consequence, at the April 1983 meeting, France agreed in principle to the adoption of the automatic matrix rate adjustment system and of CIRRs for currencies whose market interest rates had fallen below the matrix rates. Final agreement was held up for six months due to disagreements over the size of the initial cut in the matrix and the length of time for reversing this cut, but these technical matters were worked out and the reforms of October 1983 were implemented.[184]

Although the Consensus was tightened to reduce interest rate subsidies, the practice of mixed credits continued. By 1984, however, Finance Ministries in many European countries were becoming increasingly concerned with the cost of this form of export financing.[185] Most EC governments came to accept the need for greater controls on mixed credits, but France continued to view them as an acceptable practice and opposed placing further limits on their use.[186]

In 1985, the first signs of a shift in France's attitude towards export credit subsidies appeared, with the announcement by the Finance Minister that he intended to end subsidies for countries in Category I.[187] This move was in line with the Socialist government's 1986 budget goal of reducing interest rate support in a wide range of areas of the economy.[188] The most significant shift occurred, though, after the French legislative elections of 1986 which brought into office a conservative government whose programme included reducing government involvement in the economic affairs of the country and the de-nationalisation of French industries. The fact that the main benefactors of the French export credit system tended to be a few state-owned firms made export credit subsidies an inviting target for budget cuts by the new government.[189] At the same time, the OECD Secretariat's discount rate proposal softened French attitudes towards a reform of the rules on mixed credits.

At the meeting of EC Finance Ministers in early April 1986, France's request for a devaluation of the franc was approved and the EC proposal on mixed credits was worked out for presentation at the OECD later that month. At the same time the new French Finance Minister, Edouard Balladur, announced

93

a strict plan to reduce government spending, setting the goal of balancing the budget within three years. From that moment, he said, there would be a "révision des missions de l'Etat", and "une remise en cause de certaines de ses interventions qui n'ont plus leur raison d'être".[190] All of this strongly suggests, then, that the source of the shift in France's position in the export credit negotiations was more internal than it was the result of American pressure.

7. *Conclusion*

An examination of the initial bargaining positions and the agreements reached in the export credit negotiations reveals that the United States achieved most of what it set out to accomplish in the period between 1974 and 1987. However, it is incorrect to assume that the predominant position of the US in the international system was responsible for this outcome. The foregoing analysis suggests that overall power resources or even trade power resources were not mobilised by the United States in these negotiations, with the major exception of the 1982 pipeline embargo, when the attempt to link extraneous issues to the export credits issue proved to be ineffective. The distribution of power resources within the export credits issue area also fails to explain the outcome of bargaining in the OECD. Despite the fact that European export credit agencies were often better endowed and more flexible than their American counterpart, the EC moved the furthest from its original position in the negotiations.

While international institutions facilitated the reaching of agreements, they did not by and large alter the outcome of bargaining by enhancing the power of any of the participants. Variations in two unit-level variables, domestic opposition and governmental cohesion, did not explain the pattern of outcomes in these negotiations either. However, preference intensity did seem to have influenced bargaining outcomes. The apparently greater resolve of the EC member countries, France in particular, enabled the Community to block a greater restriction of subsidy practices until such a time as the preferences of Community members had shifted in favour of such restrictions. This change in interest definition, furthermore, resulted primarily from internal economic and political developments and at certain times from fluctuations in international financial markets, rather than from the direct exercise of US power.

The relatively good record of compliance with the OECD guidelines can to a large extent be explained by the mechanism of self-help, which was sanctioned by the regime, and which was facilitated by the regime's monitoring system. However, the threat that derogations might be matched by other participants did not appear to be sufficient to explain the extent of compliance, since there was always a chance that other participants would not bother to match those terms. Hence, the self-interest of participants in complying with the guidelines, primarily due to fiscal constraints, must also be regarded as an important determinant.

Notes

1 OECD, *The Export Credit Financing Systems in OECD Member Countries*, 3rd ed. (Paris: OECD, 1987), p. 7. For other comparisons of the kinds of official support given, the ways in which export credit agencies are funded, the amount of money at their disposal, and the degree of coordination with private sector sources of finance in various countries, see David P. Baron, *The Export-Import Bank: An Economic Analysis* (New York, London: Academic Press, 1983), ch.5; and Joan Pearce, *Subsidised Export Credit* (London: Royal Institute for International Affairs, 1980).

2 *IMF Survey* 13 December 1982, p. 399; *International Herald Tribune* 27 May 1980; *The Economist* 9 May 1981, 23 April 1983, 8 September 1989.

3 *IMF Survey*, 13 December 1982, p. 399.

4 OECD, *The Export Credit Financing Systems in OECD Member Countries*, 3rd ed., p. 11; *Financial Times*, 10 July 1990.

5 John E. Ray, "The OECD "Consensus" on Export Credits", *The World Economy* 9 (September 1986), p. 297.

6 GATT, *Basic Instruments and Selected Documents*, 9th Supplement (Geneva: GATT, 1961), pp. 185–188; Pearce, *Subsidised Export Credit*, p. 42; Ray, "The OECD Consensus", p. 298.

7 Participants included Austria, Belgium, Canada, Denmark, France, Germany, Ireland, Italy, the Netherlands, Norway, Portugal, Spain, Sweden, Switzerland, the United Kingdom, the United States, and the EEC. Japan joined the Group in 1964. By 1986 all OECD members except Iceland and Turkey were participants. The delegates were to be senior government officials with a major responsibility in the formulation of policies in the field of export credit insurance and foreign trade, who were to be advised by senior officials of the export credit institutions.

8 United Nations, Department of Economic and Social Affairs, *Export*

Credits and Development Financing: Part One--Current Practices and Problems (New York: UN, 1966), p. 26; OECD, *Press Release*, A(64) 37, 26 June 1964, A(64) 84, 13 November 1964, A(65) 11, 1 March 1965.

9 UN, *Export Credits*, p. 26; Ray, "The OECD Consensus", p. 301.

10 Credits of less than 5 years" duration were already regulated by the Berne Union, an organisation of government export credit agencies and private companies, established in 1934. See Pearce, *Subsidised Export Credit*, pp. 42–43, Ray, "The OECD Consensus", pp. 296–297, and John L. Moore, Jr., "Export Credit Arrangements", in *Emerging Standards of International Trade and Investment: Multinational Codes and Corporate Conduct*, ed. Seymour J. Rubin and Gary Clyde Hufbauer (Totowa, N.J.: Rowman and Allanheld, 1984), pp. 139–144.

11 Interview with OECD official.

12 *The Banker*, August 1979, p. 79.

13 By the late 1980s, the Europeans and Japanese were not opposed to admitting new Participants, in particular the "four dragons" of South-East Asia. There was never any question of expanding the membership of the ECG. Interview with OECD official.

14 *The Banker*, August 1979, p. 79. The United States in particular felt that since many GATT members were net consumers of export credits they would oppose reducing the subsidies they received. Interview with US government official.

15 The first sectoral agreement on export credits was in the shipbuilding field. This agreement was negotiated in a separate OECD working party, and is treated in Chapter 6.

16 Credit terms on which information was to be exchanged included: i) payments with contract, ii) payments on or before delivery, iii) the total length of the credit and the reasons therefore, iv) the number and amounts of installments and the periods between each, and v) any arrangements for covering local costs. For more details on how this system operates, see US, House, Committee on Banking, Finance and Urban Affairs, *To Amend and Extend the Export-Import Bank Act of 1945: Hearings before the Subcommittee on International Trade, Investment and Monetary Policy*, 95th Cong., 2nd sess., March 13, 15, 16, and 17, 1978, p. 95.

17 Participants were Austria, Belgium, Canada, Denmark, Finland, France, Germany, Ireland, Italy, Luxembourg, the Netherlands, Norway, Spain, Sweden, Switzerland, and the United Kingdom.

18 OECD, *Press Release* A(72) 28, 12 June 1972.

19 *Bulletin of the European Communities* 11–1975, pp. 47–48, 12–1975, p. 69; OECD, *Activities of the OECD in 1975*, p. 26; U.S., House, Committee on Ways and Means, *American and Foreign Practices in the Financing of Large Commercial Aircraft Sales: Hearing before the Subcommittee on Trade*, 95th Cong., 2nd sess., July 14, 1978, p. 67.

20 *New York Times* 1 November 1975; OECD, *Activities of the OECD in 1975*, p. 26; US, House, Committee on Banking, Finance and Urban Affairs, *To Extend and Amend the Export-Import Bank Act of*

1945: Hearings before the Subcommittee on International Trade, Invest-ment and Monetary Policy, 95th Cong., 1st sess., March 25 and 28, 1977, p. 20.

21 For a time this agreement was known as the "Consensus", but a later agreement (which to confuse matters even more did not contain the term "consensus" in its formal title), was and still is generally referred to as the "Consensus". In order to minimise confusion, for the rest of this study the 1976 agreement will be referred to as the Gentlemen's Agreement, while the 1978 agree-ment will be called the Consensus.

22 Marc Maindrault, "Les crédits à l'exportation", *Etudes Inter-nationales* 8 (décembre 1977), p. 633. For a detailed discussion of the negotiations between 1973 and 1976, which were both bilateral and multilateral in character, see U.S., House, Committee on Banking, Currency and Housing, *Oversight Hearings on the Export-Import Bank: Staff Report of the Subcommittee on International Trade, Investment and Monetary Policy*, August 1976, pp. 36–43; and U.S., House, Committee on Banking, Currency and Housing, *Oversight Hearings on the Export-Import Bank: Hearings before the Subcommittee on International Trade, Investment and Monetary Policy*, 94th Cong., 2nd sess., May 10 and 11, 1976, pp. 149–154.

23 By July 1976, Canada, Germany, Italy, Japan, the United Kingdom and the United States had issued these declarations. France began to implement the guidelines at the same time, but did not issue its declaration until the following year. John M. Duff, Jr., "The Outlook for Official Export Credits", *Law and Policy in International Business* 13, no.4 (1981), p. 901.

24 Interview with OECD official.

25 The classification of countries was determined by annual per capita GNP in 1974. Category I countries (relatively rich) were defined as those with a per capita GNP of over $3,000. Category II countries (intermediate) were those with a per capita GNP between $1,000 and $3,000, and those countries with a per capita GNP under $1,000 were placed in Category III. Interest rate minimums were the same for all currencies.

26 U.S., House, *Oversight Hearings on the Export-Import Bank: Staff Report*, pp. 41–42.

27 *Financial Times* 9 June 1977. After the adoption of the Gentlemen's Agreement by the original seven countries, the guidelines were adopted by Belgium and the Netherlands in July 1976, Australia in November 1976, Finland in February 1977, Sweden and Switzer-land in March 1977, Norway in April 1977, New Zealand in May 1977, and Portugal in July 1977.

28 The acceptance of the guidelines by the twenty original signatories was effective 1 April 1978. New Zealand adhered from 18 May and Australia from 1 July of that same year. Only two OECD members, Turkey and Iceland, did not participate in the Consen-sus as they did not have facilities for financing or guaranteeing export credits.

29 See next section. *OECD Press Release* A(78) 18, 31 May 1978; *OECD Observer* 91 (March 1978), p. 16; *Financial Times* 23 February 1978; Pearce, *Subsidised Export Credit*, pp. 48–49; Baron, *The Export-Import Bank*, pp. 21–22; Ray, "The OECD Consensus", p. 301; Gary Clyde Hufbauer and Joanna Shelton Erb, *Subsidies in International Trade* (Washington: Institute for International Economics, 1984), pp. 223–239.

30 *OECD Observer* 113 (November 1981), p. 14; *The Economist* 23 April 1983.

31 This international weighted average rate was to be based on the five major currencies constituting the IMF's Special Drawing Rights, that is, the US dollar, the yen, the Deutschmark, the French franc and the British pound.

32 Until the reductions introduced in October 1983 were recouped, any necessary decrease of matrix rates was to be one-half of that average rate movement, but any increase in the average rate movement was to be fully reflected in the matrix rate increases.

33 The October reduction was reversed in January 1985 because of the decline in commercial interest rates.

34 *OECD Observer* 125 (November 1983), p. 19.

35 OECD, *Activities of the OECD in 1986*, p. 19; OECD, *The Export Credit Financing Systems in OECD Member Countries*, 3rd. ed., p. 285.

36 CIRRs were to be adjusted on a monthly basis.

37 *International Trade Reporter*, 5 August 1987, p. 982.

38 *OECD Observer* 113 (November 1981), p. 14.

39 The intention behind the raising of the minimum grant element was to discourage countries from using foreign aid funds to promote exports by making such practices more expensive.

40 *Financial Times* 10 April 1984.

41 *Euromoney*, March 1986, p. 135; *Le Monde* 14–15 avril 1985; U.S., House, Committee on Foreign Affairs, *Hearings and Markup before the Subcommittee on International Economic Policy and Trade: Omnibus Trade Legislation, Vol.I*, 99th Cong., 1st sess., October 2, 1985, p. 25.

42 This definition was basically the same as the one developed in the OECD Development Assistance Committee (DAC) in 1983. *Bulletin of the European Communities* 7/8–1985, p. 83; OECD, *The Export Credit Financing Systems in OECD Member Countries*, 3rd ed., pp. 247–248, 250; Export-Import Bank of the United States, *Report to the U.S. Congress . . .*, 1985, p. 48; *Euromoney*, March 1986, p. 141.

43 The least developed countries were defined as those on the UN list of LLDCs, and *not* the Category III countries set out in the Consensus.

44 *Financial Times* 10 February, 18 March 1987; *Bulletin of the European Communities* 3–1987, p. 65; OECD, *Arrangement on Guidelines for Officially Supported Export Credits* (Paris: OECD, 1988).

45 The countries were Belgium, Canada, Denmark, France, Germany,

Ireland, Italy, Japan, the Netherlands, Sweden, Switzerland, the
United Kingdom and the United States.

46 OECD, *Activities of the OECD in 1974*, p. 20. For a copy of the text
of this agreement, see OECD, *The Export Credit Financing Systems
in OECD Member Countries*, 3rd ed., pp. 264–265.

47 At the time, most aircraft deals were worked out in US dollars.

48 Eximbank had decided unilaterally to charge this fee on all its
loans. Interview with US government official.

49 U.S., House, Committee on Foreign Affairs, *Export Credit Subsidies:
Hearing before the Subcommittee on International Economic Policy and
Trade*, 97th Cong., 1st sess., November 18, 1981, p. 24; *Financial
Times* 1 October 1982, *International Herald Tribune* 4 August 1981;
Wall Street Journal 4 August 1981.

50 *Wall Street Journal* 8 July 1985.

51 For more details, see the text of the agreement, reproduced in
OECD, *The Export Credit Financing Systems in OECD Member Countries*, 3rd ed., pp. 267–278.

52 OECD, *Activities of the OECD in 1975*, p. 26; Ray, "The OECD
Consensus", p. 303; Duff, "The Outlook for Official Export
Credits", p. 920; US, House, *American and Foreign Practices in the
Financing of Large Commercial Aircraft Sales*, p. 19.

53 This agreement came into force on 10 August 1984. *Financial Times*
25 July 1984; *Bulletin of the European Communities* 7/8–1984, p. 65;
Ray, "The OECD Consensus", p. 303.

54 James J. Emery, Norman A. Graham, et al., *The U.S. Export-Import
Bank: Policy Dilemmas and Choices* (Boulder, Col.: Westview, 1984),
p. 20.

55 Moore, "Export Credit Arrangements", pp. 162–163; Interview
with OECD official.

56 *The Banker* May 1977, pp. 126–127, January 1979, p. 81; *Financial
Times* 9 June 1977; U.S., House, *American and Foreign Practices in
the Financing of Large Commercial Aircraft Sales*, p. 67; US, Senate,
Committee on Banking, Housing, and Urban Affairs, *Competitive
Export Financing: Hearing before the Subcommittee on International Fin-
ance*, 96th Cong., 2nd sess., May 22, 1980, p. 127; Moore, "Export
Credit Arrangements", p. 156; Duff, "The Outlook for Official
Export Credits", pp. 948–950.

57 *The Banker* May 1977, p. 125.

58 Philip A. Wellons, "Banks and the Export Credit Wars: Mixed
Credits in the Sicartsa Financing", in *The Export-Import Bank at
Fifty: The International Environment and the Institution's Role*, ed. Rita
M. Rodriguez (Lexington, Mass.: D.C. Heath, 1987), pp. 186–187;
The Banker January 1979, p. 81.

59 *Financial Times* 28 November 1977, 5, 9, 10 December 1977; *Sunday
Times* 27 November 1977; *The Economist* 3 June 1978, 15 March
1980.

60 *Financial Times* 16 June, 23 October 1978; U.S., House, *American
and Foreign Practices in the Financing of Large Commercial Aircraft
Sales*, pp. 3–4, 52, 67–68, 85.

61 *The Banker* January 1979, p. 81.
62 *The Economist* 5 June 1982; *Globe and Mail* 28 June 1982; U.S., Senate, Committee on Banking, Housing, and Urban Affairs, *Subsidized Export Financing: Hearing before the Subcommittee on International Finance and Monetary Policy*, 97th Cong., 2nd sess., July 22, 1982, pp. 26–27, 40–43, 136, 178–179.
63 Export-Import Bank, *Report to the U.S. Congress . . .* , 1988, p. 4; Duff, "The Outlook for Official Export Credits", pp. 949–940; Pearce, *Subsidised Export Credit*, pp. 51–52; *Financial Times* 2 April 1985.
64 *Financial Times* 21 November 1980.
65 U.S., Senate, *Competitive Export Financing*, May 22, 1980, p. 127; Moore, "Export Credit Arrangements", p. 156.
66 *Financial Times* 28 November 1977; *The Economist* 3 June 1978; *Far Eastern Economic Review* 22 September 1978. It should be noted that Japan eventually did offer China interest rates below the Consensus minimum, arguing that it was not a case of export financing but "import" financing, which was not covered by the Consensus. *The Banker*, January 1979, p. 81.
67 One US Treasury official estimated that the US got roughly three-quarters of what it was seeking in the OECD negotiations. Interview.
68 Moore, "Export Credit Arrangements", p. 144.
69 Jordan Jay Hillman, *The Export-Import Bank at Work: Promotional Financing in the Public Sector* (Westport, Conn., London: Quorum Books, 1982), pp. 72–73.
70 Throughout most of the six rounds the US position was generally backed, although not always actively, by Canada, which shared similar interests in the export credits field.
71 *Financial Times, International Herald Tribune* 12 September 1974; *The Economist* 17 May 1975.
72 U.S., House, *Oversight Hearings on the Export-Import Bank: Staff Report*, pp. 36–43; and U.S., House, *Oversight Hearings on the Export-Import Bank*, May 10 and 11, 1976, pp. 149–154.
73 *Financial Times* 9 June, 10 December 1977; *The Economist* 5 March 1978; U.S., House, *To Amend and Extend the Export-Import Bank Act of 1945*, p. 6.
74 *Financial Times* 16 June, 17, 23, 25 October 1978; *Globe and Mail* 10, 21 June 1978; *The Times* 14 October 1978; *International Herald Tribune* 24, 25, 28–29 October 1978; *The Economist* 28 October 1978; U.S., Senate, *Competitive Export Financing*, May 22, 1980, pp. 102–104.
75 *Financial Times* 19 February, 5, 10, 12, 15, 29 March, 7, 10 May, 5 July 1982; *International Herald Tribune* 25 February, 12 March, 23 June 1982; *The Economist* 20 March 1982; *The Guardian* 6 May 1982; *Le Monde* 9–10 mai 1982; *The Banker* July 1982, p. 7.
76 *Financial Times* 14 February, 5 March, 25, 27 April, 14 October 1983; *The Banker* June 1983, p. 7; *The Economist* 23 April 1983; *Globe and Mail* 20 June 1983; *Daily Telegraph* 25 March 1983.

77 Export-Import Bank, *Report to the U.S. Congress* . . ., 1985, p. 48, 1986, p. 58.
78 *Euromoney*, March 1986, p. 141; Export-Import Bank, *Report to the U.S. Congress* . . ., 1985, p. 48.
79 Export-Import Bank, *Report to the U.S. Congress* . . ., 1987, p. 49.
80 In exchange for accepting the new discount rate, the Japanese were given an assurance that they could continue to use the 10 per cent rate for the purposes of calculating official development assistance in the DAC, so that Japan would not appear to be giving less foreign aid than it had been declaring. Interview with OECD official; Export-Import Bank, *Report to the U.S. Congress* . . ., 1986, p. 59.
81 *Financial Times* 1 October 1982; *International Herald Tribune* 4 August 1981; *Aviation Week and Space Technology* 30 May, 1983, pp. 217–220.; U.S., House, *American and Foreign Practices in the Financing of Large Commercial Aircraft Sales*, p. 19; U.S., House, Committee on Ways and Means, *U.S. Trade Policy – Phase I: Administration and Other Public Agencies: Hearings before the Subcommittee on Trade*, 97th Cong., 1st sess., 2 November 1981, p. 308.
82 *Financial Times* 13 November 1984, 11, 13 December 1984.
83 Export-Import Bank, *Report to the U.S. Congress* . . ., 1983, p. 30.
84 *Journal of Commerce* 10 January 1985.
85 *Bulletin of the European Communities* 7/8–1984, p. 65; *Financial Times* 25 July 1984; *The Banker* August 1979, p. 75; *Journal of Commerce* 10 January 1985; U.S., House, *Export Credit Subsidies*, pp. 8–9.
86 In its report to Congress for the calendar year 1984, the Export-Import Bank concluded: "By linking minimum [Consensus] rates to market interest-rate movements, these new guidelines virtually eliminate direct interest-rate subsidies in official credits to the industrialised countries and significantly reduce the subsidy to the developing countries. Such linkage has been a long-sought goal of the United States in pursuing the elimination of trade-distorting subsidies." Export-Import Bank, *Report to the U.S. Congress* . . ., 1985, p. 46.
87 *The Banker* August 1979, p. 79; *International Herald Tribune* 29 May 1980, 8, 16 October 1981; *The Economist* 10 October 1981; *Financial Times* 8, 12 October 1981.
88 *Financial Times* 14 April 1984; U.S., House, Committee on Foreign Affairs, *Review of the Mixed Credits Program: Hearings before the Subcommittee on International Economic Policy and Trade*, 98th Cong., 2nd sess., January 26, March 5, 1984, p. 4.
89 U.S., House, Committee on Ways and Means, *Certain Tariff and Trade Bills: Hearings before the Subcommittee on Trade*, 97th Cong., 1st sess., May 5 and June 15, 1981, p. 33; U.S., House, *Export Credit Subsidies*, p. 19.
90 In March 1982, the US Under Secretary of State James Buckley visited several Western European capitals and called for a "financial embargo" of COMECON, including an end to subsidised interest rates on export credits, a freeze on new export credits for

90 days, and an end to government guarantees on credits to the USSR. *Financial Times* 12, 15 March 1982; *International Herald Tribune* 12 March 1982; *The Economist* 30 March 1982.

91 *New York Times* 6 June 1982.

92 *Keesing's Contemporary Archives*, August 13, 1982, p. 31638.

93 *New York Times* 4, 7 June 1982; *Financial Times* 8 June 1982.

94 *New York Times* 7 June 1982; *Financial Times* 8 June 1982.

95 It appears that the US did not threaten to take such action at the Versailles summit, however. US, House, Committee on Foreign Affairs, *Export Controls on Oil and Gas Equipment: Hearings and Markup*, 97th Cong., November 12, 1981, May 25, August 4 and 10, 1982, p. 155; Robert D. Putnam and Nicholas Bayne, *Hanging Together: Cooperation and Conflict in the Seven-Power Summits*, Revised and Enlarged Edition (Cambridge, Mass.: Harvard University Press, 1987), pp. 137–138; *Financial Times* 8 June 1982. After 1982, the export credits issue was not mentioned in summit communiqués, except in the context of world debt problems, where recognition was given of the need for "flexibility" on the part of export credit agencies in resuming or increasing cover for countries that were implementing comprehensive adjustment programmes. *Department of State Bulletin*, July 1986, p. 9; August 1987, p. 13; August 1988, p. 51.

96 The West Europeans were concerned about the internal economic problems of the Soviet Union and about the massive Polish debt. These concerns were making them reticent to extend more credit to Eastern Europe. See Bruce W. Jentleson, *Pipeline Politics: The Complex Political Economy of East-West Energy Trade* (Ithaca, N.Y. and London: Cornell University Press, 1986), p. 181.

97 *Financial Times* 19 February, 12, 15, 29 March, 7, 10 May, 7, 8 June, 5 July 1982; *New York Times* 16 June 1982; *Le Monde* 6 février, 28 avril, 9–10 mai, 3 juillet 1982; *The Guardian* 4 May 1982; *Japan Times* 12 May 1982. See also, Putnam and Bayne, *Hanging Together*, p. 137. A tradeoff was made between Categories II and III; the US proposal of no change in the rate for Category III was adopted on the one hand, while the EC proposal of a 0.25 to 0.5 per cent increase for Category II was essentially adopted on the other with the 0.35 per cent increase for both medium- and long-term credits. The compromise would have been accepted earlier, but France delayed the EC's acceptance as a protest against the extended US sanctions. The EC also extracted a final concession from the US, moving the no derogation commitment up from 1 January 1983 to 15 October 1982. *Le Monde* 26 juin, 3 juillet 1982.

98 Assistant Secretary of Commerce, Lawrence Brady, denied that there was any link between the extension of the embargo and the policy of restricting export credits to Eastern Europe. *Le Monde* 26 juin 1982. This point is also supported by Jentleson, *Pipeline Politics*, p. 194.

99 US, House, *Export Controls on Oil and Gas Equipment*. Among the list of relatively insubstantial items in the "plan of action" which

President Reagan claimed had been accepted by allied countries in exchange for the US lifting the embargo was an undertaking to "work to harmonise our export credit policies", a phrase that closely resembled those of various communiqués issued at the end of OECD Ministerial meetings and economic summits over the preceding several years. The US continued to press its allies to stop subsidising export credits to the Soviets, to put a ceiling on overall credits to the Soviet Union, and to require a large cash downpayment for all orders placed by Soviet bloc countries. During the negotiations which led to the President's November 13 announcement, France had steadfastly rejected American proposals to end subsidised credits to the Soviet Union. France succeeded in watering down the language of the agreement, and even then denied that it was a party to the accord announced by Reagan. Britain also declared that no concessions had been made by the allies, a claim which was shared by virtually all observers at the time, despite the official Administration line. *Le Monde* 16, 19 novembre 1982; *New York Times* 3, 14, 15 November 1982; Jentleson, *Pipeline Politics*, p. 197.

100 U.S., House, Committee on Foreign Affairs, *Omnibus Trade Legislation (Volume I): Hearings and Markup before the Subcommittee on International Economic Policy and Trade*, 99th Cong., 1st sess., October 2 and 22, November 5, 1985, p. 69.
101 U.S., Senate, Committee on Banking, Housing, and Urban Affairs, *Competitive Export Financing Act of 1981: Hearing before the Subcommittee on International Finance and Monetary Policy*, 97th Cong., 1st sess., July 20, 1981, p. 47.
102 Interview with US government official.
103 *Financial Times* 15 October 1986.
104 U.S., House, Committee on Banking, Finance and Urban Affairs, *Oversight Hearing on the Export-Import Bank: Hearing before the Subcommittee on International Trade, Investment and Monetary Policy*, 96th Cong., 1st sess., May 21, 1979, pp. 71–72.
105 U.S., Senate, *Competitive Export Financing*, May 22, 1980, pp. 139–140.
106 *Business Week* 26 May 1980.
107 *Financial Times* 13 June 1980; U.S., House , Committee on Banking, Finance and Urban Affairs, *Oversight Hearings on the Export-Import Bank: Hearings before the Subcommittee on International Trade, Investment and Monetary Policy*, 96th Cong., 2nd sess., June 12 and 19, 1980, p. 53.
108 *Financial Times, International Herald Tribune, New York Times, The Times* 21 November 1980; *The Guardian* 25 November 1980.
109 U.S., House, *Review of the Mixed Credits Program*, pp. 3–4. This view was accepted by at least one independent observer, who argued that facing the threat of longer US maturities, France yielded on the 1983 agreement. Andrew M. Moravcsik, "Disciplining Trade Finance: The OECD Export Credit Arrangement", *International Organization* 43 (Winter 1989), pp. 184–186, 199.

110 *Financial Times* 9 January, 14 May 1979.

111 *Aviation Week and Space Technology* 30 May 1983, p. 217.

112 It should be noted that for countries with relatively low domestic interest rates, such as Japan and Germany, there was virtually no pressure to subsidise interest rates in export credits.

113 Letter by John A. Bohn, Jr. to Congress, reproduced in Export-Import Bank of the United States, *Report to the U.S. Congress . . .*, 1986, p. iii.

114 These figures are taken from an OECD document reproduced in, US, Senate, *Competitive Export Financing*, May 22, 1980, p. 54.

115 *Financial Times* 16 June, 17, 23, 25 October 1978; *Globe and Mail* 10, 21 June 1978; *The Times* 14 October 1978; *International Herald Tribune* 24, 25, 28–29 October 1978; *The Economist* 28 October 1978; *Far Eastern Economic Review* 24 November 1978.

116 *Financial Post* (Toronto) 24 November 1979. Interview with US government official. The US was joined by a number of other countries, including Japan, the UK, Canada, and the Netherlands, in the matching of mixed credit offers.

117 *Financial Times* 26 June 1979; U.S., Senate, *Competitive Export Financing*, May 22, 1980, pp. 104–105. In fact, it was the expanded activities of the 1970s which put Eximbank in the red in the 1980s, further constraining its leverage. Interview with US government official; *Financial Times* 28 February 1989.

118 Baron, *The Export-Import Bank*, p. 1; *Financial Times* 11 June 1981.

119 *IMF Survey*, 13 December 1982, p. 349.

120 U.S., House, *U.S. Trade Policy*, p. 53.

121 U.S., Senate, *Competitive Export Financing Act of 1981*, pp. 11–12, 20–21.

122 U.S., Senate, Committee on Banking, Housing, and Urban Affairs, *Oversight Activities of the Export-Import Bank: Hearing*, 99th Cong., 1st sess., February 5, 1985, p. 80.

123 See Moravcsik, "Disciplining Trade Finance", p. 184. By 1989, Eximbank's budgetary authorisation for direct credit lending in support of exports had dwindled to $695 million. *Financial Times* 28 February 1989.

124 *Financial Times* 13 June 1980. In May 1980, Fred Bergsten stated that if no progress were made in strengthening the Consensus, the US would attempt to reach agreement through bilateral negotiations wherever that was possible. He cited a successful example in the informal agreement on aircraft engines with Great Britain. However, this bilateral approach appeared to be a very limited tool, unlike the case of steel trade. The US could not use access to its market as a bargaining chip, since export credits were seldom used to finance exports to the United States itself, but were rather destined for third states, especially in the developing world. Also, aircraft engines were unique, in that the US and Great Britain were the only major exporters. U.S., House, *Oversight Hearings on the Export-Import Bank*, June 12 and 19, 1980, p. 53; U.S., Senate, *Competitive Export Financing*, May 22, 1980, pp. 139–140.

125 U.S., House, *Oversight Hearings on the Export-Import Bank*, pp. 81–82.
126 *Financial Times* 15, 16 November 1984.
127 *International Herald Tribune* 26, 28 November 1984; U.S., *Omnibus Trade Legislation (Volume I)*, p. 48.
128 *Financial Times* 13 March 1985.
129 U.S., Senate, *Oversight Activities of the Export-Import Bank*, p. 46.
130 U.S., House, *Hearings and Markup before the Subcommittee on International Economic Policy and Trade*, p. 47. A presidential task force report presented to Congress in early 1985 similarly concluded that the matching of interest rate subsidies on mixed credits was not effective in giving the US negotiating leverage. U.S., Senate, *Oversight Activities of the Export-Import Bank*, p. 80.
131 *Financial Times* 24 October, 13 November 1985, 10 January 1986; *Euromoney*, March 1986, p. 135.
132 Moravcsik, "Disciplining Trade Finance", pp. 200–201.
133 *Financial Times* 14 November 1985.
134 *Financial Times* 14 November 1985.
135 *Euromoney*, March 1986, p. 135.
136 *Le Monde* 25 janvier 1986; *Financial Times* 24 January 1986.
137 *Financial Times* 10 January 1986; *Euromoney*, March 1986, pp. 135, 141. One set of figures presented in Congress showed that in 1987 Japan was spending 17 times more than the US on tied aid, while France spent 12 times more and Canada four times more than the US. *Financial Times* 10 May 1989.
138 *Financial Times* 12 December 1986.
139 U.S., House, Committee on Ways and Means, *Certain Tariff and Trade Bills*, p. 33; U.S., House, *Export Credit Subsidies*, p. 19; GATT, *Basic Instruments and Selected Documents*, 28th supplement (Geneva: GATT, 1982), p. 31.
140 GATT, *Basic Instruments and Selected Documents*, 29th Supplement. Geneva: GATT, 1983. pp. 45–47.
141 After 1982, however, the no-derogation engagement lessened the need for matching.
142 U.S., Senate, *Oversight Activities of the Export-Import Bank*, p. 80; *Financial Times* 10, 13 December 1984, 14 March 1985; *International Herald Tribune* 14 December 1984; *Globe and Mail* 27 May 1985.
143 *Financial Times* 12 January, 11 June, 1979, 15 February, 1980; *The Banker*, August 1979, p. 71, August 1980, pp. 72–73; Duff, "The Outlook for Official Export Credits", pp. 907–908. For a copy of the final report, see US, Senate, *Competitive Export Financing*, May 22, 1980, pp. 16–66.
144 Moore, "Export Credit Arrangements", p. 161.
145 *Le Monde* 14–15 avril 1985; *Wall Street Journal* 8 July 1985; OECD, *Activities of the OECD in 1985*, p. 15.
146 Interview with OECD official; *Financial Times* 29 May 1986.
147 Moore, "Export Credit Arrangements", p. 159.
148 Jock A. Finlayson and Mark W. Zacher, "The GATT and the Regulation of Trade Barriers", in *International Regimes*, ed. Stephen

D. Krasner (Ithaca and London: Cornell University Press, 1983), pp. 293–296.

149 For a more detailed discussion of this aspect of the regime, see Moravcsik, "Disciplining Trade Finance", pp. 202–205.

150 *Financial Times* 10 December 1977.

151 U.S., House, *Oversight Hearing on the Export-Import Bank*, May 21, 1979, p. 71.

152 *Financial Times* 31 August 1984; *Globe and Mail* 17 September 1984.

153 Deadlines were imposed on negotiations on strengthening the Gentlemen's Agreement, on tightening the Consensus rules in 1980, and on the aircraft commonline in 1982.

154 *The Banker* June 1982, p. 7, August 1983, p. 8; Duff, p. 952; *Euromoney* March 1986, p. 141.

155 *The Times* 14 October 1978; *The Guardian* 25 November 1980, 14 October 1983; *Financial Times* 20 March 1981; *International Herald Tribune* 23 June 1982.

156 U.S., House, *To Amend and Extend the Export-Import Bank Act of 1945*, pp. 283–284; *Financial Times* 14 May 1975; Moore, "Export Credit Arrangements", p. 164.

157 U.S., Senate, *Competitive Export Financing Act of 1981*, p. 20; *New York Times* 16 June 1982.

158 U.S., Senate, *Subsidised Export Financing*, p. 5; *The Economist* 4 March 1978; *Financial Times* 12 May 1981.

159 For a more complete discussion of the activities of Eximbank during the 1970s and 1980s, see Hillman, *The Export-Import Bank at Work*; Baron, *The Export-Import Bank* (especially chapter 2); and Rita M. Rodriguez, ed., *The Export-Import Bank at Fifty*.

160 *Financial Times, International Herald Tribune, New York Times, The Times* 21 November 1980; *Financial Times* 24 November 1980; *New York Times* 28 November 1980.

161 *The Banker* April 1981, p. 23.

162 *International Herald Tribune* 8–9 May 1982; *Financial Times* 25 May, 16, 25 June, 1 July 1982; *The Guardian* 24 June 1982; *The Banker* June 1982, p. 7.

163 *Financial Times* 25 April 1983.

164 U.S., House, *Oversight Hearings on the Export-Import Bank*, June 12 and 19, 1980, p. 5.

165 U.S., Senate, *Competitive Export Financing Act of 1981*, p. 20; *The Times* 14 October 1978.

166 *Financial Times* 14 March 1985.

167 Export-Import Bank, *Report to the U.S. Congress . . .* , 1985, 1986, and 1987.

168 According to US Treasury officials, the hope of the Reagan Administration was that the selective targeting of mixed credits would bring about an international agreement to end the practice which would then permit Eximbank to "wither away". Interview.

169 Public opinion was generally unconcerned about the issue, and export credits never figured prominently in any election campaign.

170 An exception to this pattern of Eximbank presidents was William

Draper, who was strongly opposed to subsidisation and whose goal was to streamline the Bank and to bring it out of the red. Interview with US government official; *Aviation Week and Space Technology* 26 June 1981, p. 27, 7 June 1982, p. 23.

171 Interview with US and OECD officials; *Financial Times* 13 December 1984; *International Herald Tribune* 14 December 1984. See also Keith Hayward, *International Collaboration in Civil Aerospace* (New York: St. Martin's, 1986), p. 187.

172 French officials often made the point that the US was making France a scapegoat, and that American aggressiveness on mixed credits was sparked by the desire of the Administration to show Congress that it was taking steps to deal with the trade deficit, despite the minimal role of mixed credits in financing world trade. *Le Monde* 25 janvier 1986; *Financial Times* 14 November 1985; *Euromoney* March 1986, pp. 136–138; *International Trade and Finance* 16 June 1988, p. 7.

173 The ambivalence of the Administration on this issue is evident in statements about unfair trade practices. In the his economic report to Congress in 1983, President Reagan argued that America's trade problems were *not* the result of unfair trade practices of foreign countries, but when requesting funding for the war chest in September 1985, he said "I will not stand by and watch American businesses fail because of unfair trading practices abroad." *Business Week* 18 November 1985, p. 50; *New York Times* 3 February 1983.

174 U.S., House, *U.S. Trade Policy*, pp. 304–305. One independent economic study similarly concluded that the major motivation for export credit subsidisation was primarily macroeconomic, not microeconomic. Jacques Melitz and Patrick Messerlin, "Export Credit Subsidies", *Economic Policy* 4 (April 1987), p. 151.

175 U.S., House, *Review of the Mixed Credits Program*, pp. 54–56.

176 U.S., Senate, *Oversight Activities of the Export-Import Bank*, p. 79; Messerlin, "Export-credit Mercantilism", p. 390.

177 *The Banker* January 1981, p. 11; Messerlin, "Export-credit Mercantilism", pp. 385–386; Axel Wallen, "The OECD Arrangement on Guidelines for Officially Supported Export Credit: Past and Future", in *The Export-Import Bank at Fifty: The International Environment and the Institution's Role*, ed. Rita M. Rodriguez (Lexington, Mass.: D.C. Heath, 1987), p. 99; Rita M. Rodriguez, "Exim's Mission and Accomplishments: 1934–1984", in *The Export-Import Bank at Fifty*, ed. Rita M. Rodriguez, p. 19.

178 *Financial Times* 6, 15 May 1980; *The Times* 22 April 1980; *Globe and Mail* 8 September 1981.

179 U.S., Senate, *Competitive Export Financing*, May 22, 1980, p. 164.

180 Moore, "Export Credit Arrangements", p. 147; Duff, "The Outlook for Official Export Credits", p. 911; *The Banker* April 1981, p. 23; Baron, *The Export-Import Bank*, p. 306; *Financial Times* 14 October 1983.

181 *Le Monde* 26 avril 1983.

182 *New York Times* 20 January 1983.

183 Even though the cost of export credit subsidies rose from FF6.6 billion in 1980 to FF13 billion in 1982, the Socialist government appeared more concerned about the job-creating effects of large export contracts, as well as citing the benefits for developing countries. Messerlin, "Export-credit Mercantilism", p. 385; *Le Monde* 26 avril 1983.

184 At the April 1983 OECD meeting, France had wanted a 2 per cent reduction in matrix rates, which was roughly the size of the decline in world interest rates since the previous summer. The US vigorously opposed such a large reduction. However, between April and June, world interest rates moved upwards again, making a smaller cut more acceptable to the French. It appears that French officials were ready to accept the compromise plan put forward by Axel Wallen in June 1983, but President Mitterand intervened to block an agreement to express his displeasure with the US over its attempts to take over the Egyptian wheat flour market through a heavily subsidised programme targeted at traditional French export markets. *The Banker* June 1983, p. 7, August 1983, p. 8; *The Economist* 23 April 1983; *Financial Times* 27 April, 14 October 1983; *The Times, Globe and Mail* 13 July 1983.

185 Export-Import Bank, *Report to the U.S. Congress . . .*, 1985, p. 47.

186 *Euromoney* January 1985, pp. 141–142.

187 *Le Monde* 17 september 1985; *Financial Times* 19 August, 19 September 1985.

188 The government's budget was one of the toughest since the Second World War, introducing a real cut in government expenditure (not counting debt charges) for the first time. It was an attempt to pre-empt some of the programme of the conservative opposition, which was leading in the public opinion polls prior to the 1986 election, and which was making a campaign issue of the fact that the budget deficit had almost doubled between 1981 and 1985 to over 153 billion francs. In March 1986, the Socialists announced a sharp reduction of export credit subsidies to less than FF 1 billion annually, compared with roughly FF 10 billion in 1985. *Financial Times* 19 September 1985, 17 March 1986.

189 Messerlin, "Export-credit Mercantilism", pp. 397–398; *Financial Times* 15 September, 15 December 1986.

190 *Le Monde* 8 avril 1986.

Chapter Four

AGRICULTURAL TRADE

1. *The International Agricultural Market*

Conditions in the world agricultural market during the 1980s significantly deteriorated after a period of steady growth in the 1970s. From 1970 to 1980 the volume of world agricultural imports increased 53 per cent, while imports were relatively stagnant during the first half of the 1980s, rising only 7 per cent in volume and actually declining in value (see Charts 4.1 and 4.2). At the same time, agricultural production continued to increase under the influence of government incentives, creating large surpluses of many agricultural products in OECD countries.[1] Although agricultural trade picked up somewhat by the end of the 1980s, the volume of world agricultural imports increased only 18 per cent between 1980 and 1989. World food prices, which had nearly tripled between 1970 and 1980, declined by some 33 per cent between 1980 and 1987 (see Chart 4.3). Surplus production and falling prices resulted in vigorous competition for world markets among agricultural exporters, sparking numerous trade disputes. The most notable of these conflicts were between the United States and the European Community, largely over American access to the European market and competition for third markets, and between the US and Japan over American demands for a more open Japanese market.

In 1987, agricultural production in OECD countries was around 30 per cent of the world total.[2] The United States and the European Community each accounted for one-third of the total value added in agriculture in the OECD in 1985, while Japan's share was the third largest at around 16 per cent (see

Chart 4.1
World Imports of Agricultural Products
(Value)

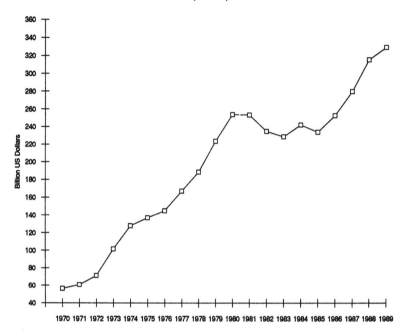

Source: FAO, *FAO Trade Yearbook*, various issues.

Table 4.1). OECD countries accounted for roughly three-fifths of world agricultural exports and two-thirds of imports during the 1970s and 1980s (see Table 4.2). The largest exporter of agricultural products during the 1970s and most of the 1980s was the United States, with an average of around 17 per cent of world agricultural exports. The agricultural exports of the EC rose gradually from 7 per cent of the world total in 1970 to 13 per cent in 1987. Canada, Australia and New Zealand each accounted for between 1 and 4.5 per cent over this period, while Japan's exports never exceeded 0.7 per cent (see Chart 4.4).

Agricultural policies affecting international trade have varied considerably from country to country. In the United States direct export subsidisation was ended in 1973 and then resumed

Chart 4.2
Indices of World Imports of Agricultural Products
(Volume)

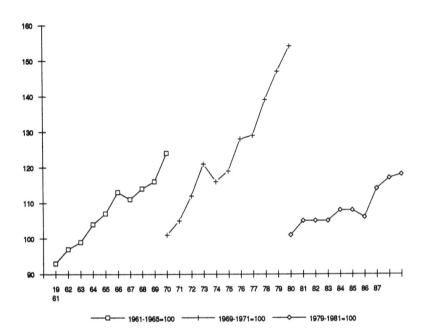

Source: FAO, *FAO Trade Yearbook*, various issues.

in 1985. During the 1980s, government intervention took several forms: credit sales, export credit loans and credit guarantees administered by the Commodity Credit Corporation (CCC); agricultural products offered as foreign aid through Public Law 480 and USAID; import quotas imposed on some products, such as sugar and dairy products; price supports for certain commodities; and deficiency income payment schemes.[3] One measure of aggregate government support in the agricultural sector is the producer subsidy equivalent (PSE), developed in the OECD. According to the OECD, the net percentage PSE for the US in all products increased between 1979 and 1986 from 14.7 per cent to 42 per cent of the gross value of agricultural production, before falling to some 27 per cent in 1989.[4]

The trade distorting aspects of the Common Agricultural

111

Chart 4.3
World Agricultural Price Index
(1980=100)

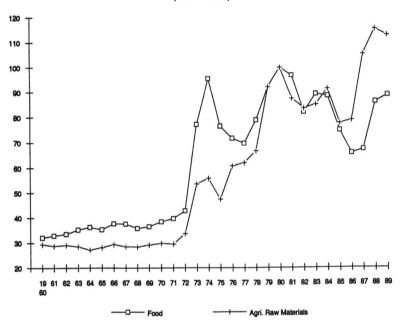

Source: IMF, *International Financial Statistics: Supplement on Trade Statistics*, 1988; IMF, *International Financial Statistics*, various issues.

Policy (CAP) of the EC have included export restitution payments, which are given to farmers to make up the difference between internal prices and world market prices, and variable import levies, which bring the price of imports up to the higher EC internal target prices. PSEs in the Community have been calculated at 44.3 per cent in 1979, 50 per cent in 1986 and 38 per cent in 1989. In Japan, the agricultural sector has been protected through import quotas, domestic price supports and import duties and levies. Agricultural budget costs have been relatively lower than in the US, since support is paid for primarily by consumers through high food prices. Between 1979 and 1986, PSEs increased from 64.3 per cent to 75 per cent, a level that was maintained for most of the rest of the 1980s.

In Canada, agricultural policies have included import quotas

Table 4.1
Shares of Total OECD Value Added in Agriculture
(Per cent)

	EC-12	US	Canada	Australia	N.Z.	Japan	EFTA-6
1960	39.8	32.0	3.6	3.1	–	9.3	12.0
1968	41.3	27.9	3.5	2.6	–	13.9	9.4
1974	37.4	30.0	4.1	2.9	0.7	14.7	10.5
1980	42.4	25.0	3.6	2.9	0.9	14.0	11.5
1985	33.8	32.7	4.1	2.5	0.8	16.1	9.2
1987	40.8	26.4	3.7	2.4	0.9	19.0	6.9

– Not available.

Source: OECD, *National Accounts: Vol. I*, various issues;
      OECD, OECD Economic Outlook: Historical Statistics, 1988.

Table 4.2
Shares of Developed Market Economies in World Agricultural
Products Trade
(Per cent of value)

	Exports	Imports
1970	58.5	71.8
1975	62.8	65.0
1980	64.7	62.0
1985	62.3	62.2
1987	66.6	68.2
1989	68.0	65.2

Source: FAO, *Trade Yearbook*, various issues.

Chart 4.4
Shares of Selected Economies in Total Agricultural Exports
(Value)

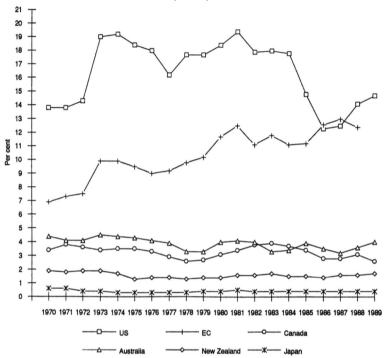

Excluding intra-EC trade. Only includes countries that were EC members during year listed.

Source: FAO, *FAO Trade Yearbook*, various issues; Commission of the European Communities; *Agricultural Situation in the Community*, various issues.

and surtaxes on certain commodities, such as dairy products, poultry and meat. In the mid-1980s subsidies were significantly increased for grain growers. The PSE level was 23.7 per cent in 1979 and rose to 49 per cent in 1986, before declining to some 35 per cent in 1989. Australia and New Zealand have traditionally been the lowest subsidisers of agriculture in the OECD. PSE levels in Australia for 1979, 1986 and 1989 were respectively 8.1 per cent, 16 per cent and 10 per cent. PSEs rose from 14.7 per cent to 33 per cent in New Zealand between 1979 and 1986, but following a major reform of agricultural policies, PSEs fell to 5 per cent in 1989, the lowest level of all OECD countries. Non-EC Western European countries have been both highly

114

protectionist and major subsidisers of agriculture. High internal prices have been maintained in these countries through a mix of import controls and export subsidies.[5]

2. Background to OECD Agricultural Trade Negotiations

The OECD has been a forum for the discussion of issues related to agricultural trade since it was created out of the old Organisation for European Economic Co-operation (OEEC) in 1960. The OECD Committee for Agriculture carried on the work of the OEEC's Food and Agriculture Committee, by discussing agricultural policies and markets, and by mandating studies on both of these topics. The Committee for Agriculture and its working parties also provided a certain degree of surveillance over agricultural trade policies through the requirement that members notify the OECD of any new restrictive measures. A series of agreements was worked out during the 1960s setting technical standards for fruits and vegetables, for the certification of seed, and for the testing of farm machinery, and a Gentleman's Agreement was concluded on whole milk powder exports.[6] In the OECD's discussions on agriculture during this period there was reluctance on the part of most members to commit themselves to liberalised agriculture trade, with the major exception of the United States. At the various OECD Ministerial meetings in which agriculture was discussed, Ministers generally recognised that problems existed, but little was done to establish any international norms which could guide national policies to remedy those problems.[7]

The predominant activity of the OECD in the field of agricultural trade, was the production of studies. The trade aspect of agriculture was given relatively little direct attention during much of the 1970s in comparison with the countless studies on domestic agricultural issues, which dealt with everything from capital and finance in agriculture to the pre-packaging of fruits and vegetables. Agricultural trade issues usually received a brief discussion in the regular reports on the agricultural policies of OECD member countries, consisting of a summary of various national measures affecting agricultural imports and exports, and of international trade agreements. The various studies on agricultural products and markets also contained brief descriptions of trade flows in those product sectors.

The main ongoing task of the Joint Working Party of the Committee for Agriculture and the Trade Committee was to examine changes in trade policies and practices of member countries, including import restrictions and export subsidies. It was also responsible for special agricultural trade studies, beginning with a study on instability in the markets for wheat and butter in the early 1970s.[8] The Joint Working Party was instructed in 1973 to carry out a study of the long term trends in the world supply and demand for major agricultural commodities, including cereals, animal feedstuffs and livestock products. Following the conclusion of that report, a more general study of instability in agricultural commodity markets was undertaken.[9]

In addition to the permanent working groups on agriculture, a number of *ad hoc* groups were established to study particular aspects of agricultural trade. An *ad hoc* Group on East-West Economic Relations and Agriculture was set up in the late 1970s to examine the agricultural policies of the Soviet Union (and later, those of Eastern European states and China), and the impact of these policies on East-West trade.[10] In 1973, the Trade Committee arranged an exchange of information and consultations on export restrictions, following the American soybean embargo.[11] In the context of the Organisation-wide project on Positive Adjustment Policies which began in 1978, the Committee for Agriculture undertook a study of the implications of different means of agricultural income support for trade.[12]

During the 1980s, the OECD stepped up its informational work on North-South agricultural trade. In 1982, the Joint Working Party began a study of the implications for OECD countries of increased agricultural trade with less-developed countries (LDCs). This report, completed in 1983, examined the effect of domestic and trade policies on OECD-LDC agriculture trade. Work was initiated in 1987 to analyse the economic impact on several LDCs of agricultural policy reform in OECD countries and in developing countries. At the same time a review was prepared of the current situation and short/medium term outlook for OECD-LDC trade relations. This review included an analysis of policy issues, actions and initiatives, as well as the positions of the two groups of countries in the Uruguay Round.[13]

A further informational activity of the OECD involved efforts to intensify the exchange of information and views on trade in particular agricultural commodities where severe imbalances in supply and demand existed. At the December 1982 OECD meeting of Ministers of Agriculture, the Committees on trade and agriculture were asked to put forward possible solutions for remedying such market imbalances. The dairy sector was dealt with first, and the Secretary-General held high-level consultations with the main milk-producing countries in March and June 1983. In 1984, high-level consultations were held on other products, such as cereals.[14]

3. Agreements on Agricultural Trade Issues

In contrast to the case of export credits, the OECD was not the main locus of international negotiations on agricultural trade. The most extensive negotiations involving OECD member countries on this issue took place in the GATT, as well as in bilateral meetings, particularly those between the US on the one hand and Japan, the EC and Canada on the other. Although participants in OECD meetings on agricultural trade repeatedly stressed that these were not negotiating sessions but rather "discussions", when viewed over a long-term perspective these talks do appear to fit the definition of negotiations set out in the introduction to this study. Certainly, the negotiations were not aimed at developing a detailed set of "rules" in the sense of the export credits Consensus. But over the years there were repeated attempts by some countries to get other countries to accept a common set of principles or norms concerning trade in agriculture which, it was hoped, would influence the making of agricultural policies affecting trade, in addition to laying the groundwork for the development of more precise rules on agricultural trade in other forums, particularly in the GATT.

The first substantial effort made to develop recommendations for action on agricultural trade by the OECD in the 1970s was contained in the report of the High Level Group on Trade and Related Problems, commonly known as the Rey report. Although this was formally an independent group of experts, it was appointed by the Secretary-General of the OECD and its recommendations were discussed by the OECD Council. Moreover, the divisions among OECD member countries were reflected in the disagreements among members of the High

117

Level Group, particularly on the issue of agricultural trade. It was this issue which gave rise to the longest discussions in the Group, the results of which were inconclusive:

> As is known, this subject has been debated for years both within the Organisation and in the other international bodies, without it having been possible so far to reconcile fully the divergent points of view held. The present examination revealed that it is still not possible to reconcile these differences.[15]

> In principle, more freedom of trade in agricultural products should not be ruled out as an objective, but at the same time it would have little meaning if it were not based on harmonising the agricultural aid and price support policies currently applied in various forms by almost all OECD Member countries. However, the opening up of agriculture to international competition raises more thorny problems than in other sectors owing to the social and political considerations underlying agricultural policies. It is hardly thinkable that it should involve the reduction of farmers' per capita incomes, and if it is to lead to an appreciable reduction in the population employed on the land, as it has begun to do, the reduction cannot be made at more than a certain speed without raising serious political problems.[16]

There were two main camps in the Group, both of whose preferences were presented in the Rey report. The first felt that the "essential principles and mechanisms" of existing agricultural policies should not be brought into question, but that the introduction of a number of limited improvements should be considered. These included adjusting prices to changing demand situations; freezing protectionist measures; relaxing import restrictions; reviewing health regulations, customs procedures and compulsory standards; seeking to regulate and avoid abuses in the use of export aids; the building of stocks; production control measures; direct payments or tax relief to small farmers; and international commodity arrangements for some products in order to stabilise markets.

The second camp accepted these measures as a first step only, and recommended more far-reaching actions based on a more market-oriented approach. This part of the Group was especially critical of price support and guarantee systems, pre-ferring direct income support for farmers, and called for an appreciable reduction of export aids. Some members of this second camp felt that agreement was needed immediately on longer-term global objectives and principles. These members called for fundamental policy reforms which would result in a substantial expansion of trade and a far greater market orien-tation to agriculture.[17] While the alternative positions presented in the Rey report did not represent a coherent set of principles acceptable to all OECD countries, the report was an important first step in the direction of establishing such principles.

For the most part, the subsequent development of norms and principles can be traced through the communiqués issued at the end of the various meetings at the Ministerial level of either the Committee for Agriculture or of the OECD Council, as well as through a number of reports published by the Organisation containing statements of principles, all of which were subject to negotiation. In April 1973, the Ministers of Agriculture affirmed the intention of their governments to approach the Multilateral Trade Negotiations with an attitude of mutual con-ciliation to improve the conditions of trade, and they pointed to the recommendations and analyses of the Rey report. The Ministers also emphasised the importance of achieving the stab-ility of agricultural markets.[18]

At the next agricultural Ministerial meeting held in February 1978, the Ministers "considered that, having regard to the inter-national impact of domestic agricultural policies, corrective mea-sures should be taken in concert" to reduce fluctuations in world commodity markets and to obtain "desired stability". They also emphasised "the need to take rapid action to establish an internationally co-ordinated system of nationally held stocks adequate to provide food security and to introduce a greater measure of stability into the international grains market in the future".[19] This concern for market stability was repeated in the communiqué approved at the 1978 Ministerial Council meeting on Positive Adjustment Policies, which stated, "More generally, it is advisable to seek improvement in the functioning of agricul-tural markets as well as in their stabilisation".[20]

The March 1980 agricultural Ministerial meeting produced more vague undertakings to ensure wider access to markets and avoid market distortions:

Ministers agreed to intensify efforts to develop a trading system for agricultural products which would facilitate a more efficient use of agricultural resources on a world-wide scale and an orderly increase in the volume of trade. In this context the primary objectives are to ensure both wider access to markets and security of supply, and to avoid trade practices that lead to market distortions. Ministers welcome the attention being given to these issues by OECD in its work on agricultural trade problems.[21]

In its consideration of international trade in June 1980, the OECD Ministerial Council agreed to intensify efforts in the agricultural sector towards the achievement of the objectives agreed to by agriculture Ministers earlier that year. The Ministers agreed that food supply and food security were high priority international objectives and stressed the need for measures to reduce fluctuations in agricultural markets.[22]

As the Tokyo Round was winding up, and with little progress made on agriculture in that forum, agreement was reached in the OECD Ministerial Council meeting of June 1979 to embark on the OECD's first comprehensive study of the problems of agricultural trade. This study, which was to pre-occupy the Joint Working Party for the next three years, focused on the relationship between agricultural trade, domestic agricultural policies and the overall economy, and was intended to contribute to the aim of improving trade flows and maintaining an open trading system.[23]

The conclusions of the final report were discussed and endorsed at the May 1982 Ministerial Council meeting.[24] In their most extensive consideration to agricultural trade up to that date, the Ministers formally recognised for the first time "that agricultural trade is affected by general economic developments and by domestic agricultural policies". This declaration was significant in that it marked acceptance of the principle that domestic agricultural policies were a legitimate subject of trade negotiations. Furthermore, the Ministers agreed "that agricultural trade should be more fully integrated within the open and multilateral trading system", and that,

the desirable adjustments in domestic policies can best take place if such moves are planned and co-ordinated within a concerted multilateral approach aimed at achieving a gradual reduction in protection and a liberalisation of trade, in which a balance should be maintained as between countries and commodities.[25]

Agreement was also reached at the 1982 Ministerial Council that the Organisation should study the various possible ways in which the aims set out in the report could be achieved "as a contribution to progress in strengthening co-operation on agricultural trade issues and as a contribution to the development of practical multilateral and other solutions".[26] Three areas were identified by the Ministers for further study: i) an analysis of the approaches and methods for a balanced and gradual reduction of protection for agriculture, and the fuller integration of agriculture within the open multilateral trading system, while taking into account the specific characteristics and role of agriculture; ii) an examination of relevant national policies and measures which had a significant impact on agricultural trade, with the aim of assisting policy-makers in the preparation and implementation of agricultural policies; and iii) an analysis of the most appropriate methods for improving the functioning of the world agricultural market.

Agriculture Ministers at the Committee for Agriculture meeting in December 1982 agreed on principles similar to those adopted at the Ministerial Council earlier that year:

> More than in the recent past, certain national policies had had the consequence of limiting the effects of world developments on the domestic agricultural sector and of exacerbating the problems in international agricultural trade. Ministers stressed the need, when formulating and implementing policies, to take into account the interests of each country and the desirability of ensuring an orderly development of the international market.[27]

The communiqué approved at the end of this meeting contained numerous statements touching on various principles of agricultural trade. The issue of market stability was referred to several times:

> The problems involved in achieving greater world market stability, including greater security of supplies and a better access to markets, had focused attention yet again on the

need for further multilateral initiatives aimed at improving the international trade situation.

The present situation called for immediate action, as the problems arising from market imbalances could have potentially dangerous consequences. Pragmatic and multilateral action was required, inspired by a sense of urgency and collective self-restraint.

The issue of food security was also dealt with in this meeting. The Ministers agreed that,

> food security considerations in developed countries, however justified, should not imply the pursuit of total self-sufficiency policies for food. Ministers agreed that food security could also be enhanced through a more open and better functioning trading system, while it could be reduced and the stability of the world economy impaired, by policies based on purely national perspectives.[28]

One outcome of the high-level consultations organised by the Secretary-General in February 1984 was an acknowledgement that a fundamental reorientation of some major aspects of agricultural policies was essential. Once again, in the absence of consensus on precisely what direction this orientation should take, the different alternatives discussed in the meetings were published. These included on the one hand the utilisation of all available productive resources while accepting the effects of the market place, and on the other hand guaranteeing prices, for social or economic reasons, but setting limits to such guarantees. There did appear to be agreement that it was necessary for all major producing and trading countries to accept responsibility for stock policies, price disciplines and restraint on credits and subsidies, both domestically and internationally.[29]

At the Ministerial Council meeting in May 1984, Ministers expressed their concern about the existence of serious international market disequilibria in a number of agricultural products, which they attributed to a large extent to domestic support policies. In a rather weakly worded undertaking, they "recognised the need to ease measures which hinder the requisite long-term adjustments and to persevere with current efforts aimed at reducing protectionism and trade distortions and at improving the functioning of international markets".[30] This theme was developed further at a special meeting of the Committee for Agriculture in March 1985, where participants concluded,

> that there was a need for concerted action by OECD Members to improve balance in markets and the climate of the international trading relations, notably by disposing of stocks in an orderly manner, maintaining or tightening production control measures and drawing up overall national strategies which would be consistent internationally.[31]

The language of the communiqué issued the following month at the Ministerial Council was considerably more vague:

> Serious tensions exist in the field of agricultural trade, particularly with respect to the generation and disposal of surpluses. Determined efforts will continue to be made to identify and implement urgently the indispensable adjustments in agricultural policies, and trade and financing practices, which are required to reduce these tensions.[32]

The Ministerial Trade Mandate (MTM) study initiated in 1982 took over four years to complete. First, an appropriate methodology for Part I of the mandate was worked out, involving the construction of a quantitative model for the agricultural sectors of several countries. This analysis of agricultural protection was intended to permit a comparison of all forms of assistance in terms of their effects on production and trade, and to evaluate the impact of reductions in the levels of this assistance on prices, production, consumption and trade. A number of assistance reduction scenarios were analysed, including a 10 per cent reduction for all commodities and countries.[33]

Part II of the MTM involved a series of country studies, which evaluated the effects of various support policies and measures on agricultural trade. The quantitative aspect of these policies and actions were measured by using the concepts of "producer subsidy equivalents" (PSEs) and "consumer subsidy equivalents" (CSEs). The qualitative aspects of agricultural and more general policies, such as taxation and transportation, were also examined in these country studies. The countries and groups of countries covered were Canada, Australia, Austria, the EEC, Japan, New Zealand and the United States.[34] Part III was largely dealt with in the context of the analyses of the principal commodities conducted under Part I, in which the impact of liberalisation measures on world markets were determined.[35]

The final report of the MTM study, *National Policies and Agricultural Trade*, was approved by the OECD Council meeting at the Ministerial level in May 1987, and the Ministers called on the OECD to update and improve the analytical tools it had begun to develop. Consequently, PSEs and CSEs were calculated for the period 1982–1986 and extended to other countries and products. A decision was also made to conduct country studies on Sweden, Switzerland, Finland and Norway. The five scenarios of protective measures reduction were repeated for the 1982–1985 period, and modifications were made to the MTM model permitting new factors to be incorporated.[36]

The May 1987 meeting marked a milestone in the Organisation's work on agricultural trade. It produced the strongest and most wide-ranging commitments yet agreed upon on this issue, not just within the OECD but in any multilateral forum. Ministers agreed to implement "in a balanced manner" a concerted reform of agricultural policies which would be based upon a number of principles. First, the long-term objective of this reform was to allow market signals to influence the orientation of agricultural production by way of a progressive and concerted reduction of agricultural support. Because this progressive correction of policies would require time, it was considered all the more necessary that this effort "be started without delay". However, it was recognised that such concerns as food security and overall employment should be considered as well in pursuing the long-term objective of agricultural reform.

Secondly, it was agreed that the most immediate need was to avoid further deterioration of existing market imbalances. To that end, the most notable commitment was "to implement measures which, by reducing guaranteed prices and other types of production incentives, by imposing quantitative production restrictions, or by other means, will prevent an increase in excess supply". Thirdly, supply control measures (including production restrictions and the withdrawal of productive farming resources) were to be implemented in such a way as to minimise economic distortions and to contribute to a better functioning of market mechanisms. Fourthly, the Ministers agreed that farm support should be sought through direct income support, rather than through price guarantees or other measures linked to production or to factors of production. Fifthly, policies which supported structural adjustment in the agricultural sector were endorsed. Finally, it was accepted that governments retained flexibility in the choice of the means necessary to fulfil their commitments to implement these principles.

The Ministers also agreed that the Uruguay Round was of decisive importance and that the Ministerial Declaration of Punta del Este furnished a framework for most of the measures needed to give effect to the principles listed above, "including a progressive reduction of assistance to and protection of agriculture on a multi-country and multi-commodity basis". In order to enhance the chances of early progress in the Uruguay Round, it was agreed that "OECD governments will carry out expeditiously their standstill and rollback commitments and, more generally, refrain from actions which would worsen the negotiating climate". Furthermore, they agreed to "avoid initiating actions which would result in stimulating production in surplus agricultural commodities and in isolating the domestic market further from international markets". Finally, the Ministers agreed to "act responsibly in disposing of surplus stocks and refrain from confrontational and destabilising trade practices".[37]

At the next OECD Ministerial Council meeting in May 1988, the Ministers reaffirmed their commitment made in May 1987, and agreed that it was imperative that policy reform efforts "be strengthened by all Member countries as a matter of urgency", in view of the limited progress made since their last meeting. They also agreed that,

> Further measures will be taken, based upon the principles agreed upon at the last Ministerial Council, to allow market signals increasingly to influence the orientation of agricultural production, by way of a progressive and concerted reduction of agricultural support as well as by all other appropriate means, while consideration may be given to social and other concerns.[38]

It was decided that work should be continued on improving and updating the PSE/CSE tool as well as the MTM model.

The Ministers mandated a study of such reform measures as quantitative limitations on production or factors of production, direct income support, other measures aimed at facilitating structural adjustment, and policies for rural development. Finally, they decided to broaden the work on the economy-wide effects of agricultural policies.[39]

No new principles or norms were agreed on at the 1989 Ministerial Council, although there were some changes in language which indicated that agreement had been reached to place greater emphasis on certain points. For example, in the Ministerial communiqué, it was agreed that reform should be achieved through "mutually reinforcing actions at domestic and international levels", underlining the importance of including domestic agricultural policy reforms in the Uruguay Round. As well, Ministers called for reductions in agricultural support and protection that were "substantial", using this word for the first time in a Ministerial communiqué.[40]

As there were no clear rules or norms devised by the OECD on agricultural trade until 1987, there was naturally little scope for any supervisory function for the Organisation prior to that date. However, at the 1987 Ministerial Council the OECD was given a monitoring role which was unparalleled in the other trade sectors for which it was responsible. The Ministers decided that the OECD would monitor the implementation of the various actions and principles agreed to during that meeting. To that end the Secretary-General was asked to submit a progress report to the next Ministerial Council held in May 1988. The Secretariat drew up a report and submitted it to the Agriculture and Trade committees in early 1988.[41] The implementation of principles and policy actions by each country was assessed generally and by product, with particular attention devoted to supply management and the orientation of policies towards the market. The report was reviewed and endorsed by the 1988 Ministerial Council, and approved for publication. At that time, the Ministers agreed that the Organisation's monitoring work would continue, and the monitoring report became a regular annual publication.[42]

4. *Impact of OECD Agreements*

While it is difficult to determine the precise impact of the informational work OECD members agreed to initiate, it is clear that the studies undertaken after 1979 facilitated discussions within the OECD on agricultural trade by clarifying certain issues such as the costs of agricultural protection and support measures, and the actual levels of these government practices and policies for each country and for the major agricultural products. In so doing, there was a more solid basis for intensifying negotiations, both within the OECD and later in other forums, on the liberalisation of agricultural trade.

An easier task is that of evaluating the impact of the commitments agreed on by Ministers to take certain actions affecting agricultural trade. Since these commitments were only adopted fairly recently, however, it is may be too early to make any definitive assessment of their impact, especially since many of the commitments were of a long-term nature. The best that can be offered at this point is a preliminary evaluation, based in the first instance, upon the surprisingly frank 1988 report of the OECD, entitled *Agricultural Policies, Markets and Trade: Monitoring and Outlook*. This report concluded that there was little evidence that countries actually did "refrain from actions which would worsen the negotiating climate" in the Uruguay Round as they said they would at the 1987 Ministerial Council. Trade confrontations continued as exporters intensified their efforts to maintain or increase their share of markets, often with the use of new or increased export subsidies.[43]

A separate report issued in May 1988 by the National Centre for Food and Agricultural Policy reached similar conclusions. The US was found to have expanded its agricultural export subsidy programme, while protection of the American sugar market was increased. Canada had doubled its direct payments to farmers since 1986, and failed to encourage market-oriented production decisions. The EEC was found to have the highest level of export subsidies in years. In virtually none of the OECD countries had agricultural support prices been lowered enough to remove their production-incentive effects, and almost everywhere PSEs were rising as a proportion of gross farm receipts.[44]

However, another report issued by the Institute for International Economics did find some signs of encouragement.

127

Japan lowered its rice support price in 1987 for the first time in over thirty years, and reduced its internal beef and dairy prices. The report also found that expenditures on subsidies to agriculture in the US were reduced from $26 billion in 1985–86 to roughly $17 billion in fiscal 1987–88. At the EC summit meeting in June 1987, European leaders confirmed the Community's commitment made in the OECD to reform the CAP, and launched internal negotiations to that end. In February, 1988, the Council of Ministers of the EC decided that increases in spending on agricultural support would be limited to no more than 74 per cent of the increase in Community GNP, and that the overall expenditure on agriculture would be limited to 1.2 per cent of Community GNP. These expenditure limits were to be achieved through cuts in domestic prices for a number of commodities, and through production quotas. The EC Council also introduced a voluntary land set-aside programme.[45] However, these measures did not address price supports, export subsidies or improving access to EC markets for exporters outside the Community.[46]

The second annual Monitoring and Outlook report carried out by the OECD Secretariat in 1989 found little concrete evidence of significant progress towards the goal of agricultural reform over the preceding year. Although levels of assistance to agriculture had fallen somewhat in 1988, this was felt to be caused largely by an increase in world prices rather than by changes in policy.[47] At the 1989 Ministerial Council, it was recognised that the role of market signals in the orientation of agricultural production was generally insufficient, that trade tensions continued to be acute and that market access had improved in only a few cases.[48] While assistance to agriculture declined for a second consecutive year in 1989, the level of assistance was still substantially above the already high levels of the first half of the 1980s, according to the third Monitoring and Outlook report. Moreover, the decline in agricultural support was again found to be predominantly the result of higher world prices and a stronger US dollar. The contribution of policy changes to the reduction in rates of assistance was considered marginal.[49]

Table 4.3
Producer Subsidy Equivalents
All Products by Country

		1979-86 (avg.)	1987	1988	1989
AUSTRALIA					
Net total PSE	US$ bn	1.07	1.10	1.23	1.25
Net percentage PSE	%	12	11	9	10
AUSTRIA					
Net total PSE	US$ bn	1.07	2.19	2.16	1.71
Net percentage PSE	%	32	48	47	39
CANADA					
Net total PSE	US$ bn	4.19	6.66	6.12	5.56
Net percentage PSE	%	32	49	42	37
EUROPEAN COMMUNITY*					
Net total PSE	US$ bn	39.87	72.95	70.48	61.49
Net percentage PSE	%	37	49	46	41
FINLAND					
Net total PSE	US$ bn	2.25	3.77	4.06	4.26
Net percentage PSE	%	58	72	73	70
JAPAN					
Net total PSE	US$ bn	21.56	35.15	36.52	33.67
Net percentage PSE	%	66	76	74	71
NEW ZEALAND					
Net total PSE	US$ bn	0.74	0.34	0.24	0.21
Net percentage PSE	%	25	14	7	5
NORWAY					
Net total PSE	US$ bn	1.71	2.53	2.66	2.55
Net percentage PSE	%	72	76	76	75
SWEDEN					
Net total PSE	US$ bn	1.64	2.53	2.45	2.72
Net percentage PSE	%	44	57	52	52
SWITZERLAND					
Net total PSE	US$ bn	2.62	4.47	4.76	4.18
Net percentage PSE	%	68	80	78	73
UNITED STATES					
Net total PSE	US$ bn	30.66	45.07	37.21	33.42
Net percentage PSE	%	28	41	34	29
OECD					
Net total PSE	US$ bn	107.38	176.78	167.91	151.01
Net percentage PSE	%	37	50	46	41

* EC-10: 1979-85; EC-12: 1986-89.

Source: OECD, *Agricultural Policies, Markets and Trade,* various issues.

5. Bargaining Positions and Outcomes

One of the striking features of agricultural trade negotiations in the OECD during the 1970s and much of the 1980s was how little movement there was in the positions of the participants. Prior to 1982, OECD members were generally grouped into two main blocs on agricultural issues. The so-called "overseas countries" (the US, Canada, Australia, and New Zealand) formed a coalition supporting trade liberalisation and a reduction of export subsidies. The EC, usually supported by other Western European countries, generally opposed this position, preferring some form of "management" of international agricultural markets (through price controls, production quotas and market sharing). Japan generally kept a low profile in these discussions, not joining either of the two groups, but not supporting any strong third position either. Its main concern was for food security, and only became vocal when it felt that its domestic production might be threatened by demands to lift import restrictions.

The United States was generally dissatisfied with the conclusions of the Rey Report in 1972, and Special Trade Representative William D. Eberle insisted that his dissenting views be annexed to the report before signing it. The US was clearly the principal advocate of fundamental agricultural policy reforms and trade expansion, and the failure of other members of the High Level Group to endorse this position was a source of disappointment to the Americans.

An analysis of the language of the Ministerial communiqués in the succeeding period reveals that the US position gradually became more acceptable to other OECD members. Certain key terms indicate which actors had the greatest success in these Ministerial meetings. "Food security" was a special concern of Japan, while references to "market stability" tended to reflect the preference of the EC. Whenever such terms as "market forces" and "trade expansion" were employed, this indicated the adoption of language put forward by the United States.

The overall pattern was for European concerns for stabilising markets to prevail through most of the 1970s, while references to trade liberalisation and to greater reliance on market forces began around 1980 and gradually shared roughly equal prominence with market stability. By 1987, the American position appeared to dominate OECD statements, although European demands for flexibility and concerns about confrontational American trade actions were also included. References to food security were a constant throughout this period, although by the 1980s the US was able to modify this principle somewhat by adding the provision that food security need not be equated with self-sufficiency and by underlining how expanded trade could promote food security.

The proposal for the Trade Mandate study originally came from New Zealand, with strong backing from the United States. Over the course of the study there was a gradual shifting of positions on the agricultural trade issue. The EC slowly came to accept the principle that agricultural reform, including a reduction of subsidies, was a necessary course of action.[50] The overseas countries pushed for the inclusion of the modelling work in Part I of the study, but the EC Commission was initially rather sceptical about this. Later, however, the Commission became one of the staunchest supporters of the MTM model. Part III of the study, on agricultural markets, was included largely at the request of the Europeans, but this part was eventually given relatively little attention as the EC became more interested in the other parts of the study.[51]

Within the context of this struggle over rather general principles and orientations, a number of more specific issues were also addressed over the years. In 1978, the United States succeeded in getting other members to accept the principle of creating an international system of nationally held wheat and rice stocks in order to try to stabilise international grain markets.[52] The US also attempted to negotiate an agreement governing the use of export credits for agricultural products, similar to other OECD export credit agreements, but this proposal was successfully resisted by other member countries.[53] At the April 1986 Ministerial Council, the US, supported by the UK, argued that the dismantling of farm subsidies should figure prominently in the next round of GATT negotiations. Agricultural trade was the most divisive issue on the agenda of the meeting, and no agreement could be reached on the dispute over the effects of the enlargement of the EC on agriculture, or on how agriculture should be handled in the GATT talks.[54]

The greatest movement in positions among OECD members in agricultural negotiations emerged in 1987. It was during this year that the opposing viewpoints most visibly collided, and that the greatest amount of bargaining activity took place. The year began with several member countries, including France and Japan, blocking the publication of the synthesis report of the Trade Mandate Study.[55] The United States, on the other hand, supported the report's publication, and was joined by Australia, Canada, New Zealand, the United Kingdom and smaller European countries in seeking a declaration for rolling back subsidies.[56] Australia was a particularly strong proponent of ending farm export subsidies, as it had been for years, and also favoured giving the OECD a strong monitoring role in the agricultural policy reform process, a role that France viewed as rather dangerous.[57]

The US was by and large satisfied with the outcome of the May 1987 Ministerial Council. Two of its major objectives were achieved, namely, agreement on the principles of reducing subsidies and decoupling farm income support from price support measures. Treasury Secretary James Baker called the communiqué "a major step forward towards multilateral agreements on agricultural reform", and USTR Clayton Yeutter said the statement was "without a doubt the most comprehensive and forward-looking" he had ever seen from an international forum.[58] Most American officials agreed that the communiqué represented a major breakthrough in agricultural trade negotiation.

A number of American objectives were not realised during the May meeting, however. First, the United States did not want to include any mention of the need for short-term measures in order to reduce tensions, since it tended to view such tensions as necessary to bring about longer-term reform, but on this point the US was virtually isolated. Secondly, the US had originally sought endorsement for the elimination of price supports, but the EC, and Germany in particular, blocked this proposal. The United States had to settle for an undertaking to reduce guaranteed prices, and reluctantly accepted the reference to quantitative production restrictions as a possible means of preventing excess supply, a reference that it had strongly opposed.[59]

A third setback for the United States was when it had to end its attempt to get the other Ministers to accept a commitment to speed up GATT farm trade talks. Earlier the US had been

132

pushing for a "fast track" approach to the GATT negotiations, in which agriculture would be placed in a separate category and results would be expected before the end of the fourth year of the Uruguay Round. It softened this demand by proposing an "early start" to agricultural negotiations, but in the face of opposition particularly from Germany and France, even this term had to be dropped.[60]

The US, along with the EC delegation, was also seeking endorsement of the new computer framework developed in the Secretariat for comparing and negotiating a wide range of farm support measures, including subsidies. In face of strong Japanese opposition, the language of the communiqué was watered down to authorise the Secretariat to "further its work by updating and improving the analytic tools it has begun to develop". The US also had to drop its proposal to urge the Venice summit meeting to "further broaden" agricultural reform talks, since the Germans, French and Italians argued that the agreement reached in Paris already went further than expected.[61] Finally, the American attempt to get Ministers to express their commitment to avoid unlimited production was dropped.[62]

Other countries also made concessions, however. Germany had resisted the inclusion of references even to the need to *reduce* price supports, but reluctantly accepted them when the role of quantitative production restrictions was acknowledged. Japan and France dropped their opposition to the publication of the Trade Mandate synthesis report, something they had opposed because the report exposed Japan and the EC as the two highest subsidisers of agriculture in the OECD. This represented a fairly major concession, since US officials had argued that publication of the report would add strong ammunition to the cause of reducing subsidies. Japanese uneasiness with this decision was indicated at the end of the Ministerial meeting when Japan expressed its concern about increasing the country's reliance on imported food, something that was an almost certain consequence of reducing agricultural support.[63]

The EC Commission appeared generally satisfied with the Ministerial statement. At the end of the meeting, Commissioner Willy de Clercq expressed his support for bringing "farm production into conformity with the reality of the world market". EC Agriculture Commissioner Frans Andriessen noted that "A few years ago it would have been impossible to have agreed on an issue as controversial as farm policy . . . Our agreement says something about the urgency of the problem worldwide".[64]

The following Ministerial Council in May 1988 produced a stalemate on the issue of agricultural trade. The US pressed the EC to accept a specific timetable for ending agricultural subsidies. The EC rejected this demand, calling it unrealistic and accused the US of damaging the negotiating climate. As a result, the US dropped its proposal but in return refused to accept a commitment not to undermine Community efforts to reduce subsidies. This proposed commitment was aimed at US plans to bring back into production farmland that had been set aside and to increase its export subsidy programme by $1 billion.[65]

6. *Explaining OECD Agreements and their Impact*

(a) Overall Capabilities

There are no clear indications that the United States used its overall power resources to pressure other participants in the OECD negotiations on agricultural trade or to enforce compliance with OECD agreements. The OECD talks were not referred to in economic summit communiqués until 1986, after which the work of the OECD was regularly given summit endorsement. In none of the summits was progress in the OECD on the agricultural trade issue a major source of controversy, nor did the US seriously attempt to make any linkages with non-trade issues. In one instance, in early 1982, a vague warning was issued by Robert D. Hormats, Assistant Secretary of State for Economic and Business Affairs, when he said "we have constantly stressed to the EC that these agricultural issues must be satisfactorily resolved or they will impact on broader US-European political and economic relations".[66] However, he gave no hint as to exactly what this impact might be, and no apparent US action was taken to follow up on this warning.

OECD Ministerial Council meetings generally ignored the agricultural trade issue until 1978, but subsequently it became a fairly major topic of discussion in most Ministerials. However, available documentation on the proceedings of those meetings does not reveal any linkage attempts at this level either. Proposals to undertake studies were seldom controversial, since

134

they were generally not viewed as threatening, and Ministerial agreements on principles tended to be the result of the gradual upward movement of discussions and agreements reached at lower levels, rather than being imposed from above by Ministers or heads of state. Hence, there was less scope for issue linkage than there would have been had proposals been introduced at the Minsisterial level.

(b) International Trade Structure

There was a relative lack of attempted linkages with unrelated trade issues in the OECD agricultural trade negotiations for the same reasons as those presented above with respect to non-trade issue linkage. When testifying before Congress in the spring of 1983, Agriculture Secretary John Block was asked if the US had any leverage to encourage Japan to open up its agricultural markets. He replied that

> The United States is a big market for Japan and they want to be sure that they can continue to have access to it. They are concerned about staying on our side and being looked upon favourably . . . I think they are very sensitive on this issue. That is the leverage we have; is their sensitivity.[67]

As was the case in negotiations on most other trade issues, Japan was certainly concerned about the possibility that the US might try to restrict the flow of imports from Japan, primarily because of the growing US trade deficit with that country. Yet the US appeared to exercise considerable restraint in using this more general trade imbalance as a bargaining chip with Japan in the OECD talks. One close observer of agricultural negotiations commented in the mid-1980s that " . . . it is somewhat odd that agricultural talks with Japan have not been functionally linked to automotive and electronic trade issues more explicitly".[68]

In the case of the EC, this underlying pressure was more or less absent, since the US was running a trade surplus with the EC in the early 1980s, and the bilateral trade deficits of the later 1980s were far smaller than those experienced with Japan. In fact, there was one vague threat made by the Community in 1982 when EC officials said that the American decision to impose import duties on sales of European steel to the US had hardened attitudes in Brussels on agriculture.[69] But the steel

135

issue did not seem significantly to affect subsequent developments in the OECD talks on agriculture.

(c) Issue Structure

There are several possible ways of measuring capabilities relevant to the issue of agricultural trade, including bilateral agricultural trade balances and the relative importance of the markets
of certain other countries to total agricultural exports, taking
into consideration the relative importance of agricultural exports
to total farm income and to total exports. In addition, the level
of financial resources available to governments for subsidising
the agricultural sector, particularly agricultural exports, may be
considered a source of bargaining power.

The more agricultural products a country imports from its
bargaining partners, presumably the more potent will be its
threats to curtail those imports, particularly if its imports represent a major share of the exporter's total market.[70] The more
dependent a country is on foreign agricultural markets generally, the more vulnerable it will be to such import restrictions.
Because of the possibility of retaliation, it is important to compare the relative dependence of the various sets of trading
partners in the negotiations. Finally, the larger a country's agricultural budget, and the greater its flexibility to increase that
budget, the more likely it will be to prevail in a subsidy war.
Level of exports as a source of power is not considered here
because an agricultural embargo would be too extreme a measure to be useful in bargaining over agricultural trade within
the OECD.[71]

Using the first of these measures, the greatest agricultural
power appears to be the EC, which during the 1970s and 1980s
imported considerably more farm products than any other
country or group of countries in the OECD. As Table 4.4 indicates, the US and Japan imported about half the amount of
agricultural products that the EC imported during the 1970s
and 1980s, while most of the remaining OECD members were
relatively small agricultural importers. In terms of straight bilateral trade balances, in 1985 New Zealand was the most vulnerable to the cut off of export markets, while Japan was the least
vulnerable (see Table 4.5). The US ran significant deficits with
Canada, New Zealand and Australia, as did the EC with

Table 4.4
Shares of Selected Economies in Total World Agricultural Imports
(Per cent of value)

	EC*	Other W.Eur.	US	Canada	Australia	N.Z.	Japan
1970	22.2	17.4	11.2	2.2	0.4	0.2	7.4
1975	23.6	5.3	7.4	2.2	0.4	0.2	8.1
1980	23.2	5.0	7.2	1.8	0.4	0.1	7.0
1985	18.3	7.1	9.9	2.0	0.5	0.2	7.2
1986	20.9	4.1	9.7	2.0	0.5	0.2	7.2
1987	21.0	4.2	8.6	1.9	0.4	0.2	7.5
1988	20.0	4.0	7.8	1.9	0.5	0.2	8.5
1989	n.a.	3.8	7.6	2.0	0.5	0.2	8.8

*Only includes countries that were members of the EC during the year listed.
Excludes intra-EC trade.

Source: FAO, *Trade Yearbook*, various issues; Commission of the European Communities, *Agricultural Situation in the Community*, various issues.

Table 4.5
Destination of Agricultural Exports 1985*
(Thousand US dollars)

Source:	Canada	US	Japan	Australia	N.Z.	EC-10	EFTA-7
Destination:							
Canada		1605068	26264	77659	84562	685021	88249
US	2150648		161146	607937	499730	4134787	432773
Japan	946300	5474733		1292253	335746	952508	153934
Australia	13886	123303	12364		149273	285620	19436
New Zealand	5548	29701	3745	78031		43934	1643
EC-10	603020	5504649	103874	955297	999190		1775759
EFTA-7	70938	916021	5364	69481	33725	3724092	
World	6951449	30188697	876090	7549606	3392217	24055887	3690279

Note: Table excludes intra-EC and intra-EFTA trade.
* Agricultural exports correspond with SITC(rev.2) O(less 03),1,21,22,232,
26(less 266,267,269),29,4.

Source: Based on statistics from OECD, *Statistics of Foreign Trade*, various issues.

Table 4.6
Destination of Agricultural Exports 1985*
(Percentage of Exporting Country's Total Agricultural Exports)

Source:	Canada	US	Japan	Australia	N.Z.	EC-10	EFTA-7
Destination:							
Canada		5.3	3.0	1.0	2.5	2.8	2.4
US	30.9		18.4	8.0	14.7	17.2	11.7
Japan	13.7	18.1		16.9	9.9	4.0	4.2
Australia	0.2	0.4	1.4		4.4	1.2	0.5
New Zealand	0.1	0.1	0.4	1.3		0.2	0.1
EC-10	8.7	18.2	11.9	14.1	29.5		48.1
EFTA-7	1.0	3.0	0.6	0.4	1.0	15.5	
World	100	100	100	100	100	100	100

Note: Table excludes intra-EC and intra-EFTA trade.
* Agricultural exports correspond with SITC(rev.2) O(less 03),1,21,22,232,
26(less 266,267,269),29,4.

Source: Based on statistics from OECD, *Statistics of Foreign Trade*, various issues.

Australia and New Zealand, and Canada with Australia. Japan had the largest bilateral deficits of all, running deficits with virtually every other OECD country.

When bilateral trade is viewed in terms of relative shares of total exports, as set out in Table 4.6, the picture is a bit different. Canada was the most dependent of all OECD countries on the American market, and was also dependent to a lesser extent on the Japanese and EC markets. Australia was the more dependent partner in all bilateral trade relationships, particularly with the US and Japan, and New Zealand was in a similar position, except that it was most dependent on the EC and the US. Japan was still in an advantageous bargaining position with Canada, Australia and New Zealand, but not with the US, and actually sent more of its total agricultural exports to the EC than the EC sent to Japan. While the EC had a distinct advantage over Canada, Japan and New Zealand in 1985, its advantage over the US was less significant.

The United States was the dependent country in all of its bilateral agricultural trade relationships, although this dependence was roughly symmetrical in the case of Japan, and to a lesser extent with the EC. However, this symmetrical relationship with the EC was relatively recent, since through the 1970s and the early 1980s, the US was much more dependent on the

Table 4.7
US-EC Agricultural Trade*

	US Exports to EC ($ billion)	(% US Agri. Exports)	EC Exports to US** ($ billion)	(% EC Agri. Exports)
1970	1.92	25.87	0.43	12.13
1971	1.87	23.73	0.45	11.14
1972	2.15	22.33	0.53	10.74
1973	4.60	25.60	1.44	16.85
1974	5.59	25.03	1.57	14.99
1975	5.65	25.35	1.44	13.02
1976	6.58	27.96	1.59	14.16
1977	6.77	27.85	1.84	13.30
1978	7.39	24.49	2.36	14.36
1979	7.87	22.04	2.59	12.79
1980	9.27	21.86	2.72	10.32
1981	9.41	21.12	2.92	10.38
1982	8.63	22.80	3.12	12.85
1983	7.61	20.44	3.32	14.49
1984	6.76	17.37	3.80	15.96
1985	5.51	18.23	4.13	17.19
1986	7.18	26.15	4.93	18.35
1987	7.57	24.55	5.20	17.06
1988	8.19	20.51	5.12	15.44
1989	7.64	17.52	5.11	14.10

* Agricultural trade corresponds with SITC(rev.2) 0(less 03),
1,21,22,232,26(less 266,267,269),29,4.
** Excludes intra-EC trade.

Source: Based on statistics from OECD, *Statistics of Foreign Trade*, various issues.

EC market than the reverse in both straight value terms and as a percentage of total agricultural exports, as Table 4.7 indicates.

The foregoing analysis is inadequate unless a number of other factors are also considered, including the importance of agricultural exports to national farm income and to a country's total merchandise exports. Charts 4.5 and 4.6 show that New Zealand and Australia were the countries where agricultural exports represented the largest proportion of farm income and total export revenue. Canada's dependence on agricultural exports for farm income was also relatively high, although farm exports as a share of total merchandise exports was slightly below the OECD average.

Japan was the least dependent on agricultural exports, both

Chart 4.5
Agricultural Exports as a Share of Agricultural Production
(Value)

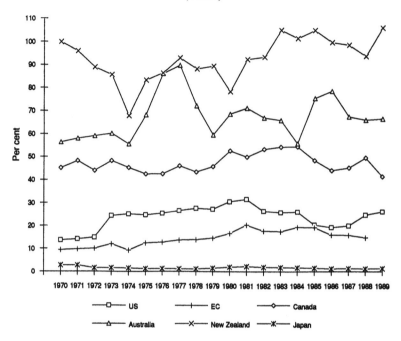

Excluding intra-EC trade. Only includes countries that were EC members during year listed.

Source: FAO, *FAO Trade Yearbook*; Canada, *Canada Yearbook*; Australia, *Year Book Australia*; New Zealand, *New Zealand Official Yearbook*; United States Department of Agriculture, *Agricultural Statistics*; Commission of the EC, *Agriculture: Statistical Yearbook* and *Agricultural Situation in the Community*; Japan, *Statistical Yearbook of the Ministry of Agriculture, Forestry and Fisheries*, various issues.

for farm income and for total export revenue, leading one to expect that it would be in a very strong bargaining position, since any restriction on farm imports from Japan by any other country would not cause a severe loss of either export revenue or agricultural income. The US was more dependent on agricultural exports in general than the EC, which, combined with the relatively greater dependence of the US on EC markets, put the EC in a significantly stronger bargaining position with the US.

Chart 4.6
Share of Agricultural Exports in
Total Exports of Selected Economies

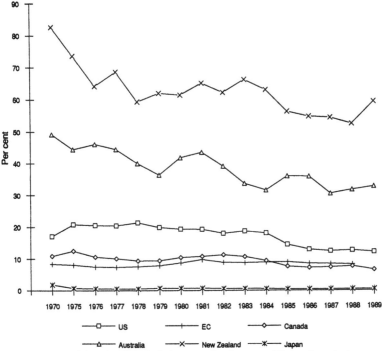

—□— US   —+— EC   —◇— Canada

—△— Australia   —×— New Zealand   —✳— Japan

Excluding intra-EC trade. Only includes countries that were EC members during year listed.

Source: FAO, *FAO Trade Yearbook*, various issues; Commission of the European Communities; *Agricultural Situation in the Community*, various issues.

In addition, the EC was less dependent on agricultural exports for total export revenue than was the US.

In the case of financial resources for a subsidy war, measurement is much more problematic. A straight comparison of public expenditure on agriculture is not necessarily helpful, because of the extensive differences in programmes and in reporting practices between countries. Also, simply comparing agricultural budgets does not necessarily indicate the ability to wage an effective subsidies war, since subsidies themselves are only one means of providing protection for farmers. For example, the US has tended to rely to a much greater extent than the EC upon direct public expenditure to assist agricultural producers. The EC countries, on the other hand, have relied much more

141

Table 4.8
Total Transfers Associated with Agricultural Policies
(in billion US dollars)

	Transfers from taxpayers (1)					Transfers from consumers (2)				
	Average 1983-85	1986	1987	1988	1989	Average 1983-85	1986	1987	1988	1989
Australia	0.6	0.4	0.3	0.2	0.3	0.4	0.5	0.4	0.4	0.4
Austria	0.5	0.4	1.0	1.0	0.8	1.2	2.2	2.8	2.6	2.0
Canada	3.2	4.4	5.6	5.7	4.3	2.8	3.6	3.6	3.6	3.5
EC-12	*22.0	31.7	38.2	45.6	41.3	*36.7	71.9	82.7	75.0	61.9
Finland		1.3	1.6	1.8	1.7		3.5	3.1	3.3	3.2
Japan	10.8	13.9	17.9	19.6	18.0	29.2	48.8	60.0	65.6	59.0
New Zealand	0.3	0.9	0.1	0.1	0.0	0.1	0.1	0.1	0.1	0.1
Norway		1.5	1.8	1.9	1.8		1.4	1.8	1.7	1.6
Sweden		0.5	0.6	0.6	0.5		3.2	2.7	2.6	2.7
Switzerland		1.1	1.7	1.8	1.8		3.8	4.5	4.7	3.9
United States	47.1	59.4	51.6	44.2	47.8	24.2	29.6	31.4	26.0	24.2
TOTAL		117.4	120.3	122.3	118.4		171.3	192.9	185.6	162.6

* EC-10

Source: OECD, *Agricultural Policies, Markets, and Trade,* various issues.

on price controls, which do not entail direct government outlays to a significant extent. If a government is already providing a large proportion of protection in the form of subsidies, it may find increasing subsidies in order to wage a trade war more onerous than would a government which spends relatively less revenue on protection.

The ease with which a country can increase its agricultural budget will also be an important factor determining subsidisation capabilities. Subsidy wars are generally only waged by countries of roughly equal national incomes, because a country with a very large GDP can usually out-subsidise countries with relatively small GDPs either by virtue of its much larger agricultural budget or because of the ability to increase that budget to the level necessary to effectively compete in a subsidies war. In the case of the OECD negotiations, the EC and the US were the only countries with large enough revenue bases to effectively prevail over other members in a subsidies war.[72]

The US and EC were fairly symmetrical in terms of the size of their respective GDPs, although the US had a slight edge

	Budget revenues (3)					Total transfers (1)+(2)-(3)				
	Average 1983-85	1986	1987	1988	1989	Average 1983-85	1986	1987	1988	1989
	0.0	0.0	0.0	0.0	0.0	0.9	0.9	0.6	0.6	0.7
	0.0	0.0	0.0	0.0	0.0	1.7	2.6	3.8	3.5	2.8
	0.0	0.1	0.1	0.1	0.1	5.9	7.9	9.1	9.3	7.8
	*0.5	0.7	0.9	1.0	0.8	*58.1	102.9	120.0	119.6	102.4
		0.1	0.3	0.1	0.0		4.8	4.4	5.0	4.9
	5.2	8.6	11.5	15.0	11.7	34.7	54.1	66.4	70.1	65.3
	0.0	0.0	0.0	0.0	0.0	0.4	0.9	0.1	0.2	0.1
		0.2	0.2	0.1	0.1		2.7	3.3	3.5	3.3
		0.1	0.2	0.2	0.1		3.5	3.1	3.0	3.1
		0.6	0.8	0.8	0.6		4.3	5.4	5.7	5.0
	1.6	0.9	1.4	1.0	0.7	69.7	88.1	81.5	69.1	71.3
		11.4	15.3	18.4	14.2		277.4	297.8	289.6	266.7

over the EC for most of the 1980s. However, as was mentioned earlier, the US was far more reliant on direct public expenditures for agricultural support than was the EC, making it difficult to surpass the EC in the total level of support it could offer its farmers (see Table 4.8). Also, most government spending on agriculture was fed into domestic programmes, and even after the introduction of an export subsidy programme in 1985, American agricultural export subsidies remained only a fraction of total EC spending on agricultural export restitutions.[73]

During the 1980s the US substantially increased its subsidisation of agriculture and by the mid-1980s was spending about twice as much government revenue on agriculture as were both the Community and the national governments of EC countries combined. Still, the EC managed to keep the overall level of support for its farmers (as measured in terms of total PSEs) well above the support received by American farmers between 1983 and 1985. The difference in support levels between the EC and the US increased steadily through the rest of the 1980s. This growing gap was due largely to the ability of the Community

143

to raise price support levels and to increase overall spending on agriculture by raising the ceiling of the EC budget, at the same time as the US was experiencing growing pressure to lower government spending in order to reduce the federal budget deficit.

This comparison of power resources specific to agricultural trade suggests that the EC was in a stronger bargaining position than the US during the 1970s and 1980s. Hence, one would not expect the US to prevail over the EC in agricultural negotiations in the OECD based on an examination of issue specific power resources. The vulnerability of US agriculture was not lost on Secretary Block in October 1983, when he told members of Congress:

> The temptation is great, and it is understandable, to fight subsidy with subsidy, to meet quota with quota, and forget budget concerns by pitting the U.S. Treasury against competitor treasuries in the world market. U.S. agriculture . . . would suffer from the distortions caused by such a confrontation. Indeed, there are no winners in a trade war.[74]

When the Reagan Administration opened up its offensive on agricultural trade many observers were skeptical about the effectiveness of such measures as subsidising exports. Following the January 1983 Egyptian wheat flour deal in which the US sold one million tons of heavily subsidised American wheat flour, a British official pointed out the vulnerability of the United States in agricultural trade when she commented,

> . . . more takeovers of the Egyptian wheat flour market, which, while they temporarily satisfy the domestic constituency, do not result in any permanent expansion of U.S. markets and are costly to operate . . . if the EC chose not to compete in an export subsidy war it might take the alternative course of cutting back on imports and using more of its grain surplus internally . . . because of its greater dependence on exports, the United States would have to pay more than the EC for a trade war.[75]

One American agricultural expert testified before Congress that the competitors losing the largest trade shares to the US in a subsidies war would be Canada, Argentina and Australia, rather than the EC.[76] Furthermore, he argued, the EC would have to spend only about a quarter of the direct subsidy cost paid by the US in order to maintain its customary export volume. He concluded that there would "be no good reason for the United States to launch a farm trade war against the European Community because the United States could very likely lose such a war".[77]

In response to the Egyptian wheat flour deal, which was targeted primarily at France, the EC stepped up its subsidised exports of unmilled wheat to Egypt, and made new sales to Iran, Syria, Libya, Algeria, China and Latin American countries. Retaliation against American soybean and corn gluten imports were also threatened by the Community, and by increasing its subsidisation of wheat flour exports, the EC was able to win a new agreement with Egypt.

Despite the criticism of this approach and the unfavourable results from the 1983 "warning shot" provided by the Egyptian wheat flour deal, in May 1985, the USDA announced its Export Enhancement Program (EEP), which authorised the Department "to use at least $1 billion worth of CCC-owned commodities as export bonuses through fiscal 1988 to make U.S. commodities more competitive in the world marketplace, and to offset the adverse effects of unfair trade practices or subsidies". The Food Security Act of 1985, which incorporated the EEP, also mandated the Targeted Export Assistance Program, which provided financial support for agricultural exports in the form of either cash or commodities and was allocated $100 million annually through 1988, and $325 million annually in the succeeding two years.[78] These programmes were set up, according to the Office of the USTR, "as a short-term tool for use in getting the EC to alter its subsidy programs". The USTR Office later reported that the EC had complained most about the EEP which was eroding EC sales to some of its markets.[79]

When asked whether the 1985 farm bill was going to put irresistible pressure on the EC to change the CAP, Under Secretary of the USDA Daniel G. Amstutz told a Congressional committee:

Well, I sure hope so, and clearly financial budgetary concerns are enormously important to them . . . The fact is that one thing the European Community can expect,

145

because of our new farm bill, is that if they continue with the same policies they have today, it is going to cost them more. Now, when we reach that point or what that point is where a financial load becomes too much, I just don't know.[80]

However, other observers were less optimistic about the effectiveness of these programmes. Former US ambassador to the EC, Robert Schaetzel, remarked,

The EC is no more apt to roll over in the face of American threats or actual retaliation than is the US . . . Before we begin to trash the Europeans we ought to consider for at least a moment where we might be vulnerable. We still have a substantial surplus in our agricultural account with the EC . . . For one, our zero binding [a GATT-negotiated zero tariff] on soybeans would become an almost irresistibly attractive target for the Europeans.[81]

In a similar vein, Fred Sanderson of Resources for the Future argued that the EEP was of little value to the US and in fact was a source of embarrassment.[82] Agricultural policy expert Robert Paarlberg also observed that while US agricultural exports did increase significantly in some of the targeted markets, overall agricultural exports did not increase much, and the volume of wheat sales actually declined by a third in the year after the EEP was initiated. The EC responded to US subsidies by either matching them with larger export restitutions or by displacing US exports in other markets like Brazil, China and the Soviet Union.[83] Nevertheless, convinced of the effectiveness of its programmes (and perhaps also becoming politically hooked on agricultural subsidies) the Reagan Administration in 1987 decided to extend the EEP once its original funding was exhausted.[84]

Although the power resources of the EC were greater than those of the US in the agricultural trade issue, it was the Community which moved closer to US demands in OECD talks, rather than the opposite. The foregoing analysis indicates that structural models are not sufficient to explain this outcome. Hence, explanations must be sought by examining other variables.

146

(c) Influence of Institutions

The fact that agricultural support talks were held in the OECD had a number of consequences. The members assembled in Paris represented the world's largest agricultural exporters, as well as the major parties to international agricultural trade disputes, ensuring that agreement reached there would have a decisive impact on a global scale. If agreement on principles could be achieved within the OECD, then the Uruguay Round negotiations might be greatly facilitated. Limiting the talks to those key actors meant that they could concentrate on the main issues dividing them, since the negotiations were less likely to be side-tracked by the concerns of other groups of countries, for whom a different set of issues might be more important. It was in part due to this that the United States used the OECD in its efforts to bring about a reduction of agricultural support.

The Secretariat played an influential role in developing concepts and conducting studies which gave greater force to the arguments of certain OECD members and which made concessions more palatable to others.[85] However, members of the Secretariat were not always entirely impartial actors. The United States saw to it that a certain number of economists, drawn from American universities and sympathetic to the American position, were assigned to the Trade Mandate project, which was being conducted by the Agricultural Directorate of the OECD. Tim Josling, for example, had already developed the PSE concept in a study he did for the FAO in the early 1970s, and by having him included in the MTM project the US was in a sense able to influence its outcome.[86] In addition to these appointments, the US cultivated a close working relationship with key Secretariat personnel during the course of the study, which may have given it a certain degree of influence over the orientation of the project.

After the May 1987 Ministerial Council, the OECD Secretariat began to monitor the agricultural policies of member countries and any changes therein. The first monitoring report, which was published in 1988, was regarded by American officials as the most hard-hitting document produced to date by the Organisation on agricultural trade.[87] This report boosted the confidence of the United States and other overseas countries in the OECD negotiation process, because they felt that any agree-

ments reached there might be taken seriously by the participants now that violations were made more visible.

In early 1987, the Secretary-General of the OECD circulated
a memo to delegations in which he warned about the danger
of agricultural trade disputes and recommended swift action to
reform agricultural policies, including a reduction of subsidies.
This memo, which was designed to stimulate debate in the
upcoming Ministerial Council, was regarded by some delegates
as generally supporting the American position and it was
pointed out that a similar study on agricultural protectionism
had recently been published by USDA. Nevertheless, much of
the memo was endorsed by the members and included in the
synthesis report.[88] In fact, the Secretariat's proposals were not
entirely supported by the United States. USTR Clayton Yeutter
opposed the scenarios presented by the Secretariat for a 10
per cent across-the-board cut in farm subsidies, saying that
agricultural negotiations should not focus on "short-term quick
fixes", but concentrate on longer-term solutions.[89]

The regular meetings of the various OECD bodies which dealt
with agriculture greatly facilitated negotiations on the issue of
agricultural support. In a sense, these were negotiations with
no discernable beginnings, since the issue had been discussed
in various forms over many years within the Organisation. But
when interest in beefing up the negotiations grew on the part
of the United States in the early 1980s, it was a relatively easy
thing to do, as the most important actors were already
assembled in the OECD and Secretariat support was available
to provide information and aid communications between the
parties. In other words, the transaction costs for these negotiations were extremely low. The regular meetings of the OECD
also permitted the US to keep up pressure on other member
countries over their agricultural support policies.

Transgovernmental contacts also played a somewhat influential role in these negotiations. By the early 1980s, the EC Commission was pushing the EC Council to agree to reform the
CAP, in view of an imminent budget crisis. The Commission
delegate at the OECD consciously sought assistance from the
Organisation in its effort to persuade the Council to accept limits
on farm spending. Even within the EC, certain departments of
national governments discretely supported attacks on their own
policies from officials of other governments. For example, the

Economics Ministry of the German government was at odds with the Agriculture Ministry, and welcomed the pressure being put on Germany to reduce its agricultural support. The Austrian government was in the midst of a farm policy review when the country studies were reaching completion. It sought to have the report on Austria published before it was approved by the OECD Council, and to have it translated into German (which is not normal a normal practice with OECD documents) in order to strengthen its hand in gaining domestic public approval of a reduction in agricultural support.[90]

Any rules, norms, or principles governing relations in the agricultural trade issue area were weak at best and non-existent at worst throughout the period under consideration. The GATT did provide for some limited restrictions on export subsidies, but did not address domestic policies which affected international trade. The most extensive principles or norms on agricultural trade were those worked out in the OECD which, up until 1987 at least, were quite vague and ambiguous. Hence, it does not appear that any international agricultural trade regime was operative which could influence bargaining in the OECD.

The broader international trade regime was not much of a constraint on the behaviour of many participants in the OECD negotiations either. Agriculture was regarded as an exception to the liberalisation norm for many countries, particularly those which placed a high priority on food security. The United States often made references to the need for progress on agriculture to prevent the erosion of the international trading system, but other countries (particularly the EC and Japan) appeared unmoved by these warnings. Ironically, the overall trade regime was in a way responsible for the relatively poor record of compliance with the agreements reached in the OECD on agriculture. The United States, the European Community and Japan were reluctant to adopt any significant reform measures while the Uruguay Round negotiations were in progress, since they preferred to wait until the final stages of the negotiations in Geneva when they could use their policies as bargaining chips.

(d) Unit-level Variables

Domestic Group Opposition There were no clear cases where the opposition of domestic groups seriously constrained the bargaining positions of governments in the OECD negotiations. Member governments generally defended the interests of domestic farm groups, and these farm groups were seldom effectively challenged by other domestic groups. The intensification of American demands in the OECD during the early 1980s, for example, resulted in large part from the pressure put on the government by American farm organisations to adopt a tougher stance vis-à-vis the trade practices of other OECD countries in view of the sharp decline in US agricultural exports. The American Farm Bureau Federation and most major commodity organisations, the American Soybean Association and the National Corn Growers Association in particular, were the principal expansionists.[91] Societal cohesion was roughly even in all OECD countries on the agricultural trade issue, due to the generally limited power of consumer groups, and transnational forces did not have much of an opportunity to influence the bargaining process.

Where domestic group opposition played a more influential role was in weakening the *impact* of OECD agreements on the policies and practices of member countries. The generally strong opposition of the farm lobby to reductions in agricultural support in most OECD countries, particularly in Europe, did not favour any rapid progress in reforming agricultural policies, and many felt that the entire Uruguay Round could be scuttled by the power of such groups.

Governmental Cohesion The greatest lack of policy-making coherence on the agricultural trade issue seemed to be within the European Community, rather than in the United States.[92] The major voice of dissent was from Great Britain (and to a lesser extent the Netherlands and Denmark), which urged its EC partners to accept a reform of agricultural policies in the direction of a greater reliance on market forces. Germany was divided internally on the agricultural issue, with the Agriculture Ministry favouring farm support programmes and the Economics Ministry pushing for greater liberalisation. However,

Agriculture tended to have the upper hand in policy making, and this influence was strengthened after the Christian Democrats, who traditionally drew strong support from the farm vote, entered into office in October 1982. Germany had been content to let France assume the leadership of opposition to reform of the CAP, until the French began to accept the need for a reduction of farm support in the second half of the 1980s, at which point the Germans became more vocal in opposing major reforms, particularly those affecting agricultural pricing policy.

The EC Commission was also an influential actor in the Community, and was instrumental in bringing about a shift in the orientation of the bloc's position on subsidies. After the Commission was won over by the modelling part of the Trade Mandate study, it supported the American effort to get the synthesis report published and to have the new computer framework for comparing the effect of changes in various farm support measures endorsed by the Ministerial Council in 1987, over the objections certain EC members (most notably Belgium and France).

Rather than weakening the EC bargaining position, internal divisions actually acted to strengthen the resistance of the Community to external political pressures to alter the CAP. The difficulties experienced in arriving at a consensus on the reform of such an important policy to the EC were apparent to other countries, and despite their impatience with the pace of change taking place in Europe, there seemed to be a certain degree of resignation among these other countries that swift change was not likely to be imposed there.[93]

There appeared to be comparatively little internal strife within the US government which could explain any weakness in the American bargaining position. The State Department, USDA, and the Office of the USTR all worked together without any significant divisions to put forward a co-ordinated position in the OECD, and there were no serious disagreements between Congress and the Administration on the objectives of the United States in international negotiations, although there were at times differences over bargaining strategies, particularly on the strength of measures to be taken against other OECD countries.[94]

Preference Intensity During the 1970s and 1980s, a considerable shift was discernable in the intensity of American preferences on the agricultural trade issue, while the preference intensity of the EC changed little over the same period. However, this increase in American commitment did not appear to outstrip European resolve, and the two parties were at rough parity in this category during the 1980s.

In the early 1970s, there was a relatively low level of concern about the agricultural trade issue in the Administration, an assessment supported by the fact that the Trade Reform Act, as originally presented to Congress in 1973, did not request specific negotiating authority with respect to agricultural trade. With the significant increase in the price of oil after 1973, the US came to rely more on its agricultural exports to help its balance of trade situation. During the Tokyo Round negotiations, there was no shortage of rhetoric among Administration officials about their strong commitment to progress in liberalising agricultural trade. For example, in 1977, Agriculture Secretary Bob Bergland told the Congress,

> We are vitally interested in ending the use of export subsidies. We think export subsidies are pernicious devices that force economic dislocation . . . We are really going to drive hard in trying to end the use of export subsidies. It will take them years to do this, if, indeed, they ever do it. We are prepared to give it some time. We must see some progress.[95]

Also, the Senior Agricultural Adviser in the Office of the Special Trade Representative assured that

> In this negotiation we intend to make a maximum effort to bring home meaningful concessions to benefit American farmers, concessions which result in expanded trade opportunities. We have made this a major objective in the negotiations, one which reflects the importance of agriculture to the U.S. economy and of agricultural exports to American farmers.[96]

Despite these expressions of determination, the Tokyo Round did not provide the kinds of discipline the United States had sought. Indeed, the US appeared to resign itself to the intractability of the problem of achieving agreement on agricultural policies, particularly on the CAP. In response to inquiries about efforts to get the Community to change the CAP, Deputy Special Representative for Trade Negotiations Alan Wolff argued, "That was unrealistic and just could not be accomplished".[97] This position seemed to be a recognition of the strength of the EC commitment to defend the CAP. The EC Council of Ministers had instructed Community negotiators to refuse to consider any proposals which called into question "the principles or mechanisms" of the policy. In 1978, perhaps as a result of declining American confidence in the MTN process, a conscious decision was made by Under Secretary of Agriculture Dale Hathaway that the OECD needed to be raised in prominence in the agricultural trade area.[98] This effort seemed to pay off to some extent with the 1979 OECD decision to launch the study on problems of agricultural trade.[99]

During the 1970s, the continuous expansion of American agricultural exports appeared to preclude any strong sense of urgency about curtailing the export subsidies of other countries. Consequently, the US did not make a major issue of export subsidies in the OECD during most of the 1970s, and there were not any significant efforts to put pressure on other OECD members through bilateral or unilateral action. However, as the United States became more dependent on agricultural exports during the 1970s, its interest in agricultural trade liberalisation also grew. The volume of US farm exports increased 40 per cent between 1970 and 1975, and grew another 67 per cent by 1980.[100]

The environment of the 1980s was quite different from that of the 1970s. US agricultural exports began to decline in 1981 for the first time in over a decade, at the same time as the country's overall trade balance was worsening. The rhetoric of a strong US commitment to agricultural trade liberalisation continued, as is demonstrated in Agriculture Secretary Block's statement before a Congressional committee:

> Our No. 1 priority in trade policy is to continue to adhere to the principle of free trade and to work until those principles are reflected in the rules for international agricultural trade. Within that priority, our most pressing task is to bring under control the use of export subsidies.[101]

In the early 1980s, the US mounted a major diplomatic offensive, as Secretary Block explained:

The decision was made early in this administration that the United States would no longer tolerate what we consider the unfair trade practices of the European Community. We focused these efforts and the USDA took the lead in developing a comprehensive interdepartmental strategy for the United States-European Community trade relations. This plan was approved at the cabinet council level, and for the first time, the United States is taking a Government-wide approach to the problems of agricultural trade with the European Community.[102]

The diplomatic offensive included raising the issue in a series of high-level bilateral meetings with the EC, with participation of the Secretaries of State, Commerce, and Agriculture and the USTR. The dispute settlement machinery of the GATT was also a part of this effort, along with an attempt to further enhance the role of the OECD. The US agricultural attaché to the OECD was upgraded to counsellor status, and the United States pushed hard for the endorsement of the report on problems of agricultural trade and for the launching of the Trade Mandate study. According to a State Department memo given to the Congress in 1983,

> In recent years, the US has sought to use the OECD to analyze the economic effects of the use of agricultural export subsidies and to clarify the linkages between domestic agricultural policies and the effects on trade in agricultural commodities.[103]

The main indication of increased American commitment was, of course, the mobilisation of resources to promote agricultural exports, through the 1983 warning shot and the 1985 Export Enhancement Program. However, as pointed out earlier, the EC was willing to match these measures in order to protect its export market share, thereby neutralising their effect. The EC remained strongly committed to maintaining the CAP up to the mid-1980s, and this commitment only wavered because of changes within the Community. Commenting on the external pressures applied against EC export subsidies, one agricultural policy analyst remarked,

> In spite of their strength, and the acrimony they generated on all sides, these pressures have not been very effective

154

in bringing about a reform of the CAP. Conflicting internal pressures and the complexity of the domestic European policy process have been such that for many years the status quo has survived.[104]

The explanations for the strong commitments of these two major actors differ somewhat. Value added in agriculture was a higher proportion of GDP in the Community than it was in the US, and the share of the workforce in the EC engaged in agriculture was twice the level in the United States. The CAP was by far the most important policy in the Community, taking up over two-thirds of the EC budget, so demands to dismantle or to radically alter the policy was bound to be strongly resisted.

In the United States, to the extent that American agricultural trade actions were seriously aimed at influencing the Europeans, the main concern was the trade deficit. The growth in the intensity of the American commitment in the agricultural trade issue area was directly related to the growth of the overall trade deficit and to the decline of agricultural exports. Agriculture was seen as an area of comparative advantage by the US, and it was felt that an increase in agricultural exports could help compensate for the decline of American exports in other sectors and for the growth of imports. It has also been suggested that the intensification of the American commitment to international agricultural negotiations was a way for the US government to deflect public criticism of its handling of the farm crisis of the 1980s, and that the hard line adopted by the US reflected the general negotiating style of the Reagan Administration.[105]

While the commitment of the United States to bring about a fundamental reform of agricultural policies in the OECD was strong, its commitment to seek the enforcement of OECD agreements on immediate policy measures was not, owing largely to its belief that short-term reforms did not contribute sufficiently to the problems of agricultural trade.

Japan's commitment to protect its farmers never wavered during the period examined here, due to the reliance of the ruling Liberal Democratic party on the rural vote, the influence of the farm lobby on the government, and the obsession with Japan's vulnerability to interruptions in the supply of imported resources. Canada, Australia and New Zealand were also strongly committed to trade liberalisation, since agriculture accounted for a relatively large share of their total exports. One indication of this commitment was demonstrated when Australia raised the question of continued defence co-operation with the United States in view of the growing subsidisation of American farm exports.[106]

(e) Changes in Interest Definition

For most OECD countries, there were no significant changes in their definition of self-interest on the agricultural trade issue. The interest of the United States in liberalising agricultural trade remained constant throughout the 1970s and 1980s, and the only major change was in the intensity of that interest. Canada, Australia and New Zealand were equally consistent in their commitment to trade liberalisation, and Japan did not change its negotiating position over the two decades. The only major shift of interest took place in Western Europe, particularly in the European Community, where proposals for a reduction of farm support gradually gained acceptance. A purely systemic analysis of this development may lead one to conclude that the EC's acceptance of the norms established in the OECD in May 1987 was the result of the successful application of American pressure, since the shift followed the introduction of the EEP. Indeed, this is a conclusion that architects of the EEP in the US government tend to support. However, like the case of export credits, a closer examination of the decision-making process in the Community reveals that the change resulted primarily from forces operating within the Community itself.

Plans for the reform of the CAP were drawn up as early as 1980, when the EC Commission recommended limiting price support guarantees to a fixed quantity. Price support expenditures had been growing so fast that they threatened to exceed the limits of the Community's budget, which according to the Treaty of Rome cannot be in deficit. Also, Great Britain was dissatisfied with its contribution to the EC budget, most of which was being spent on the CAP. No action was taken immediately because the increase in world agricultural prices had eased pressure on the budget, since smaller restitution payments would be needed to bridge the gap between Community and world prices. But with changing market conditions in 1983, the budget ceiling appeared about to be reached once again, and internal negotiations began on controlling agricultural expenditures and on the size of the budget.[107]

In March 1984 agreement was reached to increase the budget ceiling from 1 to 1.4 per cent of the VAT rate. In addition, a number of changes to the CAP were introduced, including the extension of price guarantee limits to other products, the establishment of dairy production quotas, and a slight limitation on price supports. One analyst of EC agricultural policy commented that "these proposals signaled that the era of open-ended financial commitment to support of the CAP was over".[108] However, the changes did not represent a fundamental restructuring of the CAP, and when pressure on the budget was relieved by the decision to increase the Community's revenue and by the high level of the dollar which raised the price of world agricultural products, the incentive to carry out further reforms of the CAP subsided, at least for a period of time.

After 1984, surplus production remained a problem in the Community, as self-sufficiency in many products had been reached and export markets were shrinking. With the exchange value of the dollar falling after 1985, export subsidies became more expensive for the EC and consequently, budget constraints once again stirred interest in the reform of the CAP.[109] However, in the second half of the 1980s there were new forces at play which added further impetus for the reform movement.[110] Early in 1987 an official in the Agriculture Directorate of the EC Commission commented,

> Reform of the CAP is now high on the EC's agenda. Whereas for many years there was a hesitation to deal vigorously with the agricultural problems because of the political importance of the CAP in the European construction, and the risk of undermining the policy, there is now a growing realisation that failure to reform the CAP and to control its expenditure may put at risk the development of all other policies.[111]

With the expansion of the EC membership in 1986, new pressures arose for more Community spending on rural development in Spain and Portugal, at the same time as general interest in the EC was growing in the expansion of social and regional programmes, which would compete with the CAP for Community funding. As well, France, which was one of the staunchest opponents of CAP reform, had become a net contributor to the EC budget and began to show signs of flexibility on the reduction of farm support.[112] These developments inside the Community, often reinforced by fluctuations in the world agricultural market, were the chief causes of the shift in the EC position on agriculture, explaining the eventual acceptance of the OECD's May 1987 declaration on agricultural policy, and the package of reform measures adopted in February 1988.

7. *Conclusion*

Progress in the OECD Agricultural trade talks was very slow, and the significance of agreements reached in that forum have not always been appreciated. The clearly stated acceptance by member countries that domestic agricultural policies should be subject to international discipline, and the commitment to reduce farm support were major breakthroughs in international trade negotiations, considering that the EC had until the 1980s refused to enter into any discussions which brought into question the basic tenets of the CAP. As in the case of export credit negotiations, the turn around by the Europeans followed a period of aggressive American trade actions, and the temptation is great to conclude that movement by the EC was the result of American pressure, a conclusion which would hearten proponents of the theory of hegemonic stability. However, the preceding examination of changes in interest definition reveals that the real impetus for this shift in position was internal. It was a combination of recurring strains on the EC budget, the growth of interest in competing Community programmes, mounting surpluses of agricultural products, and shifts in the distribution of benefits from the CAP which led to the gradual acceptance of the principles adopted in the OECD.

While the OECD agreements resulted from a change of interest dictated by internal developments, the *impact* of those agreements was to a large degree influenced by conditions in the world agricultural market. The rise in world prices for agricultural products lessened the budget pressures on the CAP by narrowing the difference between Community and world price levels. Hence, the sense of urgency in reforming the agricultural policy diminished, hindering efforts to institute significant short-term policy reforms, and perhaps weakening the commitment to an agreement in the Uruguay Round on long-term liberalisation.

The foregoing analysis also indicates that the issue structure model is inadequate in explaining or predicting the outcome of the OECD agricultural support talks. The EC remained predominant in agricultural trade power throughout the period under consideration, and there were no shifts in issue-specific power resources which could explain changes in the EC position. Also, a review of institutional variables suggests that while facilitating the development of the OECD agreements, they did not significantly alter bargaining positions or outcomes. A final finding of this study of agricultural negotiations is that domestic group opposition, decision-making coherence and preference intensity did not seem to be decisive in explaining bargaining outcomes. The only major variation in these three factors was the increased American resolve in the 1980s, but this did not appear to have been sufficient to produce an agreement in the OECD which satisfied American demands. However, divisions among and within the governments of EC member countries were partly responsible for the lack of significant progress by the Community in fulfilling the commitments made at the 1987 Ministerial.

Notes

1 International Monetary Fund, *Trade Policy Issues and Developments*, by Shailendra J. Anjaria, Naheed Kirmani, and Arne B. Petersen (Washington, D.C.: IMF, 1985), p. 56; Dale E. Hathaway, *Agriculture and the GATT: Issues in a New Trade Round* (Washington: Institute for International Economics, 1987), p. 8.

2 Food and Agricultural Organisation, *FAO Production Yearbook 1987*, Vol. 41, p. 105.

3 IMF, *Trade Policy Issues and Developments*, by Shailendra J. Anjaria, Naheed Kirmani, and Arne B. Peterson (Washington, D.C.: IMF, 1985), pp. 56–57; IMF, *Developments in International Trade Policy*, Shailendra J. Anjaria, Zubair Iqbal, Naheed Kirmani, and Lorenzo L. Perez (Washington, D.C.: IMF, 1982), pp. 34–35; IMF, *Issues and Developments in International Trade Policy*, by Margaret Kelly, Naheed Kirmani, Miranda Xafa, Clemens Boonekamp, and Peter Winglee (Washington, D.C.: IMF, 1988), pp. 49–52.

4 OECD, *Agricultural Policies, Markets and Trade: Monitoring and Outlook 1988* (Paris: OECD, 1988), p. 46; and OECD, *Agricultural Policies, Markets and Trade: Monitoring and Outlook 1989* (Paris: OECD,

1989), p. 90. PSE figures for other countries in this section are taken from the same sources.

5 For a complete summary of PSE levels for all OECD countries between 1979 and 1989, see Table 4.3. A more detailed comparison of agricultural support policies in various OECD countries can be found in, IMF, *Issues and Developments in International Trade Policy*, by Margaret Kelly, Naheed Kirmani, Miranda Xafa, Clemens Boonekamp, and Peter Winglee (Washington, D.C.: IMF, 1988), pp. 47–67; and OECD, *National Policies and Agricultural Trade* (Reports on Canada, United States, EEC, Australia, New Zealand, Japan, Austria, Sweden, Finland, Norway and Switzerland) (Paris: OECD, 1987, 1988, 1989 and 1990).

6 The Agreement was transferred to the GATT in the 1970s.

7 OECD *Press Release* A(62)55, 20 November 1962; A(64)14, 27 February 1964; A(65)34, 18 June 1965; A (68)68, 29 November 1968. See also, Henry G. Aubrey, *Atlantic Economic Cooperation: The Case of OECD* (New York: Praeger, 1967), pp. 66–71.

8 *Activities of OECD in 1970*, p. 3; *Activities of OECD in 1971*, p. 33.

9 *Activities of OECD in 1973*, pp. 19–28, 8–89; *Activities of OECD in 1976*, p. 49; *The Times* 12 April 1973.

10 *Activities of OECD in 1978*, p. 52.

11 *Activities of OECD in 1973*, p. 19.

12 *Activities of OECD in 1978*, pp. 52, 106.

13 *Activities of OECD in 1981*, p. 91; *Activities of OECD in 1982*, p. 54; *Activities of OECD in 1987*, pp. 44, 47.

14 *Activities of OECD in 1983*, p. 43; *Activities of OECD in 1984*, p. 41; *OECD Press Release* A(83)32, 27 June 1983.

15 OECD, *Policy Perspectives for International Trade and Economic Relations: Report by the High Level Group on Trade and Related Problems to the Secretary-General of OECD* (Paris: OECD, 1972), p. 67.

16 Ibid., p. 37.

17 Ibid., pp. 70–75.

18 OECD *Press Release* A(73)13, 12 April 1973.

19 OECD *Press Release* A(78)10, 10 February 1978.

20 *Activities of OECD in 1978*, p. 106.

21 OECD *Press Release* A(80)19 6 March 1980.

22 *Activities of OECD in 1980*, pp. 80–81.

23 *Activities of OECD in 1979*, p. 105.

24 OECD, *Problems of Agricultural Trade* (Paris: OECD, 1982), p. 132.

25 *Activities of OECD in 1982*, p. 95.

26 Ibid., p. 95.

27 Ibid., pp. 113–114.

28 Ibid.

29 *Activities of OECD in 1984*, p. 41.

30 Ibid., p. 82.

31 *Activities of OECD in 1985*, p. 43.

32 Ibid., p. 87.

33 *Activities of OECD in 1983*, p. 42; *Activities of OECD in 1985*, pp. 43–44.

34 *Activities of OECD in 1983*, pp. 42–43; *Activities of OECD in 1984*, p. 44.
35 *Activities of OECD in 1983*, pp. 42–43; *Activities of OECD in 1984*, p. 43.
36 *Activities of OECD in 1987*, pp. 43–44.
37 *Activities of OECD in 1987*, p. 94.
38 *OECD Press Release* A(88)28, 19 May 1988.
39 Ibid.
40 *OECD Press Release* A(89)26, 1 June 1989.
41 As with most published Secretariat reports, this report was fully discussed and amended by the Committee.
42 *OECD Press Release* A(88)28, 19 May 1988; *Activities of OECD in 1987*, p. 43.
43 *Activities of OECD in 1987*, pp. 46–47; OECD, *Agricultural Policies, Markets and Trade: Monitoring and Outlook 1988*, pp. 18–20.
44 National Center for Food and Agricultural Policy, *Mutual Disarmament in World Agriculture: A Declaration on Agricultural Trade*, by Twenty-Six Agricultural Trade Policy Experts from Eight Countries and Two International Organisations (Washington, D.C.: Resources for the Future, 1988), pp. 7–8.
45 Institute for International Economics, and Institute for Research on Public Policy, *Reforming World Agricultural Trade: A Policy Statement by Twenty-nine Professionals from Seventeen Countries* (Washington, D.C.: Institute for International Economics, 1988), p. 18; *Financial Times* 15 February 1988; IMF, *Issues and Developments . . . , p. 47. By April 1990, the land set-aside programme was judged to have had a negligible impact on Community production. *Financial Times* 24 April 1990.
46 IMF, *Issues and Developments . . .* , p. 47. These measures were considered insignificant by American government officials. Interviews with US government officials.
47 OECD, *Agricultural Policies, Markets and Trade: Monitoring and Outlook 1989*, pp. 12–23.
48 *OECD Press Release* A(89)26, 1 June 1989.
49 OECD, *Agricultural Policies, Markets and Trade: Monitoring and Outlook 1990* (Paris: OECD, 1990), pp. 7–20, 139–151.
50 Interview with US government official.
51 Interview with Canadian government official.
52 *OECD Observer* 91 (March 1978), pp. 4–6. This proposal was originally made to the International Wheat Council in September 1975. I.M. Destler, *Making Foreign Economic Policy* (Washington, D.C.: Brookings Institution, 1980), p. 88.
53 US, House, Committee on Agriculture and Committee on Foreign Affairs, *Review of Agricultural Trade Issues: Joint Hearing*, 98th Cong., 1st sess., April 7, 1983, p. 33.
54 *Financial Times* 18, 19 April 1986; *International Herald Tribune* 19–20 April 1986.
55 *Financial Times* 22 January, 19 February 1987.
56 *International Herald Tribune* 11 May 1987.

57 *Financial Times* 4 February 1987; *International Herald Tribune* 27 March 1987; *Globe and Mail*, 26 February 1986; Interviews with US government officials.

58 *International Herald Tribune* 14 May 1987; *Financial Times* 14, 15 May 1987.

59 Interviews with US government officials.

60 Ibid.

61 *Financial Times* 5 June 1987.

62 *International Herald Tribune* 11, 14 May 1987; *Financial Times* 14 May 1987.

63 *New York Times* 13 May 1987; *The Times* 11 May 1987; *International Herald Tribune* 14 May 1987.

64 *New York Times* 14 May 1987.

65 *International Herald Tribune* 19, 20 May 1987; *Financial Times* 20 May 1987.

66 Robert D. Hormats, "Agricultural Trade with the European Community", *Department of State Bulletin* 82 (no.2060), March 1982, p. 45.

67 US, House, *Review of Agricultural Trade Issues*, pp. 39–40.

68 Tim Josling, "Agricultural Trade among Friends: The Parlous State of U.S. Trade Relationships with the Industrialised West", in *Confrontation or Negotiation: United States Policy and European Agriculture*, ed. The Curry Foundation (Millwood, N.Y.: Associated Faculty Press, 1985), p. 196

69 *Globe and Mail* 19 June 1982.

70 The threat to curtail imports will of course be a function of the availability of alternative markets. In times of considerable surpluses in agricultural products, such as in the 1980s, such alternatives are usually difficult to find.

71 If the Reagan Administration, with its strongly-held views about the need to deal firmly with the Soviet Union, was unwilling to use the food weapon in its confrontations with that country, then it seems even more unlikely that the US would contemplate such a move in negotiations with its major trading partners and military allies.

72 Japan comes closest to the US and EC in GDP and in the size of agricultural budget, but because it is much less food self-sufficient and because it is a fairly minor agricultural exporter, it is unlikely to want to divert government revenue to try to protect or expand its export market share.

73 Robert L. Paarlberg, *Fixing Farm Trade: Policy Options for the United States* (Cambridge, Mass.: Ballinger, 1988), pp. 85–86.

74 U.S., House, Committee on Agriculture, *Review of Agricultural Exports and Trade: Hearing*, 98th Cong., 1st sess., October 18, 1983, p. 15.

75 Susan E. Brown, "Review of "The Consequences of U.S. and European Support Policies" and "Impacts of EC Policies on U.S. Export Performance" ", in *Confrontation or Negotiation*, p. 182.

76 Canada's share of world exports did drop by about 20 per cent

between 1985 and 1987, while Australia's share declined by almost the same amount. These countries were most concerned about the effect of an American-European subsidies war on agricultural prices. Australia suffered a 20 per cent loss of agricultural export revenue between 1982 and 1983, while Canada experienced a similar loss between 1984 and 1986.

77 Robert L. Paarlberg, "United States Agricultural Objectives and Policy Options", in *Confrontation or Negotiation*, pp. 233–234; U.S., Senate, Committee on Foreign Relations, *A NATO Strategy for the 1990s: Hearing before the Subcommittee on European Affairs-- Part 5*, 99th Cong., 1st sess., October 3, 1985, p. 199.

78 U.S., Senate, Committee on Agriculture, Nutrition and Forestry, *Preparing for the GATT: A Review of Agricultural Trade Issues: Hearings before the Subcommittee on Foreign Agricultural Policy*, 99th Cong., 2nd sess, June 3 and 17, July 22 and 29, August 5, 1986, pp. 413–416.

79 U.S., House, Committee on Foreign Affairs, *United States-European Community Trade Relations: Problems and Prospects for Resolution: Hearing before the Subcommittee on Europe and the Middle East*, 99th Cong., 2nd sess., July 24, 1986, p. 155.

80 U.S., House, Committee on Agriculture, *Agricultural Provision Proposals to Omnibus Trade Legislation: Hearing*, 99th Cong., 2nd sess., April 15, 1986, p. 16.

81 U.S., House, *United States-European Community Trade Relations*, p. 187.

82 U.S., Senate, *Preparing for the GATT*, p. 250.

83 Paarlberg, *Fixing Farm Trade*, pp. 93–97.

84 This suggests that the real goal of the EEP was to subsidise American farmers when the farm crisis became a major domestic political issue, rather than representing a serious attempt to force the EC to reduce its subsidy practices. *Financial Times* 6 August, 14 October 1987.

85 For example, the PSE concept was crucial in Germany's acceptance of the statement issued in May 1987, since by aggregating all different forms of agricultural support it implied that a reduction of assistance would not necessarily require Germany to eliminate its price support programme. *Financial Times, International Herald Tribune*, 13 May 1987.

86 Stefan Tangermann, T.E. Josling, and Scott Pearson, "Multilateral Negotiations on Farm-support Levels", *The World Economy* 10 (September 1987), p. 266; Interview with US government official.

87 OECD, *Agricultural Policies, Markets and Trade: Monitoring and Outlook* (Paris: OECD, 1988).

88 *Japan Times* 9 February 1987; *Financial Times* 19 February 1987; *International Herald Tribune* 27 March 1987.

89 *Financial Times* 15 May 1987.

90 Interview with US government officials.

91 Ross B. Talbot, "The Foundations of the CAP and the Development of U.S.-EC Agricultural Trade Relations", in *Confrontation or*

Negotiation, p. 37; *Globe and Mail* 19 June 1982; David Rapp, *How the U.S. Got into Agriculture* (Washington, D.C.: Congressional Quarterly Inc., 1988), pp. 63–81.

92 For a more complete discussion of agricultural policy making in the US and EC, see Michel Petit, *Determinants of Agricultural Policies in the United States and the European Community* (Washington, D.C.: International Food Policy Research Institute, 1985).

93 A more in-depth discussion of the decision-making process in the Community is found in Michel Petit, et al., *Agricultural Policy Formation in the European Community: The Birth of Milk Quotas and CAP Reform* (Amsterdam: Elsevier, 1987).

94 U.S., House, *Review of Agricultural Exports and Trade*, p. 22; *International Herald Tribune* 26 January 1982; Interviews with US government officials.

95 U.S., Senate, Committee on Finance, *Problems in International Agricultural Trade: Hearing before the Subcommittee on International Trade*, 95th Cong., 1st sess., July 13, 1977, p. 23.

96 U.S., House, Committee on Agriculture, *Export of U.S. Agricultural Commodities: Hearing before the Subcommittee on Oilseeds and Rice and the Subcommittee on Livestock and Grains*, 95th Cong., 1st sess., October 12, 1977, p. 55.

97 U.S., Senate, Committee on Agriculture, Nutrition and Forestry, *Review of the MTN: Hearing*, 96th Cong., 1st sess., May 7, 1979, p. 6.

98 Talbot, "The Foundations of the CAP", p. 41.

99 Interview with US government official.

100 Leo V. Mayer, "Agricultural Policy in a Changing Domestic and International Environment", in *United States Agricultural Policy 1985 and Beyond*, ed. Jimmye S. Hillman (University of Arizona, 1984), mimeographed, p. 140.

101 U.S., House, *Review of Agricultural Exports and Trade*, p. 14.

102 U.S., House, Committee on Agriculture, *General Agricultural Export and Trade Situation: Hearing*, 97th Cong., 2nd sess., March 9, 1982, p. 7.

103 U.S., House, Committee on Agriculture and Committee on Foreign Affairs, *Review of Agricultural Trade Issues: Joint Hearing*, 98th Cong., 1st sess., April 7, 1983, p. 33.

104 Michel Petit, "The Politics and Economics of CAP Decision Making", in *Confrontation or Negotiation*, p. 65.

105 Rapp, *How the U.S. Got into Agriculture*, pp. 149–171.

106 Rapp, *How the U.S. Got into Agriculture*, p. 158.

107 Petit, *Determinants of Agricultural Policies*, pp. 62–63.

108 Ibid., p. 63.

109 U.S., House, *United States-European Community Trade Relations*, pp. 212–213.

110 U.S., Senate, Committee on Foreign Relations, *International Trade Distortions Harming U.S. Agricultural Exports: Hearing*, 98th Cong., 2nd sess., 26 June 1984, p. 3; Petit, "The Politics and Economics of CAP Decision Making", pp. 67–68.

111 Graham Avery, "Agricultural Policy: European Options and American Comparisons", *European Affairs*, no.1 (Spring 1987), p. 69.
112 Rapp, *How the U.S. Got into Agriculture*, p. 152; IMF, *The Common Agricultural Policy of the European Community: Principles and Consequences*, by Julius Rosenblatt, Thomas Mayer, Kasper Bartholdy, Dimitrios Demekas, Sanjeev Gupta, and Leslie Lipschitz (Washington, D.C.: IMF, 1988), p. 25.

Chapter Five

STEEL TRADE

1. *The International Steel Market*

After a period of relative stability during the 1960s, the world steel market experienced considerable turbulence in the 1970s and 1980s. World steel production grew steadily up to the early 1970s, and in anticipation of further demand growth, steel companies in OECD countries continued to expand production capacity. However, the economic recessions of the decade following 1973 seriously reduced demand for steel, with the sharpest drops experienced in 1975 and 1982 (see Chart 5.1). These cyclical downturns, coupled with the emergence of new steel producers in a number of Third World countries, resulted in a major overcapacity problem. Whereas the average effective steel-making capacity utilisation in the OECD countries was around 85 per cent between 1960 and 1975, over the next decade and a half it averaged only about 70 per cent (see Chart 5.2)[1]

World steel trade has been dominated by the OECD countries, which accounted for two-thirds of world steel exports in the late 1980s, down from roughly 90 per cent in the early 1960s. As Chart 5.3 illustrates, the major exporters of steel were the EC and Japan, which consistently accounted for over two-thirds of total world exports during the 1960s and 1970s, with this joint share declining to roughly 50 per cent by the late 1980s. The respective shares of these two exporters have shifted over the past two decades, however. In the early 1960s, The EC's steel exports were 57 per cent of total world exports while Japan accounted for 11 per cent. By the 1980s, Japan and the EC each accounted for around one-quarter of world exports.

While the United States was not a major exporter of steel (its

166

Chart 5.1
World Steel Production

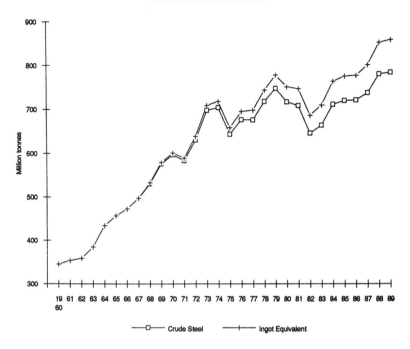

Source: OECD, *The Steel Market and Outlook*, various issues.

share of world steel exports fell from an average 8 per cent in the early 1960s to just under 1 per cent by the mid-1980s), it played a key role as the world's largest steel importer. American steel imports were an average 18 per cent of world steel imports in the 1970s and 16 per cent during the 1980s, compared with 0.3 per cent and 2.8 per cent for Japan and 10 per cent and 8.6 per cent for the EC during the same periods (see Chart 5.4). The US has also experienced the greatest import penetration of all major steel producing countries over the past twenty years. As Chart 5.5 indicates, imports grew from about 4 per cent of domestic consumption in 1960 to around 25 per cent in the mid-1980s. For the EC, the second largest importer of steel, import penetration rose from 4 per cent to about 12 per cent during the same period, while Japan did not experience significant

167

Chart 5.2
Steel Capacity Utilisation Rates

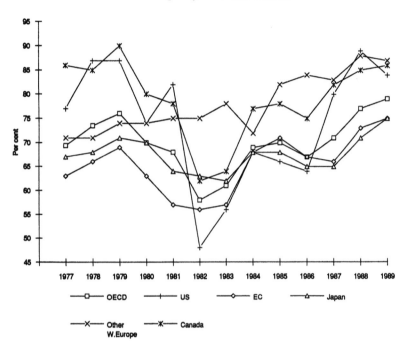

Only includes countries that were EC members during year listed.
Source: OECD, *The Steel Market and Outlook,* various issues.

import penetration until the late 1980s, with steel imports rising
to around 8 per cent of domestic consumption in 1988.

This relatively high degree of import penetration in the
United States, combined with the sharper decline in internal
steel demand and employment in the steel industry compared
with other steel-producing countries in the decade following
1973, led to strong pressure for protection from the American
steel industry.[2] The most common form of protectionism prac-
ticed by the US was the negotiation of bilateral voluntary export
restraint agreements (VRAs), although there was also some use
of tariffs and import quotas. In addition, other countries alleged
that US trade laws (particularly those dealing with anti-dumping and countervailing duties) served as protectionist measures.

Chart 5.3
Steel Exports as a Percentage of World Steel Exports

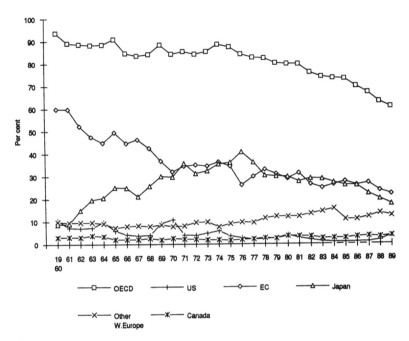

Excludes intra-EC and intra-East European trade. Only includes countries that were EC members during year listed.

Source: OECD, *World Steel Trade Developments 1960–1983: A Statistical Analysis*, 1985;
OECD, *The Steel Market and Outlook*, various issues.

The EC also experienced pressure for protection from its steel industry in the face of rising import penetration and declining internal demand. Community steel trade distortions included VRAs, but in contrast to American practice direct government subsidies were provided to the steel industry. The EC Commission also administered production quotas and set minimum prices for steel products. Government involvement in the Japanese steel industry was far less visible than it was in the American and European cases. While the Japanese government did not provide direct subsidies or impose formal import restrictions, it did offer the steel industry fiscal incentives for research and development, for plant and equipment modernisation and for product diversification. It also provided forecasts of steel

169

Chart 5.4
Steel Imports

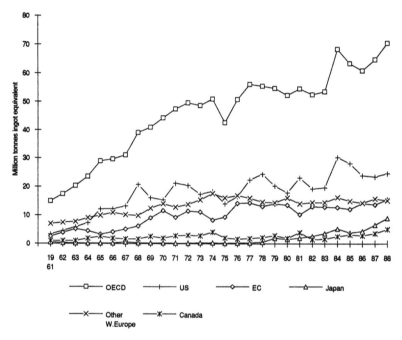

Only includes countries that were EC members during year listed.

Source: OECD, *World Steel Trade Developments 1960–1983: A Statistical Analysis*, 1985;
OECD, *The Steel Market and Outlook*, various issues.

demand which the industry used to adjust production levels,
and periodically gave "administrative guidance" to encourage
firms to reduce production or exports.[3]

2. *Background to OECD Steel Trade Negotiations*

There has been a long history of OECD involvement in the steel
industry. The OEEC had an Iron and Steel Committee from the
beginning of its existence, and its work was carried over to the
OECD's Special Committee for Iron and Steel in 1961. These
early committees were responsible for collecting, correlating
and distributing detailed information on various aspects of the
steel market, including trends in demand, investment, pro-

Chart 5.5
Steel Import Penetration
(Imports as a Percentage of Apparent Consumption)

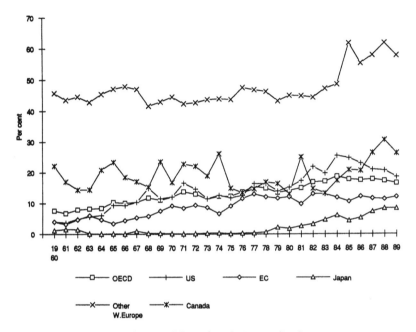

Only includes countries that were EC members during year listed.

Source: OECD, *World Steel Trade Developments 1960–1983: A Statistical Analysis*, 1995;
OECD, *The Steel Market and Outlook*, various issues.

duction capacity and international trade. Market studies were published on an annual basis beginning in 1965. The information gathered by the Secretariat was discussed by the committee and concern was often expressed about excess production capacity, but because of the steady growth in steel demand, discussions remained relatively low key and there were no major attempts to negotiate international agreements on steel trade. The Special Committee lapsed in 1970, and the responsibility for gathering and disseminating information was handed over to a working party of the Industry Committee.[4]

3. *Agreements on Steel Trade Issues*

The first significant matter raised within the OECD on steel trade in the 1970s was the request by the EC Commission for an *ad hoc* consultation on the iron and steel industry in November 1975.[5] This meeting was held within the framework of the May 1974 Trade Pledge in order to discuss the crisis in the EC steel industry.[6] The next major steel consultation was held in April 1976 to discuss American proposals for an orderly marketing arrangement to limit specialty steel exports to the United States.[7] In May 1977 the OECD Council agreed to set up an *ad hoc* Working Group on the Steel Industry to examine international steel trade issues.[8]

The exchange of information and views which had considerably increased during the consultations requested by the EC in November 1975 and by the US in 1976 intensified with the setting up of the *ad hoc* Working Group on the Steel Industry.[9] During the first meeting of the Working Group, participating countries were asked to prepare statements on the supply and demand situation in their internal steel markets and on the main problems experienced by their steel industries. In addition, the Secretariat was asked to prepare a report on short- and long-term developments in supply and demand, as well as on trends in the pattern of international steel trade.[10]

During the Working Group's second meeting in September 1977, agreement was reached to set up an information system permitting member governments to follow current and long-term trends in the steel industry.[11] In late November of the same year members agreed upon the details of this information system, which was intended to give early warning of crisis conditions and to guide investment decisions. Data was to be provided on worldwide production capacity, monthly crude steel production, new orders and order book positions, employment levels, imports, exports, as well as domestic and export prices. Governments were to notify the Working Group of any new measures likely to affect production levels or trade in steel, and to provide information on major investment projects and rationalisation schemes.[12]

The first major understanding reached on steel was contained in a communiqué issued after the November 30, 1977 Working Group meeting, which came to be known as the "OECD Steel

172

Consensus". Three main principles were laid down by which joint or individual efforts to deal with the steel crisis were to be guided. Top priority was to be given to the restructuring and modernisation of the steel industry. Members of the Working Group agreed to avoid shifting the burden of adjustment from one producing nation to another.

The second principle agreed upon was that any immediate government measure should be consistent with the longer-term need to rationalise the world steel industry and with the "free and fair flow of international trade". In particular, it was agreed that no solution to the fundamental problems of the steel industry could be found by recourse to quantitative restrictions. The third principle of the agreement was that no nation could be expected to absorb for lengthy periods large quantities of imports at "unjustifiably low prices" to the detriment of domestic production and employment. However, any measure designed to deal with such imports were to take into account "customary patterns of trade".[13]

After meeting several times during 1977 and 1978 the *ad hoc* Working Group recommended on 21 September 1978 that a permanent Steel Committee be set up to deal with all aspects of the world steel industry's problems.[14] This recommendation was approved by the OECD Council, which created an OECD Steel Committee on 26 October 1978. In addition to a number of informational activities, the Steel Committee was charged with examining government steel trade measures and a range of domestic policies affecting the steel sector. The Committee's work was to be assisted by a Working Party.

The stated objectives of the Committee were as follows: to ensure that trade in steel remained as free of distortion as possible and to that end encourage a reduction of trade barriers; to enable governments to take prompt crisis measures in close consultation with their trading partners; to facilitate structural adjustment in the steel sector; to ensure that measures affecting the steel industry took into account their impact on related industries and on general economic policies; to avoid encouraging economically unjustified investments while recognising legitimate development needs; and to facilitate multilateral co-operation in order to anticipate and prevent problems. The Committee was originally composed of 20 OECD member governments plus the European Community, and was permitted to invite non-OECD countries with substantial steel interests to participate in the work of the committee.[15] After declining an invitation to participate in the Steel Committee, the Government of Mexico agreed to the establishment of a Liaison Committee in early 1982 in which occasional exchanges of information and views on steel developments were held between Mexico and the Steel Committee.[16]

The Council decision setting up the Steel Committee in 1978 included a group of "Initial Commitments" by participating governments. Among these commitments was the agreement that no steel crisis trade actions should be inconsistent with GATT provisions, and that any actions that were taken should be as limited and temporary as possible and should be appropriate to the causes which led to their introduction. In a re-phrasing of the third principle of the Steel Consensus, it was agreed that steel crisis actions should not severely disrupt traditional trade flows established under normal conditions of competition. Reference was also made to price guidelines (such as the US Trigger Price Mechanism and the EC Basic Price System) which were deemed appropriate only during crisis periods, and which were to be removed as conditions improved.[17] A set of guidelines was also established for setting the level of trigger prices.

Participants also agreed to abstain from competition in the granting of export credits and to make sure that export credit policies affecting steel plant and equipment were fully consistent with the Arrangement on Guidelines for Officially Supported Export Credits.[18] Regarding adjustment policies, the Participants agreed that in order to avoid restrictive trade measures by other countries, domestic policies to sustain steel firms during crisis periods should not shift the burden of adjustment to other countries by artificially stimulating exports or displacing imports. In a related area, participants agreed to provide effective programmes for steel worker re-adaptation away from facilities affected by structural adjustments into alternative employment. Finally, it was agreed that any action to restrict steel trade should be reported promptly to the Steel Committee and be subject to consultation with affected parties.[19]

When it was established in 1978, one of the main functions of the Steel Committee was intended to be the development of multilateral objectives or guidelines for government policies. However, no further explicit agreements were reached within the Committee after the Initial Commitments, and rather than try to develop "rules" constraining the behaviour of participating countries, the Committee's work seemed to concentrate more on quietly influencing government decisions affecting the steel industry and trade through the exchange of views and information.[20]

The Steel Committee's monitoring role was set out in the Council Decision of 1978. One of the Committee's stated functions was to "regularly review and assess government policies and actions in the steel sector in the light of the current situation, agreed multilateral objectives and guidelines, the GATT and other relevant international agreements".[21] In particular, the Committee was directed to examine: the impact of government measures on trade flows; the restructuring of the steel industry; policies for the re-adaptation of labour; domestic policies to sustain steel production and stimulate steel demand in times of crisis; domestic pricing and supply; and government export credits for steel plant and equipment.[22] In addition to reporting any new steel trade measures to the Steel Committee, participants also agreed to report periodically on the status and rationale for maintaining such actions. A continuous information system was set to gather data on steel production, consumption and trade, which also facilitated the monitoring of compliance with various OECD commitments.

In practice the monitoring of the policies and practices of participants was quite successful. Participants generally co-operated in providing the Committee with the information requested, permitting a clearer picture of the progress made in complying with the principles set out in the Steel Consensus and Initial Commitments. For example, Steel Committee meetings generally began with statements by delegates of "recent policy developments", where recent problems and new and evolving government measures were announced. In addition to this on-going reporting system, a more comprehensive review of government measures affecting steel trade (domestic adjustment measures) was agreed upon in November 1979 and was completed in early 1981. Another review of steel policies since 1980 was launched in 1984 and completed in 1985. These country-by-country "progress reviews" were conducted in a manner similar to the economic surveys carried out by the Economic Policy Committee, with two countries serving as rapporteurs for each country examined. One area of difficulty, however, was in the monitoring of prices. Because the collecting of price data was so time consuming, it was found that by the time this information was put together it was out of date. Consequently, the OECD carried out relatively little statistical monitoring of steel prices.

4. *Impact of OECD Agreements*

Assessing compliance with OECD principles and commitments on steel trade is problematic, largely because of the looseness of the wording of many of the undertakings. For example, one of the Initial Commitments was that steel trade actions taken by governments should be as limited and temporary as possible and should be appropriate to the causes which led to their introduction. Clearly, what is "appropriate" or "as limited and temporary as possible" is open to interpretation, making it almost impossible to determine whether countries have complied or not. Nonetheless, there are a number of specific undertakings within the Steel Consensus and the Initial Commitments in which it is possible to gauge at least to some degree the record of compliance of participating governments. As the Steel Consensus and Initial Commitments were to a large extent targeted at the United States and the European Community, the following assessment will focus principally on those two parties, with the performance of Japan also evaluated where appropriate.

Steel Consensus Principles

1. "Priority attention must be given to the long-term need of restructuring and modernisation of the steel industry"

While it is difficult to determine whether these goals were truly given priority by a government, it is clear that most participants in the Steel Consensus (particularly the less efficient producers) did make considerable capacity cuts in the steel industry. As Table 5.1 illustrates, steel production capacity in the OECD was reduced by over 13 per cent between 1977 and 1989, representing more than 75 million tonnes of capacity. Among the largest producers, the US reduced capacity almost 30 per cent over this period, while the EC reduced its capacity by about 19 per cent if its membership is held constant for this period. Japan's capacity, after rising somewhat in the early 1980s, returned to about the 1977 level by the late 1980s.[23] Despite this apparent progress, the problem of overcapacity in OECD countries did not improve in the decade after the adoption of the Steel Consensus. Capacity utilisation rates fell from an average 74 per cent in 1978 to 58 per cent in 1982, before recovering to 71 per cent in 1987 and 79 per cent in 1989 (see Table 5.2). On the other hand, if it were not for the capacity cuts that were made, these utilisation figures would have been much lower.

As mentioned in the Introduction, "compliance", for the purposes of this study is above all a question of whether governments actually carried out the policies promised in the OECD context, regardless of whether those policies turned out to be effective or not (ie. irrespective of whether the problem of overcapacity was actually resolved or not). Assessing compliance with the first Steel Consensus principle is complicated first of all by the fact that the term "restructuring" meant different things to different countries. The EC interpreted restructuring as meaning above all the reduction of steel-making capacity through plant closures, while publicly, at least, the US government seemed to believe that the problem of excess capacity would be resolved with an upturn in the world economy, and placed more emphasis on the modernisation of steel production facilities. Japan's restructuring programme was aimed largely at improving production efficiency and product quality.[24]

The second difficulty in evaluating the impact of this commitment is that because OECD member countries had different conceptions of the proper role of government in the economy, restructuring involved different tasks for different governments. In the EC, where government intervention in the industry was a fairly widespread practice, evidence that governments gave priority to restructuring would include the reduction or termination of subsidisation programmes and of other forms of government assistance to the steel industry, such as price and production controls, and the negotiation of VRAs, all of which tended to slow the restructuring process. For the United States government, which did not provide direct subsidies to the steel industry, an indication that priority was given to restructuring would be the refusal to protect the US steel industry from

Table 5.1
Crude Steel Production Capacity
(million tonnes)

	OECD	US	EC-10	Japan	Other W.Europe	Canada	Australia and N.Z.
1977	566.0	147.7	202.1	151.8	41.3	15.8	8.7
1978	561.1	143.2	203.5	151.3	44.3	17.5	8.7
1979	573.2	141.9	204.7	156.6	45.7	17.6	8.7
1980	570.1	137.9	203.1	158.1	43.8	19.9	8.7
1981	574.2	139.7	200.0	159.6	43.3	18.9	8.7
1982	568.3	139.8	195.7	157.8	43.9	19.2	9.2
1983	555.6	136.6	190.9	156.7	44.3	20.1	7.1
1984	533.0	122.7	177.8	156.0	50.8	19.2	7.0
1985	522.8	121.1	169.5	154.1	52.3	18.7	7.1
1986	510.1	116.1	164.9	150.9	52.3	18.7	7.2
1987	497.9	101.7	165.2	151.0	54.2	17.9	7.9
1988	496.4	101.6	166.8	149.4	53.0	17.7	7.9
1989	489.3	105.1	163.9	143.3	51.0	17.9	8.2

Source: OECD, *The Steel Market and Outlook*, various issues;
OECD, *The Iron and Steel Industry*, various issues.

Table 5.2
Capacity Utilisation Rates
(Per cent)

	OECD	US	EC*	Japan	Other W.Europe	Canada	Australia and N.Z.
1977	69	77	63	67	71	86	87
1978	74	87	66	68	71	85	90
1979	76	87	69	71	74	90	95
1980	70	74	63	70	74	80	90
1981	68	82	57	64	75	78	91
1982	58	48	56	63	75	62	72
1983	61	56	57	62	78	64	83
1984	69	68	68	68	72	77	94
1985	70	66	71	68	82	78	96
1986	67	64	67	65	84	75	97
1987	71	80	66	65	83	82	82
1988	77	89	73	71	88	85	90
1989	79	84	75	75	87	86	89

* 1977-1981=EC-9; 1982-1985=EC-10; 1986-1989=EC-12.

Source: OECD, *The Steel Market and Outlook*, various issues.

foreign competition, thereby permitting the closure of inefficient production facilities and encouraging modernisation.[25]

Using the indicators discussed above, the record of compliance with the first principle of the Steel Consensus was not entirely positive. Subsidisation of the steel industry in the European Community actually increased in the early 1980s, although in 1980 the EC Commission put considerable pressure on Community member states, when it laid down rules for member government aids to the steel industry, approving subsidies only if they were degressive, temporary, and contributed directly to the restructuring of the steel sector.[26] The US International Trade Commission was not satisfied with the application of these rules, finding in 1985 that subsidies offered by EC governments went beyond what was needed to enable the closure of excess capacity.[27] From the end of 1985, however, state aids to the steel industry were generally prohibited in the EC except for government support for plant closures, research and development and environmental protection.[28] Restructuring was also delayed by the imposition of mandatory minimum prices from 1977 to 1985 and of production quotas between 1980 and 1988.[29] Although these measures were ended by the late 1980s, the programme of VRAs with foreign suppliers continued unabated from its beginning in 1978 through the end of the 1980s.

In the United States, restructuring and modernisation were also delayed by safeguard actions and by the numerous VRAs entered into with countries exporting steel to the US. The import quotas imposed on specialty steel were continued after the adoption of the Steel Consensus, as was the Orderly Marketing Arrangement (OMA) concluded with Japan in 1976. A carbon steel VRA was negotiated with the EC in 1982, and was renewed and extended to additional steel products in 1985. In 1984, the US government decided to negotiate further VRAs with other steel exporting countries, and by the late 1980s some 29 such arrangements had been concluded. These arrangements were renewed for an additional two and a half years from October 1989.[30]

Although the text of the 1982 US-EC carbon steel VRA defended the arrangement as necessary to permit restructuring in accordance with the first OECD Steel Consensus principle, US steel companies were later criticised for not using the respite provided by this and other VRAs to modernise plant and equipment, and for instead using their increased profits to invest in other sectors.[31] In October 1984 the Congress made renewal of VRAs with foreign steel suppliers conditional upon the re-investment of profits by the domestic steel industry in plant modernisation and worker retraining.[32] However, the Reagan Administration was not eager to monitor progress in these areas or to enforce this condition, in part because it regarded such action as excessive government intrusion in the private sector.[33]

The US was also accused of using its trade laws in an effort to protect an inefficient American steel industry. For example, in 1980 the EC Commission contended that the anti-dumping suits filed by steel companies were contrary to the Steel Consensus principle on restructuring and modernisation.[34] American countervailing duty and safeguard actions were equally criticised as means of delaying or avoiding necessary measures for the modernisation of the steel industry.

The Carter Administration made some effort to follow the first Steel Consensus principle in 1980 when it reinstated the Trigger Price Mechanism (which had been suspended earlier that year) for a five year period, but warned that it could terminate the system after three years if the steel industry did not make adequate progress in restructuring.[35] However, the Administration was somewhat slow to implement the recommendations put forward by the Solomon Task Force on the Steel Industry in 1977 which included plans to provide incentives for steel plant and equipment modernisation by expanding trade adjustment assistance, easing environmental regulations, reducing rail-freight rates, providing loan guarantees and tax benefits.[36] One recommendation was adopted in March 1978 when the Economic Development Administration set aside $100 million to be used to guarantee up to $500 million in private loans to help the US steel industry.[37] Another recommendation was carried out when the Treasury Department reduced the time over which steel companies could depreciate equipment in August 1979.[38]

It was not until just before the 1980 election that further recommendations were acted upon by the Carter Administration. These included delaying the deadline for compliance with environmental standards, a further acceleration of depreciation tax write-offs and more liberal tax credits for the steel industry.[39] The Reagan Administration dealt with the problems of the steel industry in the context of a general reform of tax, environmental and regulatory policies aimed at revitalising the American economy as a whole.

Despite the impediments to restructuring posed by government policies, the US and EC did register major capacity reductions in the decade following the Steel Consensus. Japan's production capacity, in contrast, did not decline during this period, and actually increased in the early 1980s. However, since it was already a low-cost producer of steel in 1977, it may be argued that there was less of a need for capacity cuts in that country. On the other hand, capacity utilisation in Japan averaged only 67 per cent from 1977 to 1988, and by the end of the 1980s its utilisation rate was about the same as that of the EC. As was mentioned earlier in this section, the Japanese government did not play a highly visible role in the restructuring efforts of the steel industry, although it did help firms somewhat with tax incentives and low-interest loans from the Japan Development Board for diversification. However, some observers have blamed the Japanese government for complicity in the maintenance of a national steel cartel which allegedly prevented reductions in capacity from being made.[40]

2. "No solution for the fundamental problems of steel industries can be found in reliance on quantitative restrictions."

Compliance with the second principle of the Steel Consensus is perhaps the easiest to gauge because of the high visibility of quantitative restrictions. The first violation of this principle was committed by the EC Commission, which proposed in December 1977 the negotiation of bilateral deals with supplier countries covering both prices and quantities of steel imports to the Community.[41] Over a dozen bilateral arrangements were negotiated in 1978 and renewed annually through the end of the 1980s.

The United States also disregarded this principle by negotiating VRAs with a number of countries in the 1980s.[42] In July 1983, the US imposed a combination of quotas and tariffs on all imported specialty steel products for four years, an action which was condemned by the EC Commission in the Steel Committee as a violation of the Steel Consensus. The specialty steel restrictions were extended for another 27 months in July 1987.[43] Import quotas were unilaterally imposed by the US in 1984, 1985 and

1986 in order to pressure European countries to bring various steel products into the 1982 US-EC agreement.[44]

3. "Any measures designed to deal with [dumping practices] should take into account customary patterns of trade".

This principle was targeted at the United States, since there had been a flood of anti-dumping petitions filed by American steel producers against European imports in 1977. After the Steel Consensus was adopted, the Carter Administration, which had previously encouraged American steel producers to file anti-dumping suits, set up the Trigger Price Mechanism (TPM) in exchange for an agreement by these producers to drop their anti-dumping petitions. This move helped to reduce the climate of uncertainty that the rash of anti-dumping suits had created for European companies, who were reluctant to export to the US for fear of facing heavy penalties if found guilty of dumping.[45] Under the TPM, European steel products maintained their share of the American market in 1978, although this share declined somewhat in 1979.[46]

When the US Steel Corporation broke its 1978 accord with the Administration by filing anti-dumping suits against European steel exporters in March 1980, the Carter Administration attempted to put pressure on the American steel industry by suspending the TPM, arguing that the industry could not enjoy protection through both unrestrained anti-dumping action *and* the TPM. This action led to a fall in European steel exports to the US due to the renewed uncertainty and fear of prosecution under anti-dumping laws. The EC Commission claimed in the Steel Committee meeting in April 1980 that both the anti-dumping suits and the suspension of the TPM called into question the Steel Consensus principle of taking customary trade flows into account, and in late September the Carter Administration restored the TPM, which permitted a recovery of Europe's share of the US steel market in 1981 to a level close to that of 1978.[47]

In January 1982, following a surge in European steel exports to the US, several American steel companies filed anti-dumping and countervailing duty suits against European producers. The Reagan Administration reacted as the Carter Administration had in 1980 by suspending the TPM system, although this time the action was followed by a considerable jump in the EC's share of the American steel market, due largely to the high level of the dollar. Once again the EC denounced the anti-dumping actions as contrary to the Steel Consensus.[48] Rather than revise the TPM, the Reagan Adminjistration preferred to attempt to negotiate a bilateral arrangement with the EC. The carbon steel agreement concluded in October 1982 set the market share for 11 EC steel products at 5.75 per cent, a level slightly higher than that of the five years preceding the Steel Consensus, meaning that traditional steel trade flows between the EC and US were effectively maintained.

Initial Commitments

A.1 "No [steel crisis] trade actions should be inconsistent with GATT provisions."

The US TPM and EC Basic Price System (BPS) did not appear to constitute violations of GATT provisions, since they effectively tolerated a certain amount of dumped steel and provided for normal process of investigation and adjudication for steel products that were suspected of being dumped. The question of whether or not these devices were consistent with the GATT was never clearly resolved because no complaint of violation was ever officially lodged. In the case of US specialty steel quotas, although the EC did not agree with the US interpretation of the situation and took retaliatory action, the US appears to have followed all of the Article XIX procedures, including notifying the GATT of its actions. GATT provisions on subsidies were vague enough that the steel subsidies offered by EC member states did not seem to have violated them.

The various unilateral actions taken by the United States arising from the 1982 carbon steel arrangement (such as the ban on steel pipe and tubes in November 1984, the ban on all EC carbon steel products except pipe and tubes in November 1985, and the quotas on EC semi-finished steel) were notified to the GATT by the Reagan Administration, which claimed that the 1982 pact permitted the US to take such action. However, the carbon steel agreement itself was inconsistent with GATT provisions and the parties failed to file a copy of the agreement with the GATT Secretariat. Indeed, all of the VRAs negotiated by the US and the EC constituted significant breaches of GATT principles, particularly Article XI, which generally prohibits quantitative trade

183

restrictions, and Article XIII, which stipulates that any restrictions that are exceptionally permitted must be applied on a non-discriminatory basis.[49]

A.2 "When actions are necessary they should be as limited and temporary as practicable and appropriate to the causes which led to their introduction".

The most immediate steel crisis trade actions taken after the adoption of the Initial Commitments were the American TPM and the Community's Basic Price System (BPS). From its introduction in early 1978, the BPS was intended to last three months, and ended for those countries which concluded a VRA with the Community. However, it continued into the late 1980s for those countries which were not covered by VRAs.[50] As was mentioned earlier, EC price controls and operating subsidies were terminated in 1985, as were production quotas in 1988.

In the case of American crisis measures, the tariffs and quotas imposed on specialty steel in 1983 were degressive, with tariffs decreasing and quotas rising over a four-year period.[51] These measures were renewed, however, for a further 27 months in 1987. The TPM was intended to last only until an expansion of the world economy eliminated the problem of surplus capacity. After its suspension and re-introduction in 1980, the expiry date was made much more definite. The TPM was to last no more than five years, but was terminated by the Reagan Administration in 1982.[52]

Perhaps the most pervasive crisis measure was the negotiation of VRAs, arrangements which proved very difficult to bring to an end. In the decade which followed the adoption of the Initial Commitments most of the steel traded within the OECD area was covered by VRAs, which in virtually every case were renewed at the end of their term.[53] In addition, many of these VRAs were not degressive. The VRAs negotiated by the United States fixed quotas at a certain percentage of domestic consumption, while those initiated by the EC typically set fixed quantitative levels which were not lowered over the life of the agreements.[54]

A.3 "All actions should be reported promptly to the Steel Committee and in conformity with GATT rules, to the GATT. The status and rationale for maintaining such actions should be reported periodically to the Steel Committee. Participants agree to consult on any trade action of interest to another participant."

This commitment appears to have been fulfilled to the satisfaction of most Steel Committee members. New measures were regularly reported at Steel Committee meetings in the presentations of "recent policy developments".[55] However, GATT officials were not entirely satisfied that they had received complete notification on the VRAs negotiated by the US and the EC.[56]

A.4 "When taking action under domestic law and procedures to deal with serious difficulties of its industry, a participant shall take into account the concerns of trading partners that traditional trade flows established under normal conditions of competition not be severely disrupted."

This commitment was a weaker version of the third principle of the Steel Consensus, since it permitted the United States to claim that traditional EC exports to the US had not been established under "normal conditions of competition" due to subsidisation and the control of prices in the Community. In any case, since the 1977 version of this commitment was generally respected, there were no complaints that the 1978 commitment had been violated.

A.5 "Price guidelines . . . should be expeditiously removed or liberalised as conditions improve."

The conditions referred to in this commitment were substantial excess capacity in exporting countries, widespread price cutting by many exporters, and low capacity utilisation, profits, sales, investments and employment in the domestic industry. Since there was little improvement in most of these areas in the decade following 1978, the US and the EC could not be accused of violating this commitment by continuing the TPM and Basic Price System as long as they did. The EC ended its mandatory minimum price guidelines in 1985 even though substantial surplus capacity remained and other conditions had not significantly improved.

A.6 "Price guidelines should neither exceed the lowest normal prices in the supplying country or countries where normal conditions of competition are prevailing, nor exceed the sums of

185

the full costs of production (including overheads) and profit, as determined over a reasonable period of recent time, in the supplying countries; delivery costs to the importing market and import duties may be included in the event that price guidelines are established on a delivered basis."

In the cases of the EC basic price system and the American TPM, this commitment appears to have been respected.

B. "Participants in the Steel Committee recall their determination to abstain from destructive competition in official support of export credit; they agree that policies in the field of export credits for steel plant and equipment will be fully consistent with the Arrangement on Guidelines for Officially Supported Export Credits and contribute to the avoidance of competitive subsidisation of such exports."

Steel plants were brought into the Consensus on Export Credits in February 1978, and despite complaints of non-compliance periodically made by the US steel industry and echoed within the Congress, in general this commitment appeared to have been respected. Long-term export credits for steel plants and equipment declined rather steadily throughout most of the 1980s, rising slightly only in 1985. The US, however, felt that the Consensus was too permissive in steel plant exports, and the Carter and Reagan Administrations pressed within both the Steel Committee and in the Participants Group for an agreement to further reduce or even end all official support for steel plant and equipment exports.[57]

C. "Domestic policies to sustain steel firms during crisis periods should not shift the burden of adjustment to other countries (eg. by artificially stimulating exports or by artificially displacing imports). Domestic measures should not prevent marginal facilities from closing in those instances where the facilities cannot become commercially viable within a reasonable period of time."

The EC was alone among the three major steel traders in developing clear-cut domestic policies to sustain steel firms. One way of determining whether or not this commitment was observed is by examining steel trade statistics in the period following the creation of the Steel Committee. EC steel exports

Chart 5.6
Steel Exports as a Percentage of Production

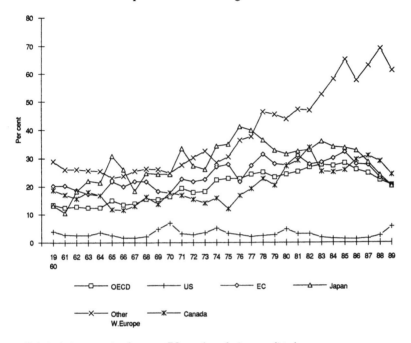

Only includes countries that were EC members during year listed.

Source: OECD, *World Steel Trade Developments 1960–1983: A Statistical Analysis*, 1985;
OECD, *The Steel Market and Outlook*, various issues.

as a percentage of world steel exports declined from 33 per cent to 24 per cent between 1978 and 1988.[58] Thus, although domestic policies may have had some impact on the pace of adjustment, they were not significant enough to reverse the trend of the declining world share of EC steel exports. Whether or not exports were being artificially stimulated may also be indicated by examining the trend in steel exports as a percentage of production. As is illustrated in Chart 5.6, EC steel exports as a percentage of production declined from 31 per cent in 1978 to 23 per cent in 1988, despite the increase in the membership of the Community.[59]

On the import side, statistics show that steel import penetration in the EC actually declined 4 per cent between 1978 and

187

1987, while it increased for the OECD by over 20 per cent, indicating that there was a greater than average displacement of imports in the EC (Chart 5.5). While it can be argued that *any* policies aimed at sustaining an industry in crisis periods will necessarily displace imports (and stimulate exports), VRAs appear to have been far more important in reducing import penetration than were domestic policies.

D. "Participants in the Steel Committee agree to make every effort to provide effective programmes for steel worker re-adaptation away from facilities affected by structural adjustments into alternative employment. To this end, they will periodically exchange information of the effectiveness of policies and programmes to assist steel workers and communities."

Evaluating the impact of this commitment is made somewhat difficult because re-adaption policies in the steel industry are often indistinguishable from a country's overall labour policies. Consequently, the Steel Committee at times found that this question was better treated by the Manpower Committee of the OECD. Nevertheless, the Steel Committee did periodically mandate studies on the question of steel worker re-adaptation programmes in which governments shared information, and changes in these programmes were presented during Steel Committee meetings in the discussion of "recent policy developments".

After 1978 the EC Commission did decide to contribute funds towards re-adaptation aid for steel-workers in a number of Community countries, although the amount of this aid was substantially reduced in 1984, provoking criticism from the ECSC Consultative Committee.[60] Assistance for retraining was increased by the Commission in 1988 to encourage further capacity cuts.[61] The Japanese government also provided funding for worker retraining in 1978, and in 1982 the integrated steel-makers became eligible for these funds.[62] In the United States, re-adaptation assistance was not targeted specifically at steel-workers, but steel-workers were eligible for the more general funding made available through such programmes as the Economic Development and Assistance programme and the Trade Adjustment Assistance programme, the latter of which was cut back sharply by the Reagan Administration.[63] Under the 1984 Trade and Tariff Act, the primary responsibility for worker

188

retraining was expected to be borne by the steel industry and paid for out of company profits.[64]

E. "Any action to restrict trade in steel-making materials should be reported promptly to the Steel Committee and be subject to consultation with affected parties."

This commitment was apparently respected to the satisfaction of all Steel Committee members.[65]

In summary, the Initial Commitments appear to have been largely respected by the major steel trading nations to which they were particularly targeted. Of the three Steel Consensus principles, one was clearly violated and another appeared to have been only partially respected. The most flagrant violation was the negotiation of VRAs by the EC and the US, which impeded progress toward restructuring, constituted quantitative restrictions, were inconsistent with GATT provisions, were not temporary, and were not always fully reported to the appropriate international bodies.

5. Bargaining Positions and Outcomes

The first major steel trade proposal made by the United States in the OECD during the 1970s was an attempt in April 1976 to get its major foreign specialty steel suppliers (Japan, the EC, Sweden and Canada) to accept in principle the need for orderly marketing arrangements to limit specialty steel imports into the US. The American delegates met with a fairly solid front of opposition from the other countries involved, although after the meeting Japan agreed to negotiate an OMA with the United States. The US unilaterally imposed import quotas and higher tariffs on the remaining suppliers two months later.[66]

At the end of April 1977 the United States proposed that the OECD set up a special study group on steel trade and that the group produce a report within a month. On this procedural matter the United States was more successful, since the OECD Council agreed to set up an *ad hoc* Working Group on May 11, although the Japanese expressed reservations over the terms of reference and scope of the new body. The United States insisted that the consideration of any issue should be permissible in the group, and further argued that the group's report should be launched without any prior agreement on how it was to be

189

used.[67] Again, on these procedural matters the US received satisfaction.

Regarding the nature of discussions in the Working Group, the US rejected French proposals for negotiations on a multilateral market-sharing agreement along the lines of the multifibre arrangement (MFA), a proposal which was reportedly not opposed by other EC countries or by Japan.[68] The United States was interested in formulating multilateral rules on safeguards for steel which, if injury were found, would allow governments to impose temporary import restrictions. It was hoped that an accord among OECD countries would later be introduced in the MTN negotiations in Geneva, but the American proposal was apparently blocked by Japan and the EC.[69] Three issues of immediate concern topped the American agenda for the bilateral and trilateral talks held in Paris parallel to the July 1977 Working Group meetings: the alleged dumping of Japanese steel in the US market, steel mill construction and protectionist policies in developing countries, and the question of a suspected diversion of Japanese steel exports to the US as a consequence of the EC-Japanese VRA concluded in 1975.[70]

Within the Working Group itself, the US seemed most interested in focusing attention on government involvement in the steel industry (such as government subsidisation of the steel industry, and voluntary restraint agreements which diverted steel products to the US market) in order to make other countries aware of the repercussions of this involvement on the US steel industry.[71] To this end, in the September 1977 Working Group meeting the US proposed the setting up of a steel trade monitoring system, which was also intended to detect impending problems before they became serious.[72] This proposal was accepted, although the EC and Japan refused to give the US assurances that their steel products would not be sold in the American market at what the US government considered to be dumped prices.[73] At the end of the meetings the US delegate, Deputy Special Trade Representative Richard Heimlick expressed his disappointment with the talks and their outcome, and predicted that the monitoring body would "fall short of our objectives".[74]

While the US was emphasising the problem of dumping in the Working Group (as a result of a flood of anti-dumping petitions by US steel producers and because of Congressional

190

pressure), the EC Industry Commissioner Viscount Davignon was putting forth a proposal for discussions on structural problems in the world steel industry.[75] His restructuring proposal included co-ordinated action to phase out old steel plants in the US and EC and to limit the growth of new capacity in Japan and the developing countries, as well as retraining schemes for laid-off workers.

The Steel Consensus adopted in November 1977 seemed to offer something for every major participant. The undertaking to avoid shifting the burden of adjustment from one producing nation to another addressed American concerns about the assistance given the steel industry by EC governments and European concerns about the protectionist objectives underlying US anti-dumping action and import restrictions like the specialty steel quotas and tariff increases. The priority given to restructuring appeared to satisfy the Europeans, and particularly helped Commissioner Davignon to persuade Community governments to accept capacity reductions. The second principle also seemed to accommodate both US and EC preferences. The need to rationalise the world steel industry seemed to be an allusion to American (and later European) concerns about growing excess production capacity resulting in part from new capacity being built in developing countries, and the reference to "fair" trade was intended to appease protectionist forces in Congress and in the US steel industry. The proscription on quantitative restrictions was clearly aimed at the specialty steel quotas imposed by the US in 1976, but also satisfied American concerns over VRAs such as the one concluded between the EC and Japan. This principle also strengthened the Carter Administration's hand in opposing the import quota legislation that had been introduced in Congress.

The third principle of the Steel Consensus was of particular interest to the United States, since the Carter Administration was focusing on the issue of steel pricing at the time, but also catered to European and Japanese concerns that the proposed TPM programme should preserve their traditional shares of the American market.[76] Finally, the inclusion of information on steel prices in the new monitoring system, and the commitment by participants to notify the Working Group of government measures likely to affect production levels or trade in steel (ie. subsidies) met American objectives in the OECD discussions.

After the November 30 meeting, the chief US delegate, Deputy Assistant Secretary of State William Barraclough was quoted as being "highly satisfied" with the agreement.[77]

After the adoption of the Steel Consensus, a US priority became the creation of a permanent steel committee within the OECD. The US steel industry was continuing to call for steel sector discussions in the Multilateral Trade Negotiations (MTN), a move opposed by the EC and Japan, but also by US trade negotiators, particularly the president's Special Trade Representative Robert Strauss. An OECD steel committee was seen as a more acceptable alternative which would at least partially satisfy American steel producers and not interfere with the Administration's objectives in the MTN.[78] Through the spring of 1978 a series of trilateral meetings among senior officials of the US, EC and Japan was held to negotiate the setting up of an OECD steel committee.[79] The US was interested in a permanent body which would monitor steel prices and how they were related to production costs, subsidies, and "unfair" trade practices. American negotiators also proposed that OECD nations reduce the export of steel production facilities to developing countries, and that major steel producing countries in the Third World be invited to join the committee.[80]

Most of the American objectives were met in the 26 October Council decision establishing a steel committee. The EC countries, which were eager to prevent protectionist pressure in the US steel industry from spreading to other sectors and perhaps jeopardising the MTN, supported the committee's creation, although they withheld their approval until they were assured that the last of the outstanding anti-dumping cases against European steel producers had been lifted.[81] The US successfully pressed for a change in language in Commitment A.4 of the Initial Commitments (a re-phrasing of the third principle of the Consensus) which stated that domestic actions to assist the steel industry should take into account traditional trade flows. This commitment was qualified by the phrase "established under normal conditions of competition", which the US interpreted as meaning that traditional trade flows could be disrupted if they were established as a result of dumping or subsidies. This represented something of a setback for the EC Commission which had been claiming that the third principle of the Consensus gave the EC the right to its traditional share of the US market, regardless of dumping or subsidisation practices.[82] Japan had strong reservations about inviting developing countries to participate, but finally gave in to pressure from other OECD members, particularly from the United States.[83]

The major point on which the US was not fully satisfied was the subsidisation of export credits for steel making equipment sold to developing countries. The US tried to get stronger language in Commitment B, but was unsuccessful.[84] Subsequent attempts to convince other participants to reduce or eliminate export credit subsidies for LDC steel plants in Steel Committee meetings over the next decade were blocked by the Europeans and Japanese, who prevented the adoption of any measures other than requesting the Secretariat to collect data and to prepare studies of the practice.[85] At one stage in the discussions in 1986 and 1987, the United States proposed that official export credit support for steel plants be prohibited altogether, but after failing to receive sufficient acceptance of this proposal, the US modified its stance by calling for significant reductions in *subsidised* export credits. The United States was largely successful in resisting pressure from other OECD members to change its policies and practices in the steel sector. At various times in OECD meetings the US was urged to change the "sales below cost" criterion in its anti-dumping legislation and to terminate its quotas on specialty steel, both of which it refused to do.[86]

In summary, while most American objectives in the OECD appear to have been attained in the steel sector, on a least three major issues American attempts to persuade other participants were unsuccessful: gaining acceptance from the EC, Sweden and Canada in 1976 of the need to negotiate OMAs in specialty steel; obtaining guarantees from the EC and Japan not to dump steel in the American market using the US government's definition of dumping in 1977; and getting an agreement to reduce or eliminate export credit subsidies for steel plant equipment sales to LDCs beginning in 1978.

6. Explaining OECD Agreements and their Impact

(a) Overall Capabilities

There is no clear evidence of any country overtly linking the various steel issues raised in the OECD to non-trade issues, either to force acceptance of commitments or to ensure that OECD commitments were respected. The OECD steel trade talks were apparently not discussed at any of the economic summit meetings, and even at the OECD Ministerial Councils, steel trade was only on the agenda in 1978 when a decision was made to set up the Steel Committee. Thus, the distribution of overall power resources does not seem to offer an adequate explanation for the outcome of bargaining in the OECD with respect to steel or for the impact of OECD agreements.

(b) International Trade Structure

Despite the fact that the US had greater overall trade power capabilities than Japan and the EC (at least, during the early 1970s and after 1982), it did not attempt to draw on that power by linking progress in OECD steel trade talks or the implementation of OECD commitments to other trade issues. The EC Commission, on the other hand, displayed a greater assertiveness in OECD talks than a simple international trade structure model could account for, making both veiled and more open threats of retaliation in other industrial sectors and in agricultural products in response to American protectionist action in the steel sector.[87] At the OECD Steel Symposium held in 1980, Viscount Davignon, while denying that he was threatening the United States, warned that US protectionism on steel could touch off a trade war. The EC Commission warned the US more directly in the April 1984 Steel Committee meeting that the Fair Trade in Steel Act introduced in Congress risked igniting a trade war between the EC and the United States.[88]

The only clear cases where trade issue linkages were actually carried out were those undertaken by the EC in retaliation for unilaterally-imposed quantitative restrictions on steel imports by the United States. However, these linkages, which were made in accordance with GATT provisions, did not succeed in convincing the US to abandon its restrictions on specialty steel imports.[89]

(c) Issue Structure

In the case of steel trade, issue-specific bargaining power derives largely from market access. The US steel industry was

194

far less dependent on access to the markets of the EC and Japan than the European and Japanese industries were on access to the US market. Tables 5.3 through 5.5 indicate that during the period from 1977 to 1988, the EC purchased an average of 9.3 per cent of total US exports, while Japan purchased only 1.8 per cent. Because of the relatively low level of American steel exports, these purchases represented only 0.2 per cent and 0.02 per cent respectively of total US steel production. Over the same period, the American market accounted for an average 18 per cent of total EC steel exports and 17 per cent of total Japanese steel exports, representing 5 per cent and 5.7 per cent respectively of domestic steel production. The EC Commission was particularly concerned about maintaining access to this market because of the fear that reductions in exports to the US would affect certain European producers more severely than others, resulting in renewed price competition within the EC.[90]

As a result of this pattern of steel trade, the US was in a position to curtail steel imports unilaterally (which it in fact did in some cases) without much concern about being similarly closed out of the steel markets of other countries. With this bargaining power capability, there was no need for the US to link the steel issue to other issues in order to get its way on the various proposals opposed by other OECD members. While the US did effectively use this capability to impose bilateral agreements on most of its steel trade partners, including the EC and Japan, it is curious that it did not make the same effort to obtain agreements within the OECD closer to its preferences, particularly an agreement on one issue that could not be dealt with through bilateral arrangements – the subsidisation of export credits for steel-making facilities.

In only one instance was the threat of unilateral steel trade action by the US successful in OECD discussions. The US threat to impose import quotas unilaterally unless its major foreign suppliers of specialty steel agreed to negotiate an orderly marketing arrangement in 1976 was effective only in the case of Japan, while the other major suppliers refused to give in to the American demand.[91] Issue-specific power capabilities were not mobilised to enforce respect for OECD principles and commitments on steel trade because the two parties with the greatest capabilities, the US and the EC (which were the two largest importers of steel in the world), were themselves the main

195

Table 5.3
Destination of US Steel Exports

	As % of Total Steel Exports		As % of Steel Production	
	EC	Japan	EC	Japan
1960	23.9	2.6	0.9	0.1
1965	4.8	0.4	0.1	0.0
1970	43.8	0.3	3.0	0.0
1975	4.0	0.1	0.1	0.0
1976	14.1	0.3	0.4	0.0
1977	8.1	0.5	0.2	0.0
1978	6.4	2.1	0.2	0.0
1979	6.8	0.8	0.2	0.0
1980	10.4	0.8	0.5	0.0
1981	5.5	0.3	0.2	0.0
1982	5.2	0.6	0.2	0.0
1983	9.1	0.9	0.1	0.0
1984	7.9	0.0	0.1	0.0
1985	8.8	0.0	0.1	0.0
1986	16.5	0.0	0.3	0.0
1987	14.8	7.4	0.2	0.1
1988	12.5	8.3	0.3	0.2

Source: OECD, *The Steel Market and Outlook,* various issues;
        OECD, *World Steel Trade Developments 1960–1983: A Statistical Analysis,* 1985.

violators of these principles through their negotiation of VRAs on steel.

(d) Influence of Institutions

The size and composition of the *ad hoc* Working Group or of the Steel Committee did not appear to have strongly influenced the nature of the steel agreements negotiated in the OECD or their impact on the policies and practices of member countries. This is somewhat surprising, since the OECD included the countries accounting for the vast majority of US steel imports.

Table 5.4
Destination of EC Steel Exports

	As % of Total Steel Exports		As % of Steel Production	
	US	Japan	US	Japan
1960	12.8	0.6	2.6	0.1
1965	23.0	0.0	5.0	0.0
1970	25.3	0.0	4.5	0.0
1975	13.5	0.0	3.8	0.0
1976	12.4	0.0	2.7	0.0
1977	22.3	0.0	6.1	0.0
1978	20.1	0.0	6.3	0.0
1979	15.3	0.0	4.3	0.0
1980	12.2	0.0	3.3	0.0
1981	17.8	0.0	5.6	0.0
1982	18.8	0.0	3.7	0.0
1983	16.7	0.0	5.9	0.0
1984	19.2	0.7	4.2	0.1
1985	18.8	0.2	6.0	0.1
1986	19.6	0.5	5.5	0.1
1987	17.1	0.5	4.7	0.1
1988	20.0	1.1	4.6	0.2

Source: OECD, *The Steel Market and Outlook*, various issues;
   OECD, *World Steel Trade Developments 1960–1983: A Statistical Analysis*, 1985.

It might have been expected that the US would prefer to negotiate a multilateral steel agreement with its major suppliers on
rules covering subsidisation, dumping and safeguard measures,
or at least an arrangement along the lines of the MFA (which
involved a larger number of parties than the Steel Committee),
instead of numerous bilateral arrangements.

Even more than in the cases of export credits and agricultural
trade, OECD Secretariat officials attempted to be as neutral as
possible in dealing with steel trade issues, and did not play any
singnificant role in the socialisation of delegates or by participating in transgovernmental coalitions. Where the Secretariat was

Table 5.5
Destination of Japanese Steel Exports

	As % of Total Steel Exports		As % of Steel Production	
	US	EC	US	EC
1960	19.5	0.0	2.6	0.0
1965	42.2	1.7	13.0	0.5
1970	29.9	6.0	7.3	1.4
1975	18.0	6.1	6.3	2.1
1976	19.7	4.9	8.1	2.0
1977	20.7	5.1	8.3	2.1
1978	18.7	2.6	6.8	1.0
1979	18.5	2.3	6.1	0.7
1980	18.2	2.1	5.7	0.8
1981	19.7	0.5	6.4	0.2
1982	16.4	1.1	5.4	0.2
1983	12.5	1.0	4.4	0.3
1984	18.8	1.0	6.4	0.3
1985	17.1	1.0	5.7	0.3
1986	13.9	1.9	4.6	0.6
1987	15.5	0.9	4.4	0.3
1988	16.6	1.3	4.1	0.3

Source: OECD, *The Steel Market and Outlook,* various issues;
OECD, *World Steel Trade Developments 1960–1983: A Statistical Analysis,* 1985.

somewhat more active, however, was in influencing the agenda of steel meetings in the Organisation. For example, sensing that the steel trade situation was deteriorating after the 1976 specialty steel import restrictions imposed by the US, Secretariat officials decided to draft a report on world steel trade problems in early 1977. This report subsequently formed the basis of discussion in the *ad hoc* Working Group.[91] In addition, the February 1980 Steel Symposium was held on the suggestion of Secretariat officials after comments by some Steel Committee participants that the steel was a world-wide and not just an OECD problem. The Symposium was intended to bring together a number of parties which were not participants in the Steel Committee, including representatives of non-OECD countries, trade unions, and steel industries, in addition to OECD country representatives.[92] While the Secretariat was sometimes pro-active in preparing studies and in proposing the Symposium, these actions were not significant either in determining the outcome of the OECD discussions, or in influencing the impact of agreements reached in those discussions.

The permanent forum provided by the OECD permitted the United States to keep the issue of subsidised export credits for steel plants on the table for many years in the hopes that a breakthrough would eventually be reached, although as has been seen, it did not exert the same degree of pressure that it did on general export credit and agricultural issues. By the end of the 1980s there was still no agreement on the issue, which had been the subject of American proposals for over a decade.

On the basis of available information there are no examples of transgovernmental coalitions being formed which enabled other member countries to resist American proposals in the OECD on steel trade. However, there is an example of a transgovernmental coalition aimed at changing the practice of direct subsidisation of the EC steel industry. The EC Commission welcomed repeated American calls in the OECD for Community member countries to reduce or eliminate these subsidies, demands which were in line with the Commission's own preferences. These American demands may have facilitated the Commission's move in 1986 to ban direct subsidies and to limit other forms of subsidisation of the steel industry by EC member states. While American delegates at times agreed with the criticism made by other delegations about legislation proposed in the US Congress (such as the Fair Trade in Steel Act), they did not make much use of those criticisms in the OECD when opposing the legislation.

Although there were extensive transgovernmental contacts in the OECD, there is little evidence to indicate that these contacts resulted in significantly altered perceptions of self-interest by delegates, at least not any which were strong enough to change the policies or practices of member governments. In fact, an examination of the positions of various participants in OECD steel discussions reveals that there was very little change in the positions of any countries, although delegates did often appear

199

to have gained a greater awareness of each other's problems and views.[94] OECD rules tended to be not so much a product of hard bargaining where countries altered their positions, giving up some demands in exchange for the acceptance of others, but were rather a collection of the diverse proposals put forward by each of the major parties who were seeking to address some particular domestic objective.

It is not clear that a multilateral "steel trade regime" has ever existed since 1945. The only rules, norms, principles or decision-making procedures aimed specifically at steel at the multilateral level were those set out in the Steel Consensus and Initial Commitments. If these two agreements can be considered to constitute a steel trade regime, then it was a very weak regime, since it did not appear to have had a major influence on subsequent discussions in the OECD or on the policies and practices of member governments. Some of the commitments contained in these agreements were likely to be carried out by governments in any case, whether other countries complied or not (for example, restructuring). Others came to be disregarded by most participants (the proscription on quantitative restrictions), or were simply a restatement of rules established in other forums (GATT rules, Consensus on Export Credits), while on still others there was fairly widespread disagreement over interpretations of established principles (maintaining traditional steel trade flows).

About the only principle or rule valued enough to influence the subsequent behaviour of participants in the OECD talks was the need to consult with one another on steel trade measures. In fact, after 1978 these consultations and exchanges of information came to dominate Steel Committee discussions. The only noticeable change in the already weak multilateral steel regime was its further weakening by the trend towards a bilaterally-negotiated steel trade order. The influence of this trend was to virtually eliminate bargaining in the OECD, with the exception of the export credits issue. As a result, there was little opportunity for further bargaining in the OECD to influence the steel regime, which by the 1980s was a network of bilateral regimes operating outside of any apparent multilateral rules or norms.

The influence of the overall trade regime on what little steel trade bargaining there was in the OECD and on the impact of commitments agreed upon there was also limited. None of the principles and commitments agreed on in the OECD were inconsistent with GATT rules, although there were often disagreements over the interpretation of these rules (such as on dumping and safeguard measures). A major concern of OECD members, at least rhetorically, was the condition of the general international liberal trading regime. The possibility of trade wars and of a proliferation of protectionist measures was often cited as a reason for exercising constraint in steel trade policy. One of the motivations behind European support for the creation of the Steel Committee as expressed by an EC official was the fear that if the steel problem were not resolved then protectionism could spread into other sectors and jeopardise the MTN.[95]

The US government obviously had a similar concern, since one of the reasons it decided to introduce the steel issue into the OECD in the first place was that the steel industry and the steel caucus in Congress had threatened to hold up the MTN unless there was some kind of international action on steel trade.[96] As well, at various times in Steel Committee meetings the US delegation agreed with other members that certain steel trade measures proposed in the Congress were protectionist and could lead to a trade war, and pledged itself to oppose these measures.[97] With respect to the negotiation of VRAs, however, the influence of the overall trade regime was weak. Most steel trade came to be regulated by these arrangements, which were inconsistent with the principles of multilateralism, non-discrimination and liberalisation.

(e) Unit-level Variables

Domestic Group Opposition   There were no discernible cases where resistance from major domestic groups weakened the American bargaining position in OECD talks. Indeed, the US steel industry, backed by its steel-workers, had been calling for the use of multilateral forums such as the OECD to regulate steel trade as early as 1975, and many of the US proposals in the OECD were actually in response to the demands of the American steel industry.[98] If anyone was resisting a more aggressive stance in the OECD, it was not domestic groups but the Administration itself. The EC Commission played a similar restraining role in the bargaining position of Community governments and domestic groups calling for a harder line in OECD discussions.[99]

Domestic groups were not particularly successful in influencing the pattern of government compliance with OECD commitments either. In the United States, the steel industry for the most part preferred to use trade laws to deal with import competition, rather than have the government arrange quantitative import restrictions. Ironically, the application of US trade laws was not proscribed by the OECD agreements, even though these laws on imports were often more trade-restricting than quantitative restrictions, which had been discouraged by the Steel Consensus. The steel industry forced the government to grant it protection from imports by resorting to trade laws, but the Administration was able to convince the industry to accept quantitative restrictions and to abandon legal action against imported steel.

VRAs were generally preferred by the Administration, because they were generally less restrictive than the legal process was proving to be, they did not lead to retaliatory trade actions from America's trading partners and they were fully controlled by the executive branch, unlike anti-trust and countervailing duty suits. Thus, in a sense, the American violation of the second principle of the Steel Consensus occurred regardless of the preferences of domestic groups. Opposition from other domestic groups, steel consuming industries in particular, was not effective in preventing quantitative restrictions from being imposed, although in 1989 pressure from these groups may have contributed to the Administration's decision to extend VRAs for another two and a half years instead of the five years requested by the steel industry.[100]

In the European Community, the steel industry and steel-workers generally supported the negotiation of VRAs by the Commission, while consumer groups were unable to oppose these restrictions effectively. Domestic group opposition was not effective in preventing the EC from giving priority to restructuring in accordance with the first Steel Consensus principle. An in-depth study of the restructuring efforts in the steel industry concluded that attempts by steel-workers in both the EC and the US to oppose plant closures had generally failed.[101]

Governmental Cohesion Lack of coherence in US steel trade policy making does not provide an adequate explanation for the inability of the United States to get its way on some issues in OECD steel trade talks, nor does it explain the pattern of compliance (and noncompliance) with the OECD commitments. American initiatives leading to the adoption of the Steel Consensus and Initial Commitments were part of an attempt by the Carter Administration to take control of steel trade policy-making, at a time when the Steel Caucus in the Congress was introducing legislation for the imposition of import quotas.[102] However, differences between the executive and legislative branches did not weaken the bargaining position of the US in the OECD talks, and if anything probably strengthened it, since other delegations were aware that an alternative to a multilateral agreement was unilateral American import restrictions. While the Congressional Steel Caucus was pushing for immediate action to remedy the US steel industry's plight, there were few major criticisms by the Caucus about the Administration's handling of the issue in the OECD.[103]

Any divisions which existed within the EC on steel trade policy were not sufficient either to weaken the EC bargaining position in the OECD talks, or to alter the impact of OECD commitments on EC policy and practices. The major division had been between Germany and the Netherlands on the one hand, who were traditionally opposed to government intervention in the form of state aids or production quotas, and France, Italy and Belgium, who favoured such measures. As the severity of the steel crisis increased, however, these differences eroded and interventionist programmes were generally accepted as necessary.[104] The authority of the EC Commission over steel policy under the Treaty of Paris was also such that it could preside over a fairly coherent Community policy, in marked contrast to the case of shipbuilding, as will be seen in the next chapter.[105] Indeed, a high-ranking OECD Secretariat official, John Marcum, once commented that steel was the only industry in which the European Community behaved as one country instead of ten or twelve small countries, usually speaking with one voice at Steel Committee meetings.[106]

Preference Intensity The most persuasive explanation for the

United States' lack of success in obtaining an agreement on certain of its demands in the OECD, particularly on steel plant export financing, seems to be the relatively limited commitment to these objectives and, indeed, to the whole multilateral approach to the steel problem. Evidence of this lack of commitment is seen in the absence of attempts to link these demands to other trade issues, and in the failure to use access to the US market for steel products as an instrument of pressure. The bilateral and unilateral measures taken by the United States on steel trade were not generally tied to progress in the OECD, which indicates that successive Administrations (with the possible exception of the Carter Administration) had more faith in, and even a preference for, bilateral and unilateral instruments than they did for a multilateral approach. The Carter Administration appeared to have the strongest commitment to the OECD, largely due to its disdain for quantitative restrictions, whether imposed unilaterally or negotiated bilaterally.[107]

The introduction of proposals in the OECD by the US appeared to be a way of deflecting industry and Congressional pressure for action on steel imports. The US steel industry had made numerous demands for a multilateral approach to the problem between 1975 and 1978, preferably an agreement negotiated under the auspices of the GATT, along the lines of the MFA.[108] When this pressure was at its most intense in 1977 and 1978, the Administration pushed for agreements like the Steel Consensus and the Initial Commitments, although it was opposed to the kind of market-sharing arrangement demanded by the industry and Congress.[109] But once the US steel industry lost interest in sectoral multilateral negotiations on steel, the Carter Administration seemed content to allow the Steel Committee to settle into a routine without attempting to introduce any new multilateral measures. Thus, the OECD may have been more of a safety valve for the Administration, rather than an approach to which it was strongly committed.

After 1980, the Reagan Administration displayed a preference first for unilateral measures, such as the enforcement of US trade laws, and then later for bilaterally-negotiated VRAs to cope with the steel industry's problems.[110] The issue of official support of export credits for plant and equipment sold to developing countries could not be resolved unilaterally or bilaterally, however, so the US continued to urge Steel Committee members to reach some kind of understanding to reduce or eliminate this support. Yet while the US proved fairly persistent in its efforts to obtain an agreement on export credits in the Steel Committee, it was not willing to push hard enough to force other members to accept its demands.

The limited commitment of the US is also evident in the lack of attention devoted to American demands in the OECD at the highest political levels. In the early years of the Steel Committee, the US sent high-level officials to the meetings in Paris, but after 1982 lower-level officials tended to represent the United States.[111] The lack of concern about violations of the OECD commitments by other countries, and indeed its own disregard for the commitments on quantitative restrictions and restructuring, also demonstrated the relative disinterest of the United States in the OECD process.

The main explanation for the lack of commitment of the US to the OECD in the area of steel trade was the realisation by the Administration that the steel industry in the United States was fundamentally uncompetitive in the international marketplace. The Administration wanted to avoid taking forceful action against other countries, since this could harm more efficient American producers in other sectors through possible retaliation, place unnecessary strain on the international trading system and weaken alliance solidarity. The US position on steel within the OECD was in marked contrast with the resolve displayed in the agricultural and export credits talks, since the US believed that it had a strong comparative advantage in agricultural and capital goods exports. The US was never a major exporter of steel during the 1970s and 1980s, however, so the government was not as interested in pushing for free trade for steel as it was for the other two groups of products. American government action on steel trade in general was both reluctant and reactive, and it was only because of the aggressive use of American trade laws and pressure from the Steel Caucus in Congress that the Administration turned to the OECD in the first place, and then turned to bilateral agreements when the OECD agreements failed to placate the steel industry.

The commitment of the EC to its objectives in the OECD talks, on the other hand, appeared quite strong. Governments in the Community were very active in supporting the steel industry, where the American government had only been reactive. While the EC was much more directly involved than the US in encouraging the industry to restructure, in the area of quantitative restrictions it was at least as culpable as the US. The Community imposed VRAs on foreign suppliers as well as requesting such arrangements for their own exports to the United States. Despite the fact that these bilateral arrangements were clearly inconsistent with the Steel Consensus, they were not generally criticised in Steel Committee meetings, since the EC and other parties to VRAs were more interested in maintaining or increasing their share of the US market through these bilateral deals than they were in challenging the principle of VRAs.[112] The EC (as well as Japan) resisted American attempts to reduce or eliminate subsidised export credits on steel plant exports because it exported more of these facilities than the US and valued the contribution of these large exports to its trade balance.

(f) Changes in Interest Definition

There was no major shift in the definition of interest concerning steel trade among any of the major actors in the OECD during the 1970s and 1980s. The EC remained committed to restructuring the steel industry, while protecting it from foreign competitors, at least as long as the United States continued to do the same. Neither the EC nor Japan were willing to accept American definitions of dumping, and the US remained steadfast in resisting calls to change this definition. The American government continued to give in to industry demands for protection from imports, while Japan accepted the growing competitiveness of newly industrialising countries in the steel market, and permitted the growth in steel import penetration. The only discernable change was one of approach rather than of interest. The high profile given to the OECD by the United States under the Carter Administration came to an end when the Reagan Administration took office and adopted a more unilateralist and bilateralist approach to steel trade policy.

7. Conclusion

In contrast to the vigorous and protracted bargaining activity within the OECD in the areas of export credits and agriculture, negotiations on steel were much more subdued and short-lived. The only time any intense bargaining activity took place on steel was in the late 1970s, when the Steel Consensus and the Initial Commitments were worked out. After that the only activity that resembled negotiation was on the issue of the financing of steel plant exports. However, the parties were locked into a stalemate on this issue. A pattern set in of the United States demanding controls on the practice while other countries blocked any agreement, and after more than a decade of talks there was no real movement on the issue.

In many ways the steel trade talks in the OECD can be described as a failure. Although many differences and disputes remained among parties in the Steel Committee, and the problem of surplus production capacity persisted, there were no serious attempts to formulate additional collective guidelines after 1978, despite the Committee's mandate to do just that. Those guidelines and principles that had been agreed upon were often disregarded, and the most important of those violations were seldom even discussed, let alone penalised.

The most perplexing aspect of the OECD steel trade talks is that despite the clear predominance of the United States in terms of issue-specific power capabilities, it did not mobilise its resources (as it had attempted to do in the cases of agriculture and export credits) to bring about an agreement on steel plant export financing, on an internationally-accepted definition of dumping, or on a multilateral export restraint agreement similar to the MFA. The US also failed to enforce respect for OECD guidelines and principles. The most plausible explanation for this is that the US government was not strongly committed to its objectives in the OECD, to the whole OECD process in the steel trade area, or to free trade in steel.

Alternative explanations are not satisfactory in explaining the pattern of outcomes in the OECD talks. Because the US was predominant in terms of steel trade bargaining power, it did not need to link other issues to progress on steel, so the overall capabilities and international trade structure models are not relevant here. International institutional variables did not generally play a decisive role, although one of the chief reasons that the US insisted on setting up the Steel Committee was to protect its objectives in negotiations on the general international trade regime. However, once the Tokyo Round was concluded, concern for the trade regime no longer strongly influenced subsequent OECD discussions or the implementation of OECD commitments.

The two other unit-level variables considered in this study did not provide adequate explanations either. The European Community was remarkably unified on the steel trade issue in the OECD, and those disagreements that existed between Congress and the Administration in the US did not weaken the American position in the talks. Also, there was no resistance to the objectives of delegates in OECD talks from domestic groups which could explain why any party failed to prevail. Pressure from domestic groups was more influential, at least indirectly, in determining the impact of OECD norms on government policies and practices. While the American government opted for quantitative restrictions despite the preference of the steel industry for enforcement of trade laws, without pressure from the industry the government would probably not have felt compelled to take any protective action at all.

Notes

1 Robert Ballance, "Industry-specific Strategies in a Protectionist World," *Intereconomics* 20 (November/December 1985), pp. 277–278; OECD, *The Steel Market and Outlook*, various years; OECD, *The Iron and Steel Industry*, various years.

2 Between 1973 and 1983 US apparent steel consumption declined some 34.4 per cent while apparent consumption in the EC fell 22.6 per cent and in Japan it fell 18.2 per cent. During thr same period employment levels in the steel industry fell 47.3 per cent in the US, 37.4 per cent in the EC and 17.8 per cent in Japan. IMF, *Trade Policy Issues and Developments*, by Shailendra J. Anljaria, Naheed Kirmani, and Arne B. Petersen (Washington: IMF, 1985), p. 117.

3 For a more in-depth discussion of EC and Japanese steel policies, see Thomas R. Howell et al., *Steel and the State: Government Intervention and Steel's Structural Crisis* (Boulder and London: Westview Press, 1988).

4 Interview with OECD official; *OECD Observer*, No.16 (June 1965), pp. 36–37; No.20 (February 1966), pp. 34–36; No.26 (February 1967), pp. 10–11; No.32 (February 1968), pp. 16–20; No.39 (April 1969), pp. 12–14; *OECD Press Release* A(63)75, 6 December 1963; A(67), 2 March 1967.

5 *OECD Press Release* A(75)44, 14 November 1975.

6 The Trade Pledge was a declaration issued at the 1974 OECD Ministerial meeting and intended to head off the adoption of beggar-thy-neighbour policies in the wake of the 1973 oil crisis.

Member countries committed themselves to avoid imposing import restrictions and export controls, artificially stimulating exports, or competing in official support of export credit. In addition, they agreed "to consult with each other, making full use of the general procedures of consultation within OECD, in order to assure that the present Declaration is properly implemented." *Activities of OECD in 1974*, pp. 81–82.

7 *The Times* 30 March 1976; 6 April 1976; 7 April 1976; *Financial Times* 7 April 1976. U.S., President (Ford, 1974–1976), "Import Relief Determination Under Section 202(b) of the Trade Act: Memorandum for the Special Representative for Trade Negotiations, March 16, 1976", *Federal Register*, Vol. 41, March 18, 1976, p. 11269.

8 *The Times* 12 May 1977; *New York Times* 19 May 1977.

9 *OECD Press Release* A(75)44, 14 November 1975; *Bulletin of the European Communities*, 10–1975, pp. 41–42, 11–1975, p. 52; *Financial Times* 28 October 1975, 7 April 1976; *The Times* 7 April 1976; *Le Monde* 24 octobre 1975.

10 *Financial Times* 21 July 1977.

11 *Financial Times* 1 and 10 October 1977.

12 *Financial Times, New York Times* 1 December 1977; *The Times* 19 December 1977.

13 *OECD Press Release* A(77)54, 30 November 1977.

14 OECD, *Activities of the OECD*, 1977, p. 67; *Financial Times* 21 July 1978, 22 September, 9 June 1978; *Bulletin of the European Communities*, 2–1978, pp. 64–65.

15 The original participants included Australia, Austria, Belgium, Canada, Denmark, Finland, France, Germany, Greece, Ireland, Italy, Japan, Luxembourg, the Netherlands, Norway, Spain, Sweden, Switzerland, the United Kingdom and the United States. Portugal became a member in 1979 as did Turkey in 1983.

16 The Liaison Committee met about twice a year at the end of Steel Committee meetings. Interview with OECD official; OECD, *Activities of the OECD*, 1983, p. 59.

17 The Trigger Price Mechanism (TPM) was a device introduced in late 1977 to deal with the flood of anti-dumping suits in the United States. The TPM set minimum "trigger prices" for steel products, based on Japanese steel production costs, which were considered to be among the lowest at that time. Imports entering the US above the trigger prices were given immunity from anti-dumping litigation, while those entering under the trigger price were subject to government investigation and possible prosecution. The EC's Basic Price System was a similar mechanism introduced shortly after the TPM.

18 See chapter 3.

19 *OECD Press Release* A(78)43, 27 October 1978.

20 Interview with OECD official.

21 *OECD Press Release* A(78)43, 27 October 1978.

22 Ibid.

23 OECD, *The Steel Market* and *The Iron and Steel Industry*, various years.
24 U.S., House, Committee on Ways and Means, *Administration's Comprehensive Program for the Steel Industry: Hearings before the Subcommittee on Trade.* 95th Cong., 2nd sess., January 25 and 26, 1978, pp. 10, 24–27; *Bulletin of the European Communities*, 6–1978, p. 14; OECD, *Steel in the 80s: Paris Symposium* (Paris: OECD, 1980), p. 157.
25 In the case of Japan, where government was traditionally much less involved in the steel industry, indicators of compliance with this principle cannot readily be presented.
26 *Bulletin of the European Communities*, 2–1980, p. 40; 3–1981, pp. 87–88. The aids code was substantially strengthened in 1981. Decision 257/80/ECSC OJ 1980 L29 and Decision 2320/81/ECSC OJ 1981 L228.
27 *Financial Times* 18 April 1985.
28 *Bulletin of the European Communities*, 10–1985, pp. 12–13;11–1985, p. 36; *Financial Times*, 17 July, 31 October 1985; *International Herald Tribune*, 24 January 1986; Walter H. Goldberg, *Ailing Steel: The Transoceanic Quarrel* (Aldershot: Gower, 1986), p. 116; Howell et al., *Steel and the State*, pp. 65–71; *OECD Observer*, No.103 (March 1980), p. 8.
29 A report of an independent committee of "Wise Men" appointed by the EC Commission concluded in late 1987 that production quotas had discouraged companies from making necessary plant closures. Howell et al., *Steel and the State*, pp. 89–91; *Financial Times* 26 November 1987.
30 *New York Times* 26 July 1989.
31 Michael K. Levine, *Inside International Trade Policy Formulation: A History of the 1982 US-EC Steel Arrangements* (New York: Praeger, 1985), pp. 117 and 129. The Trade and Tariff Act of 1984 called on the steel industry to reinvest its cash flow in the steel industry in return for the negotiation of VRAs. Gary Clyde Hufbauer and Howard F. Rosen, *Trade Policy for Troubled Industries* (Washington: Institute for International Economics, 1986), p. 39.
32 IMF, *Trade Policy Issues and Developments*, p. 38.
33 Stephen Woolcock et al., *Interdependence in the Post-multilateral Era* (Cambridge, Mass.: Center for International Affairs and University Press of America, 1985), pp. 53–54.
34 *Financial Times* 18 April 1980; *Bulletin of the European Communities*, 4–1980, p. 73.
35 Hugh Patrick and Hideo Sato, "The Political Economy of United States-Japan Trade in Steel", in *Policy and Trade Issues of the Japanese Economy: American and Japanese Perspectives*, ed. Koza Yamamura (Seattle and London: University of Washington Press, 1982), p. 212.
36 U.S., House, *Administration's Comprehensive Program for the Steel Industry*, pp. 4–38.
37 *New York Times* 23 March 1978.
38 *New York Times* 21 August 1979.

39 *New York Times* 1 October 1980.
40 Howell et al., *Steel and the State*, pp. 233–239.
41 *Financial Times* 20 December 1977.
42 *International Herald Tribune* 6, 28 July 1983; *Bulletin of the European Communities*, 7/8–1983, p. 58. The US had previously imposed import quotas on Community and Swedish specialty steel from 1976 to 1980. A bill to restrict imports of specialty steel was introduced in the Congress in 1982. U.S., Senate, Committee on Finance, *Import Relief for the Specialty Steel Industry: Hearing before the Subcommittee on International Trade*, 97th Cong., 2nd sess., September 29, 1982, pp. 7–8.
43 *International Herald Tribune* 6, 28 July 1983; *Bulletin of the European Communities*, 7/8–1983, p. 58; IMF, *Issues and Developments in International Trade Policy*, by Margaret Kelly, Naheed Kirmani, Miranda Xafa, Clemens Boonekamp, and Peter Winglee (Washington, D.C.: IMF, 1988), p. 70.
44 *Financial Times* 29 November, 11, 29, 31 December 1984; *International Herald Tribune* 8 August 1985, 28–29 June 1986; *Globe and Mail* 3 May, 19 September 1984, 30 November 1985.
45 Ingo Walter, "Protection of Industries in Trouble--the Case of Iron and Steel," *The World Economy* 2 (May 1979), pp. 160–161; Matthew J. Marks, "Remedies to "Unfair" Trade: American Action Against Steel Imports" *The World Economy* 1 (January 1978), pp. 228–229; Robert Crandall, "The EC-US Steel Trade Crisis", in *Europe, America and the World Economy*, ed. Louis Tsoukalis (Oxford: Basil Blackwell, 1986), p. 21; *Le Monde* 25 mars 1980.
46 OECD, *World Steel Trade Developments 1960–1983* (Paris: OECD, 1985).
47 *Bulletin of the European Communities*, 4–1980, p. 73; *Financial Times* 22 March 1980.
48 *Financial Times* 14 January 1982; *New York Times* 12 January 1982; *Le Monde* 15 janvier 1982; *The Economist* 15 May 1982; *Bulletin of the European Communities*, 1–1982, p. 41.
49 Interview with GATT official.
50 Kent Jones, *Politics vs. Economics in World Steel Trade* (London: Allen and Unwin, 1986), p. 162; *Financial Times* 20, 31 December 1977, 12 April 1978.
51 *International Herald Tribune* 6 July 1983.
52 U.S., House, *Administration's Comprehensive Program for the Steel Industry*, p. 23; *New York Times* 1 October 1980; Patrick and Sato, "The Political Economy of United States-Japan Trade in Steel", p. 212.
53 Jones, *Politics vs. Economics*, p. 162.
54 Interview with GATT official.
55 Interview with OECD official.
56 Interview with GATT official.
57 U.S., Senate, Committee on Banking, Housing and Urban Affairs, *Trade and Technology in the Steel Industry: Hearing before the Subcom-*

mittee on *International Finance*, 96th Cong., 1st sess., November 19, 1979, pp. 29, 37, 38, 55, 56; Interviews with OECD and US officials.

58 The steel exports of all OECD countries as a percentage of world steel exports declined from 82 per cent in 1978 to 64 per cent by 1988. This pattern held for the other two major OECD steel producers, with the share of world exports declining from 30 per cent to 21 per cent for Japan, and from 2.3 to 1.6 per cent for the United States.

59 The figure for all OECD countries in the late 1980s was slightly lower than in 1978, after rising somewhat in the mid-1980s. The American export/production ratio rose from 2.4 per cent in 1978, to 4.8 per cent in 1980, before declining to 1.3 per cent in the mid-1980s and then recovering to 2.4 per cent in 1988. Japanese exports fell from 36 per cent of production in 1978 to 25 percent in 1988.

60 *Bulletin of the European Communities*, 7/8–1979, p. 35; 3–1981, pp. 87–88; 6–1981, pp. 17–19; 12–1983, p. 21; 10–1984, p. 19; 9–1985, p. 37; 10–1985, p. 13.

61 IMF, *Issues and Developments in International Trade Policy*, 1988, pp. 70–71.

62 Howell et al., *Steel and the State*, p. 236.

63 OECD, *Steel in the 80s*, p. 164; Walter, "Protection of Industries in Trouble", p. 171; Hufbauer and Rosen, *Trade Policy for Troubled Industries*, 1986, p. 37.

64 IMF, *Trade Policy Issues and Developments*, p. 38.

65 Interview with OECD official.

66 *The Times* 30 March 1976; *International Herald Tribune* 6 April 1976; *Financial Times, The Times, New York Times* 7 April 1976; *Financial Times, New York Times* 8 June 1976. OMAs for specialty steel were negotiated with Canada and Sweden in 1983.

67 *Financial Times, International Herald Tribune* 3 May 1977; *The Times* 4, 12 May 1977, *New York Times* 19 May 1977; *Japan Times* 9 July 1977; *The Times, Financial Times* 21 July 1977.

68 *New York Times* 29 September 1977; Walter, "Protection of Industries in Trouble", pp. 184–185.

69 Walter, "Protection of Industries in Trouble", pp. 183–184.

70 *New York Times* 19 May 1977.

71 Ibid. In particular, the US was concerned that the EC Commission's plan to raise minimum steel prices within the Community would result in EC producers dumping steel in the American market.

72 *New York Times* 29 September 1977.

73 This refusal stemmed in large part from differences over the definition of dumping between the US on the one hand and the EC and Japan on the other. The US was hoping to have commitments from other OECD members to stop what it considered "unfair trade practices", but settled for the idea of an early-warning monitoring of these practices instead.

74 *New York Times, Financial Times*, 1 October 1977.

75 *Financial Times, New York Times* 4 November 1977; *The Times* 7 November 1977.

76 Levine, *Inside International Trade Policy Formulation*, pp. 31–32.

77 *New York Times* 1 December 1977.

78 Robert S. Walters, "The U.S. Steel Industry: National Policies and International Trade", in *The Emerging International Economic Order: Dynamics, Processes, Constraints, and Opportunities*, ed. Harold K. Jacobson and Dusan Sidjanski (Beverly Hills, London, New Delhi: Sage, 1982), p. 119.

79 The meetings included Strauss, Davignon, and Amaya, the Deputy-Minister of MITI.

80 *The Economist* 29 April 1978; *Japan Times* 12 May 1978; *The Times, International Herald Tribune, Financial Times* 7 June 1978; *Financial Times* 9 June 1978.

81 *International Herald Tribune, The Times, Financial Times* 7 June 1978; *The Times* 9 June 1978.

82 Interview with OECD official; Levine, *Inside International Trade Policy Formulation*, pp. 31–32; *Bulletin of the European Communities*, 1–1982, p. 41.

83 *Financial Times* 22 September 1978.

84 U.S., Senate, *Trade and Technology in the Steel Industry*, pp. 5, 7, 10.

85 Interviews with OECD officials, and with US and Canadian government officials; *Bulletin of the European Communities*, 1–1984, p. 54; *AP-Dow Jones Dispatch*, 26 January 1984; *New York Times* 26 December 1983; US, Senate, *Trade and Technology in the Steel Industry*, pp. 2, 4–10, 30; *Financial Times* 6 January 1984.

86 *Japan Times* 23 September 1977; *New York Times* 7 July 1983; *Le Monde* 20 juillet 1983; *The Guardian* 21 July 1983; U.S., House, Committee on Ways and Means, *Problems of the U.S. Steel Industry: Hearings before the Subcommittee on Trade*, 98th Cong., 2nd sess., April 26, May 2, 8, June 20 and August 3, 1984, pp. 121–122.

87 Patrick and Sato, "The Political Economy of United States-Japan Trade in Steel", pp. 219, 221, 224, 235; Ballance, "Industry-specific Strategies", p. 279; Kiyoshi Kawahito, "Japanese Steel in the American Market: Conflict and Causes", *The World Economy* 4 (September 1981), pp. 229–250; Walters, "The U.S. Steel Industry", pp. 118–119; Hideo Sato and Michael W. Hodin, "The U.S.-Japanese Steel Issue of 1977", in *Coping with U.S.-Japanese Economic Conflicts*, ed. I.M. Destler and Hideo Sato (Lexington, Mass.: D.C. Heath, 1982) p. 52; *New York Times* 23 June 1982; *Financial Times* 18 October 1983, 14 January 1984, 30 March 1985, 15 January 1986.

88 *Financial Times, The Times* 29 February 1980.

89 OECD, *Costs and Benefits of Protection* (Paris: OECD, 1985), p. 94; Howell et al., *Steel and the State*, p. 532; Levine, *Inside International Trade Policy Formulation*, p. 15.

90 *The Economist* 15 March, 29 May 1982.

91 *Financial Times* 7 April 1976; *The Times* 29 April 1976; *The Times, International Herald Tribune* 19 May 1976; *Financial Times, Inter-*

national *Herald Tribune, New York Times* 8 June 1976; *Financial Times* 12 June 1976.

92 Interview with OECD official.

93 Interview with OECD official; *Activities of the OECD*, 1979, pp. 73–74.

94 Interview with OECD official; *New York Times* 30 March 1981; U.S., Senate, Committee on Banking, Housing and Urban Affairs, *Economic Conditions in Specialty Steel Industry: Hearing*, 97th Cong., 2nd sess., January 5, 1982; OECD, *Steel in the 80s*, p. 242. The Solomon report noted that the US had carried on a frank and extensive dialogue with the EC, Japan and other countries on the nature of the problems of the world's steel industry and the implications of alternative measures for dealing with them: "The proposals made here have benefited from understandings gained through these consultations". While the OECD is not mentioned explicitly, it is reasonable to assume that the Organisation is largely referred to here, as Treasury officials were active in OECD steel discussions prior to and during the drafting of the Solomon report. Transgovernmental contact established in the OECD influenced both the nature of the report and the reaction of other OECD members to the TPM system. The US was eager to gain support for, or at least acceptance of, the system in these discussions. U.S., House, *Administration's Comprehensive Program for the Steel Industry*, p. 23; Sato and Hodin, "The U.S.-Japanese Steel Issue of 1977", pp. 55–56.

95 *International Herald Tribune* 7 June 1978; Jones, *Politics vs. Economics*, pp. 86–113, 128.

96 *The Economist* 29 April 1978; *International Herald Tribune* 7 June 1978; Sato and Hodin, "The U.S.-Japanese Steel Issue of 1977", p. 51.

97 *New York Times* 28 February 1980; *AP-Dow Jones Dispatch* 26 January 1984; Walters, "The U.S. Steel Industry", pp. 118–119; *International Herald Tribune* 1–2 March 1980.

98 Patrick and Sato, "The Political Economy of United States-Japan Trade in Steel", p. 208.

99 In 1975 the Commission turned to the OECD to help deflect pressure from European steel-makers for unilaterally imposed steel import quotas. The Commission's stance in the OECD discussions were criticised as being inadequate by the steel industry as well as by the French government. *The Times* 23 October 1975.

100 *New York Times* 15 February, 19 March, 29 May, 26 July 1989.

101 Hudson and Sadler, *The International Steel Industry*, pp. 61–107.

102 Woolcock et al., *Interdependence in the Post-multilateral Era*, p. 39; Jones, *Politics vs. Economics*, p. 118; Levine, *Inside International Trade Policy Formulation*, p. 12.

103 See for example, U.S., Senate, *Trade and Technology in the Steel Industry* and House, *Problems of the U.S. Steel Industry*. See also the statement of Congressman Charles A. Vanik at the 1980 OECD Steel Symposium. OECD, *Steel in the 80s*, p. 242.

104 Woolcock et al., *Interdependence*, pp. 30, 33; Ray Hudson and David

Sadler, *The International Steel Industry: Restructuring, State Policies and Localities* (London and New York: Routledge, 1989), pp. 35–36.

105 Howell et al., *Steel and the State*, pp. 60–71.

106 *International Herald Tribune* 24 January 1986.

107 Matthew J. Marks, "Remedies to 'Unfair' Trade", p. 228; Sato and Hodin, "The U.S.–Japanese Steel Issue of 1977", pp. 45, 66; Patrick and Sato, "The Political Economy of United States–Japan Trade in Steel", p. 209; Stephen Woolcock, "Iron and Steel", in *The International Politics of Surplus Capacity*, ed. Susan Strange and Roger Tooze (London: Allen and Unwin, 1981), p. 73.

108 *Financial Times* 16 October 1975; *The Economist* 24 January 1976; *International Herald Tribune, Financial Times* 3 May 1977; *The Economist* 14 May 1977; *New York Times* 26 May 1977; *Financial Times* 30 September 1977; *Financial Times* 17 February 1978; Patrick and Sato, "The Political Economy of United States–Japan Trade in Steel", p. 208; U.S., House, *Administration's Comprehensive Program for the Steel Industry*, pp. 80, 107, 112, 114; Walter, "Protection of Industries in Trouble", p. 183. President Ford had attempted to pursue sectoral steel discussions in the MTN in 1976, but these efforts failed largely because of opposition from Japan and the EC, but also perhaps due to the disinterest of American trade negotiators. Walters, "The U.S. Steel Industry", p. 119; *International Herald Tribune* 20 May 1977.

109 Sato and Hodin, "The U.S.-Japanese Steel Issue of 1977", p. 51; Walter, "Protection of Industries in Trouble", 184–185; Walters, "The U.S. Steel Industry", p. 119.

110 In early 1982, the Reagan Administration's approach to the Steel Committee was presented to the Congress. The Administration's objective was a longer term one of influencing the attitudes and policy responses of other members, while immediate term problems were to be dealt with unilaterally by enforcing US trade laws (ie. anti-dumping and countervailing duty procedures). U.S., Senate, *Economic Conditions in Specialty Steel Industry*, p. 11.

111 Interview with US government official.

112 Interview with Canadian government official.

Chapter Six

TRADE IN SHIPS

1. *The International Shipbuilding Market*

The world shipbuilding market was highly volatile during the 1970s and 1980s, creating major difficulties for the industry in OECD countries. During a long period of uninterrupted growth in demand for ships during the 1960s, production capacity was built up in Europe and Japan with the expectation that this trend in demand would continue into the 1970s. New orders for ships dropped significantly after 1973, however, due to economic recession and the slower growth in demand for petroleum which hit tanker sales.[1] World production of ships peaked in 1975 at 36 million gross register tons (grt), with total production capacity standing at 39 million grt. By 1979, ship production was only around 12 million grt, resulting in considerable excess shipbuilding capacity.

Unstable demand persisted in the 1980s, with annual production averaging only 16 million grt during the first half of the 1980s, in contrast with the yearly average of nearly 30 million grt between 1970 and 1975. A major reason for this situation was that the volume of world trade, which had more than doubled between 1965 and 1975, was only slightly above the 1974 level in 1985. Despite capacity reductions of 20 per cent by the mid-1980s, world excess capacity was still estimated at around 40 per cent.[2]

This sharp drop in overall demand for ships was accompanied by a major shift in the shares of producing countries in the shipbuilding market. Western European countries had traditionally dominated world shipbuilding prior to the 1960s, but with the rise of Japanese production their share of the market

Chart 6.1
World Ship Production

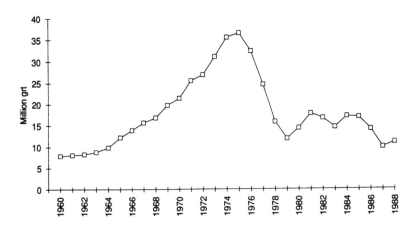

Source: UN, *Industrial Statistics Yearbook,* various issues.

declined from over 60 per cent in the early 1960s to an average
of just over 40 per cent during the 1970s, and to around 15
per cent in the mid-1980s. Japan has been the largest national
producer of ships since 1956, accounting for between 40 and
50 per cent of world production since the mid-1960s, with a
temporary decline to around 33 percent in the late 1970s.

North America has been a rather minor producer of merchant
ships, accounting for only about 4 per cent of world production
during the 1960s and 1970s, and less than 2.5 per cent in the
first half of the 1980s. Throughout the 1970s a number of new
arrivals on the world shipbuilding scene were building up their
production capacity. While relatively insignificant in the 1960s,
by the early 1980s these new producers, which included countries like South Korea, Taiwan, Brazil and China, accounted for

217

Chart 6.2
Shares of World Ship Production

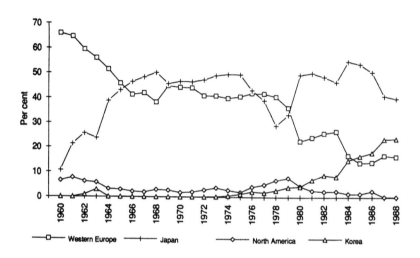

Only includes countries that were EC members during year listed. 1960–64 = ISIC 384103 and 384104B; 1965–89 = ISIC 3841–13B and 3841–16B.

Source: UN, *Industrial Statistics Yearbook,* various issues.

over 25 per cent of world shipbuilding capacity. By 1981, South Korea had become the world's second largest shipbuilding nation after Japan.

The pattern of world trade in ships generally followed that of world ship production. Total world ship exports increased steadily through the 1960s and early 1970s, peaking in the mid-1970s, bottoming out in 1979, followed by a decade of uneven growth. Together, Japan and Western Europe dominated the export side of world trade in ships, although Western Europe was the world's largest exporter throughout the 1960s, 1970s and 1980s. Western European countries accounted for over 50 per cent of world ship exports from 1967 to 1977, and an average 42 per cent from 1977 to 1987. Japan's share of world ship

218

Chart 6.3
Market Economy Ship Exports

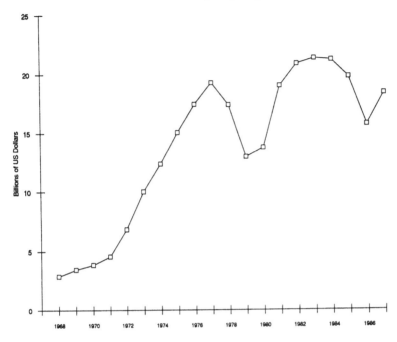

Source: UN, *International Trade Statistics Yearbook*, OECD, *Statistics of Foreign Trade*, various
issues.

exports averaged 39 per cent and 33 per cent during the same
two periods. North America accounted for just 3 per cent of
world exports during the 1970s, a share which increased slightly
to 5 per cent in the first half of the 1980s. Korea was the major
non-OECD ship exporter, and its share of world exports rose
from an average of less than 3 per cent in the second half of the
1970s to over 25 per cent in 1985. However, its share declined
dramatically in the following two years.

The ranking of ship importers varied greatly from year to
year, but the largest importers over time were naturally the
countries with major shipping concerns. The countries of the
European Community collectively comprised the largest import
market over time, followed by the Scandinavian countries,

Chart 6.4
Shares of Market Economy Ship Exports

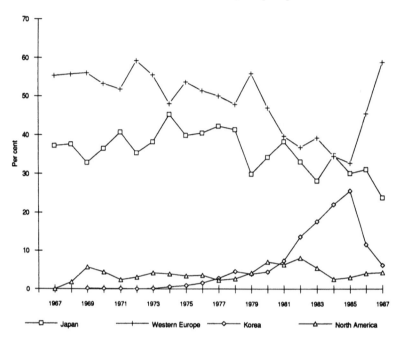

Includes intra-Western European trade.

Source: UN, *International Trade Statistics Yearbook*, various issues; OECD, *Statistics of Foreign Trade*, various issues.

Panama, Liberia, Singapore, Korea, Japan, the Bahamas and the United States.

The crisis in the shipbuilding sector in the traditional producing countries led to an intensification of government measures to protect national industries. Trade distortions in shipbuilding have tended to take the form of subsidised export credits, direct subsidies to shipbuilders, taxation measures, government procurement policies, and financing for investment and research, rather than tariffs, quotas or other border restrictions.[3] In 1983, the OECD estimated that the total of all subsidies offered for shipbuilding was around $5 billion on ship sales of some $20 billion.[4]

Because Western European countries suffered the most severe

decline in ship orders after 1973, they experienced the greatest
pressure for government assistance in this sector.[5] One of the
most heavily protected markets for ships was the United States.
The Jones Act of 1920 required that all national coastal shipping
(that is, merchandise transported by ship between points in the
US) be confined to vessels built in the United States and owned
by American citizens. The US government also provided differential construction and operating subsidies (in which the
government financed the difference between US costs and
foreign costs) for American-built ships involved in the foreign
trade of the United States. The result of this policy was that the
American shipbuilding industry enjoyed almost total protection
in the market for domestic trading vessels and a high degree of
protection for ships under the US flag that were used for foreign
trade.[6]

2. Background to OECD Shipbuilding Negotiations

The OECD first gave serious attention to the shipbuilding sector
in early 1963 when an *ad hoc* working party of the Industry
Committee was set up to study measures of government assistance to the shipbuilding industry in each OECD country. This
study was launched due to concern over the growing competition among shipbuilding nations in the granting of government
assistance to the industry, at the same time as production
capacity appeared to be surpassing demand.[7] After the study
of 17 member countries was completed in 1965, steps were
taken to set up a permanent body within the Organisation to
deal with the shipbuilding issue. On 24 May 1966 the OECD
Council decided to set up a body which came to be known
as Council Working Party Six on Shipbuilding, to work out
"recommendations directed to a progressive reduction of factors
which distort normal competitive conditions in the shipbuilding
industry", and to keep the situation in the industry under
review.

The first meeting of the Working Party took place in July 1966
and included representatives from Belgium, Denmark, France,
Germany, Greece, Italy, Japan, the Netherlands, Norway,
Sweden and the United Kingdom. Spain joined the Working
Party in 1967, as did Finland in 1970 and Ireland in 1973. The
Commission of the European Communities began to participate

221

in Working Party meetings in 1970.[8] The United States was invited several times to join the Working Party but repeatedly refused, until the end of the 1980s.[9] The early work of Working Party Six concentrated on the issue of government credit for the sale of ships, an area where competition among industrialised countries was particularly fierce.

3. *Agreements on Shipbuilding Issues*

Three principal agreements were negotiated within the OECD to deal with various aspects of trade in ships. The first of these was the Understanding on Export Credits for Ships adopted by the OECD Council on 30 May 1969. This Understanding set limits on the export credit terms offered by 13 participating governments to help finance the sale of ships produced by national shipyards.[10] The minimum net interest rate allowed by the Understanding was 6 per cent, the maximum repayment period was set at 8 years and a minimum downpayment of 20 per cent of the purchase price was required. On 16 December 1970 the OECD Council increased the minimum interest rate to 7.5 per cent effective from 1 January 1971. At the same time, participating governments stated that they would endeavour not to increase incentives for shipowners to place their orders in their home country.

The terms of the Understanding were further hardened by a decision of the OECD Council on 18 July 1974 which raised the minimum interest rate to 8 per cent, reduced the maximum repayment period to 7 years and increased the minimum downpayment to 30 per cent of the purchase price.[11] As of 1 December 1979 the terms were softened, with a return to the original 20 per cent minimum downpayment and an increase in the maximum repayment period to 8.5 years.[12] Participants in the Understanding agreed that the minimum interest rate of 8 per cent "should remain the rule", but that "some flexibility may, however, be necessary for some countries".[13] The EC considered that this minimum interest rate could include credit insurance premiums and banking charges, but that the minimum interest rate net of all charges would not be permitted to fall below 7.5 per cent. The revised Understanding extended its coverage to the conversion of ships in addition to the construction of new ships.

Finally, in July 1981 the Understanding was again revised to extend the repayment period for liquified natural gas tankers to 10 years, and to apply the terms of the Understanding to ship conversions weighing more than one thousand gross register tons. At the same time, new rules of procedure were established for prior notification of decisions taken by governments that contravened the terms of the Understanding for exceptional reasons or in order to match terms offered by other countries.[14]

After the Understanding on Export Credits for Ships had been negotiated in 1969, the OECD Council instructed Working Party Six to "concentrate on the removal of obstacles to normal shipbuilding competition" other than export credits.[15] Negotiations in the Working Party resulted in a General Arrangement for the Progressive Removal of Obstacles to Normal Competitive Conditions in the Shipbuilding Industry, which was adopted by the Council in October 1972 and came into effect on 1 November of that same year. In this General Arrangement, Japan and ten Western European countries agreed to reduce progressively measures of assistance to the shipbuilding industry with the objective of eliminating them entirely by 1 November 1975.[16]

In 1976 participants in the General Arrangement reaffirmed their intention to implement the terms set out in 1972, but changed the date by which they intended to eliminate government assistance to 1 November 1978. The General Arrangement was revised in early 1983 to remove any target dates for the elimination of measures of assistance. The Council Resolution of 23 February 1983 introducing the revised General Arrangement set out the aim of eliminating these measures "at the earliest possible moment", but there was no reference to their complete elimination in the text of the Arrangement itself.

The third shipbuilding agreement negotiated in the OECD was the General Guidelines for Government Policies in the Shipbuilding Industry, acknowledged by the Council on 4 May 1976. In this document members of the Working Party stressed the need for *all* shipbuilding nations to contribute to the reduction of world shipbuilding capacity, and agreed that "appropriate national policies should be devised to deal with the problems of adaptation in each shipbuilding country" based on the principles of "solidarity, fairness and responsibility".[17] The General Guidelines called on members: to give priority to the reduction of shipbuilding capacity; not to take any measures

223

which would disturb the "adaptation process of the industry"; to make sure that industry practices remained "in a framework of fair competition", particularly with respect to pricing; and to refrain from taking measures that would help to create new shipbuilding capacity. The document explicitly stated that compliance with the guidelines was not obligatory and did not limit the right of members to take measures set out in other shipbuilding agreements concluded in the OECD. Finally, it emphasised that the Guidelines provided only a general framework for government policies, while practical solutions "must continue to be sought by governments at an accelerated pace" within this framework.

The General Guidelines were revised in 1983, although no fundamental changes were introduced. The revised document called for the "appropriate adjustment" of shipbuilding capacity, rather than the "reduction" of capacity, as recommended in the original text. A new guideline was introduced in which Working Party members were to watch that the market was not disturbed by the "premature reactivation of capacities which are presently removed from the new building of merchant ships".

Each of the three major agreements on shipbuilding contained provisions for the monitoring of policies and practices of the participating governments. Under the Understanding on Export Credits for Ships, a participant was authorised to obtain information from any other participant on the terms of official support for a ship export contract in order to determine whether the terms contravened the Understanding. Participants undertook to supply all possible information with all possible speed. In addition, the Understanding permitted any participant to ask the Secretary-General to act on its behalf in requesting information from other participants and to circulate the information to all participants. Participants were required to give prior notice to all parties to the Understanding whenever more favourable terms were granted within the context of their foreign aid programmes, for "exceptional reasons", or in order to match terms offered by other countries (participants or non-participants) which contravened the terms of the Understanding. Each participant was also required to notify the Secretary-General of its export credit system and of the means by which the Understanding was being implemented.

The provisions for monitoring compliance with the General Arrangement were virtually identical to those for the Understanding. The information to be supplied upon request included measures of assistance to shipbuilding in force and progress made in their reduction. No provision was made for foreign aid, but prior notice and an explanation to the Working Party was required whenever a participant delayed a reduction it had offered to make or retracted a reduction already made for "imperative reasons". Participants were also required to give prior notice along with an explanation before matching assistance measures offered by other countries which were incompatible with the General Arrangement. In both cases, the Working Party was required to review the action either at its next scheduled meeting or at a specially convened session. Apart from the review of these special cases, the Working Party was required to review at least once a year progress being made in the reduction of measures of assistance to the shipbuilding industry. Among the measures reviewed were export credit facilities, thereby permitting a regular monitoring of the Understanding on Export Credits for Ships.

The General Guidelines also provided for certain rule-supervisory activities. The original agreement called for participants to keep each other informed on the progress of their national policies every six months, but this was revised in 1983 when participants agreed simply to "keep each other rapidly informed".[18] The Working Party's sub-Group on Supply and Demand was instructed in 1976 to monitor regularly the trend of shipbuilding capacities, in addition to the trend in new orders, order books and ships completed.[19] In November 1977, agreement was reached to begin calculating production and capacity in terms of Compensated Gross Register Tons (CGRT or CGT), which took into account the extra work involved in constructing more sophisticated ships.

4. Impact of OECD Agreements

Of the three agreements on shipbuilding negotiated in the OECD, the one which had the most direct impact on member country policies and practices was the Understanding on Export Credits for Ships. This agreement was by and large respected by participating governments, even through the most difficult periods of the shipbuilding crisis.[20] The terms set out in the Understanding were incorporated into the laws of the European Communities, and the EC Commission monitored the export credit policies of EC member countries to ensure that these terms were respected.[21]

While numerous complaints regarding isolated cases of non-compliance were made over the years, largely by shipbuilding industry representatives, many of these complaints were unsubstantiated, and there did not appear to have been any serious allegations of systematic or prolonged violations by governments.[22] In general, participating governments were willing to resist domestic pressure from unions, shipbuilders and shipowners to exceed the limits of the Understanding.[23] Concern was often expressed over the credit terms offered to developing countries by governments participating in the Understanding, although provisions were made in the agreement for shipbuilding credit extended as part of a country's foreign aid programme.[24]

In contrast to the relative effectiveness of the Understanding on Export Credits for Ships, compliance with the General Arrangement was much weaker. While governments generally showed a willingness to limit their subsidisation of the shipbuilding sector in the first half of the 1970s, as the crisis situation in shipbuilding began to be felt, governments generally *increased* the level of state aids to the industry.[25] Some countries offered direct assistance to shipbuilders, but more often aid was indirect, such as subsidies given to shipowners for the purchase of new vessels.[26] European countries were the first to increase the subsidisation of shipbuilding. Even countries which had traditionally rejected any significant subsidisation of the industry, such as Germany, Denmark, Sweden and Italy, finally broke down as the crisis wore on and began offering government support in one form or another.[27] Japan repeatedly criticised European countries for the proliferation of subsidies throughout 1977 and 1978, which it claimed were inconsistent with the General Arrangement. But in 1979, Japan itself resumed its practice of offering credit on preferential terms to Japanese shipowners.[28]

The EC Commission attempted throughout the 1970s to reduce government aid to shipbuilding, but met resistance from Community member countries. After the General Arrangement was adopted in the OECD, the Commission sent a proposal to the Council of Ministers for a Third Directive on Aid to Shipbuilding in October 1973. The proposal, which was not approved by the Council until July 1975, called for the prompt reduction of shipbuilding subsidies and an information mechanism on investment subsidies in the sector.[29] In March 1978, the Council approved a Fourth Directive, which stipulated that aid should not be granted for investments which increased production capacity, and that any aid had to be tied to the introduction of restructuring plans, be extended for limited periods, and be progressively reduced. It was pointed out that all the provisions of the Directive were consistent with OECD arrangements to restore normal conditions of competition in the world shipbuilding market.[30]

Under the Fifth Directive, adopted in April 1981, restrictions were also imposed on assistance to shipowners, and it was make more difficult for nationalised firms to have operating losses paid for by governments.[31] By 1984 the Commission had reluctantly agreed to suspend the goal of ending all subsidies for Community shipyards by the end of the year, acknowledging that the governments of EC member countries would not accept the phasing out of assistance programmes with the industry still in crisis.[32] The Commission even proposed that governments be permitted to increase subsidies, as long as such increases were tied to reductions in production capacity. A 17 per cent ceiling on subsidies imposed by the EC was allowed to expire in 1984, and afterwards subsidy cases were settled on an individual basis, with many going well above the former ceiling.[33]

The Sixth Directive, which took effect in January 1987, did not represent much progress in the effort to reduce subsidies. The goal of this Directive was to concentrate aid on specialised production in the most efficient yards of the Community, and to impose a uniform ceiling on all cases. The ceiling was set at 28 per cent of *cost*, rather than being based on contract value as in earlier Directives. Because ships were generally sold below cost, the new ceiling was estimated at 39 per cent of average price which, according to the British Minister of State for Industry, constituted a "substantial" increase for British shipbuilders.[34] The Commission argued that this amount of subsidy was necessary to bridge the gap between European costs and the prices being offered by Far Eastern producers, who were considered by some to be practicing predatory pricing.[35] The ceiling was reduced somewhat to 26 per cent at the beginning of 1989.[36]

In the case of the General Guidelines, considerable efforts were made by OECD governments to reduce shipbuilding capacity after 1976. Shortly after the Guidelines were adopted, the governments of Sweden and Holland announced plans to reduce capacity by 30 per cent.[37] In November 1976, the Japanese Ministry of Transport issued guidelines to 40 major shipbuilding companies (representing over 90 per cent of the domestic market) to reduce manhours worked in 1977 to 72 per cent of the 1974 level, and to 65 per cent of that level in 1978.[38] The Shipbuilders' Association of Japan announced in January 1978 that Japanese shipbuilders planned to scrap up to 50 per cent of capacity by the end of 1979, and in November of that year the Japanese government announced its own plan to cut back shipbuilding capacity 35 per cent by the end of March 1980.[39] In July 1978 the Spanish government reached agreement with its shipbuilding industry and trade unions to reduce shipbuilding capacity by 50 per cent over the following five years.[40]

The EC was slower to act on the General Guidelines, saying that it was not willing to curtail capacity until it had some sort of guarantee that Japan would not take a larger share of new orders.[41] Although the Commission of the European Communities drew up a plan for a 46 per cent reduction in production capacity in late 1977, it was unable to obtain the support of a number of key EC member governments.[42] By 1978 the EC Commission was attempting to impose capacity reductions on member states by linking its approval of member country requests for shipbuilding subsidies to progress in capacity cuts.[43] This linkage was made explicit in the Fourth, Fifth and Sixth Directives on Aid to Shipbuilding, although the size of capacity reductions was not specified and the Commission did not set reduction targets.[44] Nevertheless, the EC Commission estimated that the Community had cut capacity by 48 per cent between 1975 and 1985, and it was estimated that a further 27 per cent of capacity would be reduced by the early 1990s. Japan reduced capacity by 35 per cent between 1976 and 1986, and in the 1987–1988 period cut back a further 24 per cent. The Nordic countries were estimated to have cut between 50 and 60 per cent of capacity from 1976 to 1986.[45]

A matter of some controversy regarding compliance with the General Guidelines concerned the distribution of new ship orders among OECD countries. Western European countries claimed that a "tacit agreement" had been reached in 1976 in which Japan and themselves were to share evenly new orders won in the OECD area.[46] While new orders were in fact shared more or less along those lines until 1979, in 1980 Japan increased its share of new orders to roughly 50 per cent of the world total. However, it would be difficult to treat this trend, which continued through 1986, as a violation of the General Guidelines because there is no evidence that Japan ever agreed to Europe's interpretation of that document. Indeed, Japan stated on numerous occasions after the General Guidelines were adopted that it could not accept a market sharing arrangement with Western Europe, while claiming that it had no intention of exceeding 50 per cent of the world market after 1980. In early 1981 Albert Grübel, the chairman of the Working Party since 1974, stated that he found no justification for criticisms that Japan had violated any commitments.[47]

5. Bargaining Positions and Outcomes

Understanding on Export Credits for Ships In the field of ship-building, the European Community played a role similar to that played by the United States in the three other sectors examined in this study. It was the EC which took the initiative in proposing most of the measures adopted by the OECD, as well as one that was not. In the 1960s, at a time when credit competition among OECD countries was growing, the EC put forward proposals for limiting the terms of export credits for ships, which led to the adoption of the 1969 Understanding. The original EC proposal called for a maximum repayment term of 8 years and a minimum downpayment of 15 per cent of the purchase price. The EC later proposed repayment terms of either 7 or 10 years, depending on the value of the order. Sweden preferred stricter terms, including a repayment period limited to 7 years and a 33 per cent minimum downpayment. Japan called for an 8 year repayment period and a 20 per cent downpayment. Greece, which was a major importer of ships, was generally opposed to putting limits on export credit terms.

The United Kingdom proposed that prior notification be given for all government assistance measures, while France preferred that only derogations from the agreement be subject to prior notification. A number of countries, including Sweden, Norway and Germany, wanted agreement to be reached on all forms of government assistance, and not just on export credits, although they later accepted the Understanding as a first step in that direction. The compromise proposal presented by Japan was ultimately adopted in 1969. In 1971 France called for an increase in the minimum downpayment from 20 per cent to 30 per cent, a proposal which was opposed by Britain.[48]

At the April 1978 Working Party meeting, some European countries suggested that the terms of the Understanding should be eased, along the lines of the export credit guidelines for aircraft, and that an attempt be made to get third countries to adopt the Understanding and possibly the General Arrangement. However, Japan was reluctant to accept this proposal, which would be directed at developing countries, since it was interested in fostering diplomatic and trade links with those countries and did not wish to antagonise them over the shipbuilding issue.[49]

At the Working Party meetings held in July and November 1978, Germany and France pressed other Working Party participants to ease the credit terms of the Understanding. Germany enjoyed interest rates that were lower than in most other countries and wanted to be able to benefit from this advantage, while France was seeking a way to ease the growing crisis in its shipbuilding industry. However, other participants rejected this proposal, and countered with a proposal to further tighten credit terms, arguing that any softening of terms would be both expensive and unlikely to generate a significant increase in orders.[50]

Efforts to ease the credit terms of the Understanding were given a boost when Spain announced its intention to withdraw from the agreement at the March 1979 Working Party meeting. Spain had been advocating a 0.5 per cent reduction in the minimum interest rate, a reduction in the minimum downpayment to 20 per cent, and an extension of the maximum repayment period by one and a half years. Agreement was finally reached to meet all of these demands in October 1979, although it came too late to prevent the Spanish from withdrawing from the Understanding.[51]

Unlike the OECD Consensus on export credits, where interest rates were constantly renegotiated, the minimum interest rate allowed by the Understanding remained at 8 per cent (with an exceptional 7.5 per cent rate adopted in 1979 for European countries) through most of the rest of the 1980s. In 1987, Japan proposed that commercial interest rates be introduced into the Understanding, along the lines of CIRRs in the Consensus. This proposal was supported by the Nordic countries, while France and Italy were reluctant to accept it.[52]

General Arrangement   Since the late 1960s, Japan had cautiously supported the principle of abolishing state aids to shipbuilding, although it opposed the "offer and reciprocity documents" proposed by Britain, France and Italy, which would give in detail the forms of state aid that governments were prepared to phase out and the measures that each government would like other nations to abolish.[53] Within the EC, Germany was the strongest supporter of removing state aid to shipbuilding, since it had one of the least subsidised industries in the Community.[54] There was not much strong opposition to the proposal for the General Arrangement, which was introduced at a time when demand for ships was steadily climbing, and when the maintenance of state aids seemed increasingly unnecessary.

At the September 1980 Working Party meeting, the OECD Secretariat put forward a proposal to eliminate by 1985 all direct government assistance to the shipbuilding industry, and to reduce this assistance by 20 per cent by the beginning of 1982. This suggestion was in line with the EC Commission's proposed Fifth Directive on Shipbuilding, but as the attitude of the Community towards ending subsidies was changing, there was insufficient support for the Secretariat plan.[54] When the Commission realised that its own objective of ending subsidies by 1985 would have to be suspended, it favoured the removal of target dates from the General Arrangement when the agreement was revised in 1983.[55]

General Guidelines   The 1976 General Guidelines were very

231

much a European initiative, inspired by the simultaneous decline in the European share of new orders and the increase in Japan's share.[56] At the December 1975 Working Party meeting, the EC asked Japan to reduce voluntarily its shipbuilding capacity, and the EC Commission sent an "oral démarche" to the Japanese Foreign Ministry prior to the meeting, underlining the seriousness of its request.[58]

Following the adoption of the General Guidelines, the EC Commission, in a communication to the Council of Ministers, recommended that the Community should "negotiate, on the basis of a common position, any measures required within the OECD to achieve the targets of the General Guidelines".[59] In particular, the Commission wanted an agreement on a balanced reduction of shipbuilding capacity among Working Party participants.[60] However, by the autumn of 1976 the EC, under increasing pressure from the shipbuilding industry, turned the focus of its efforts from a sharing of capacity reductions to the sharing of new orders.

Market Sharing   There was not a great deal of controversy over the three agreements on shipbuilding that were reached in the OECD. Once each of these agreements was proposed, the details were usually worked out fairly quickly.[61] The most intensive bargaining on the shipbuilding issue was therefore not in negotiations for the agreements, but over demands for a fourth agreement which was never concluded. The EC had been trying as early as 1972 to get the Japanese government to agree to prevent Japanese shipbuilders from enlarging their share of the world shipbuilding market. The EC Commission made a reduction of government assistance to shipbuilding conditional upon an agreement on the sharing of supply and demand among Working Party members.[90]

In addition to demanding that Japan reduce its shipbuilding capacity at the December 1975 Working Party meeting, the EC requested that Japan share orders with European shipyards, and that it agree to the setting of floor prices for shipbuilding contracts.[63] The Community intensified its demands for a market sharing agreement at the October 1976 Working Party meeting. The Commission called for a more even distribution

232

of new shipbuilding orders between Western Europe and Japan, while the Japanese stuck to their forecasts, in which Japan would take 50 per cent of world orders by 1980.[64]

Besides the disagreement over market share targets, the Europeans and Japanese held opposing views over how market shares should be measured. Japan preferred to use gross register tonnage, while the Europeans proposed the use of compensated gross register tonnage, which would take into account the movement of the Japanese industry into more sophisticated ships. If a simple gross register tonnage measurement were used, it was felt that this would understate the actual work and value involved in Japanese shipbuilding.[65]

At the December 1976 Working Party meeting, the EC made a formal proposal for an equal sharing of new orders between Western Europe and Japan, beginning in January 1977 and lasting through the end of 1978. This proposal, which was supported by Spain, Portugal, and the Nordic countries, also called for monthly notifications of orders placed in producing countries. The Japanese delegation reserved its position, and later a Ministry of Transport spokesman said that Japan could not accept the proposal since it ran counter to the principle of free trade.[66] At a high-level bilateral meeting between the EC and Japan in Tokyo in late December and at the January 1977 Working Party meeting, Japanese officials told the Europeans that Japan was not convinced of the appropriateness of market sharing, although they did agree to hold monthly information exchanges on new shipbuilding orders. The Europeans accepted Japan's proposal that the length of order books, which took into account order backlogs and cancellations, should also be subject to regular monitoring on a quarterly basis.[67]

At the Working Party meeting held on 8 February 1977, Japan pledged that it would raise the price of all exported ships, and would urge Japanese shipyards to limit their exports to those Western European nations whose shipbuilding industry was in a particularly difficult situation. Japan also announced that it was prepared to further reduce production if it exceeded the average rate of the preceding three years by making further cuts in manhours worked in shipbuilding. However, the Japanese delegation continued to reject as unworkable the European market sharing proposal. The EC accepted the Japanese proposals as "a useful beginning", and a European delegate stated that the Community maintained its market sharing objective, but that it viewed this more as a negotiating yardstick than as a rigid objective.[68] The Japanese Ministry of Transport subsequently ordered Japanese shipbuilders to raise prices for all overseas customers by at least five per cent, and the Japanese Shipbuilders' Association declared that it would not accept any new orders from West Germany for the time being.[69]

Western European representatives claimed at the next Working Party meeting in March 1977 that the 5 per cent price increase was inadequate, and sought a further price increase from Japan. The Japanese delegation rejected European demands, arguing that the 5 per cent increase was in addition to the anticipated inflation rate of 8 per cent, and that an appreciating yen would further reduce Japanese ship exports.[70] At the Working Party meetings held in May and June 1977, both sides stood by their positions, with the Europeans repeating their expressions of disappointment with Japan, and the Japanese refusing to take any further action.[71] At the June meeting, however, Japan lifted its reservations over subsidy schemes introduced by several European countries to cope with difficulties facing shipyards, but urged that these measures be temporary and not interfere with free competition in the long term. Both the Japanese and Europeans expressed concerns over growing competition from shipbuilders in the developing countries, and a study was initiated on the role and development of the industry in those countries.[72]

At the following meeting in November 1977, the EC blamed Japanese expansion in part for the problem of overcapacity, although it acknowledged Japan's export restraint measures. The EC requested that Japan not weaken the effect of these measures by lowering interest rates in export credits or by denominating contracts partially in dollars. The EC also asked Japan to reduce shipbuilding capacity and to revise its shipbuilding forecast for 1980 of 6.5 million tonnes, which represented 50 per cent of anticipated world demand. In addition, the EC expressed its support for the OECD as the best framework for solving international shipbuilding problems.

Japan responded at the meeting that it would maintain its recently announced measures and that it would avoid any action which could compromise their effectiveness. In the longer term, Japan confirmed that it did not intend to increase its market share, but refused to make any specific commitment on capacity reductions, arguing that market forces would bring about this reduction naturally. Japan rejected demands for a further reduction in its share of the world shipbuilding market, arguing that the Japanese industry was facing difficult conditions and had been curtailing operations at a much faster pace than the shipbuilding guidelines set by the Ministry of Transport in November 1976. The Working Party chairman, Albert Grübel, remarked after the meeting that the Japanese response to European demands on the 1980 forecast was not entirely negative, since Japan had told the Working Party that the 6.5 million ton figure was not inflexible and that there was no feeling that Japan must construct that volume of ships by 1980. The Japanese did agree on a formula for calculating compensated gross register tonnage beginning in January 1978.[73]

At the April 1978 Working Party meeting, Japan, joined by Sweden, criticised the proliferation of shipbuilding subsidies in Europe and the lack of restructuring plans. A disagreement also emerged over how to deal with the perceived threat from Third World shipbuilders. A report by the Secretariat suggested that additional meetings take place outside the context of the OECD, which would include industry representatives from the developing countries. The leader of the Japanese delegation, Shinichi Yanai, said after the meeting that Tokyo was taking a negative attitude toward the proposal, since Japan and several other countries were concerned that formal contacts with developing countries on shipbuilding could prejudice the North-South dialogue in other forums.[74]

The director of the shipbuilding division of Japan's Ministry of Transport, Tadashi Mano, announced at the November 1978 Working Party meeting that Japan would not renew its 5 per cent price increase after it expired at the end of December. Mano told other delegations that Japan was no longer prepared to damage its competitiveness while European governments were supporting their shipbuilding industries with increasingly heavy subsidies. This announcement was criticised by European governments and by the EC Commission, although at the same time Mano offered a preview of capacity cuts planned by Tokyo. Japan, with some support from Italy, once again rejected European proposals to involve certain developing countries in Working Party discussions.[75]

While the distribution of new orders (measured in CGRT) between Japan and Western Europe had been relatively even in 1978 and 1979, by 1980 the Japanese were increasing their share of world orders. During the first half of 1980, Japan took over 53 per cent of new orders, compared with 20 per cent by Western European countries and 27 per cent by the rest of the world. At the Working Party meeting in late September 1980, European delegates called upon Japan to reduce its share of the world shipbuilding market. The EC Commission asked Japan to exercise greater vigilance in its domestic measures, in order to ensure that the commitments entered into in the OECD, aimed at avoiding an unfair distribution of the burden of the shipbuilding crisis, continued to be respected.[76] Japan pointed out in March 1981 that many of its orders had come from South-East Asian shipowners, who had been traditional clients of Japan, and that there was little evidence that European shipowners were ordering large numbers of Japanese ships. The EC delegation repeated its accusation that Japan had violated a tacit 1976 agreement to share orders, and pressed the Japanese to reduce its share of the market. In view of the increasing share of Third World producers in the world shipbuilding market, Working Party members discussed the idea of involving South Korea in its meetings.[77]

Growing Korean ship production became a major concern of the Working Party in 1982, and in November of that year Korean shipbuilders sat as observers at the Working Party meeting for the first time. Both the Japanese and the Europeans were concerned about the expansion of South Korean shipbuilding capacity, which they viewed as being stimulated by government subsidisation and by export financing that was more generous than that allowed by the OECD Understanding.[78]

As demand for ships slumped in the early 1980s, Western European governments renewed their complaints about the increasing Japanese share of the shipbuilding market, and the EC called on Japan to respect its commitments. The Japanese replied that they had already reduced capacity by 35 per cent and that the slump in orders for the Europeans should be blamed on third countries. New demands were now being made from Europe that the Japanese press Korea to moderate its drive to take new orders, which had contributed to the decline in world ship prices by 30 per cent over the preceding two years.[79]

At the April 1984 Working Party meeting, European delegations continued to criticise Japan's dominant position in the
world shipbuilding market, and said that Japanese shipbuilders
must reduce production facilities, reduce operating hours and
raise prices. Japan finally gave in to European demands to put
pressure on Korea, and in October 1984 Japan and Korea agreed
not to expand their ship output during the current crisis.[80] In
November 1986, a Liaison Group was set up between the Working Party and South Korea, intended to enable the members of
the Working Party and the Koreans to exchange views and
explain their policies to each other.

After several years of increased government subsidies had
failed to improve the order book situation of European shipyards, the EC Commission resumed its attack on Japanese and
South Korean shipbuilders. Having failed to secure an agreement to share the shipbuilding market evenly with Japan, the
Community's share of world production fell dramatically while
Japan succeeded in holding on to roughly 50 per cent of the
market. By the late 1980s, the EC was desperately trying to hold
on to the modest share it still had and to prevent European
shipbuilding from disappearing altogether. The principal
obstacles to this, in the view of the Community, were the low
prices being charged by Far Eastern producers. At this point
the main EC objective became the reduction of the spread
between prices charged by the EC and its competitors.[81]

In the spring of 1988, the Commission began bilateral talks
with Japan aimed at stabilising trade in ships, bringing about a
"fair" reduction in capacity, restoring prices to a "normal" level,
and introducing transparency with regard to prices, subsidies
and financing.[82] After negotiations between senior officials of
the Commission and Japanese government in Tokyo and
Brussels, a five point accord was reached. The agreement under-
lined the grave situation in world shipbuilding, which was seen
as resulting from persistent overcapacity, government subsidisation, and prices falling below profitable levels. Consequently,
Japan and the EC agreed to work together to clarify the basis
on which prices were set and to help restore prices to profitable
levels.

The agreement included a provision to hold regular meetings
on how to bring these goals about, and an invitation was made
to other shipbuilding nations, particularly Korea and Finland,

to join in the accord. The EC continued to pursue a pricing and production agreement with Japan and Korea following the April accord, but failed to secure any specific commitments from those two countries.[83] By the end of the 1980s, the pricing issue became less prominent in Working Party discussions, even though the Community continued to complain that its industry was suffering from unfair pricing practices. Once again, the Community was unsuccessful in getting Japan, as well as Korea, to accept its demands on shipbuilding.

6. *Explaining OECD Agreements and their Impact*

(a) Overall Capabilities

In OECD negotiations on shipbuilding the two principal parties were Japan on the one hand, and the EC, generally allied with other Western European countries, on the other. As was pointed out in the Chapter Two, military power does not have much direct relevance in the relations between these two because of their relative isolation from one another in military matters. Instead, their relations are dominated by economic concerns, so any calculation of the relative overall power of these actors must be restricted to their respective economic power, particularly in the area of trade.

(b) International Trade Structure

Despite the predominance of the EC over Japan in trade power capabilities, the EC failed in its efforts to get Japan to accept a market sharing arrangement. In fact, there appears to be only one case where the EC resorted to the tactic of linking its demands on shipbuilding to an unrelated trade issue. Faced with Japanese intransigence in 1977, the EC Commission began discussing the possibility of penalising Japan in other trade areas.[84] Japan's general trade surplus with the EC was a source of tension at the time between the two, and on 4 February 1977 the Commission imposed a provisional 20 per cent anti-dumping duty on Japanese ballbearings. The Commission stressed that such actions could become more frequent if Japan did not adjust her trade practices.[85] Four days later, at the Working Party Six meeting, Japan announced that it would raise the price of all exported ships and would urge Japanese shipyards to limit their exports to those Western European nations whose shipbuilding industries were in a particularly difficult situation.[86]

Despite these conciliatory moves, Japan continued to resist European demands that it share new orders equally with the EC, and did not abandon its objective of producing 50 per cent of the world's ships by 1980, a target which had been vigorously opposed by the Europeans. However, the EC did not attempt any further linkages with other trade issues after 1977.

(c) Issue Structure

Japan's exports of ships to the EC and to EFTA countries far exceeded those countries' exports of vessels to Japan throughout the 1970s and 1980s. The European Community recognised its advantage in ship trade capabilities, and made numerous attempts to manipulate it. As early as 1972 the EC had been trying to prevent Japan from enlarging her share of the world shipbuilding market, warning Japan in one Working Party meeting that the Community would not tolerate a monopoly situation in the market. Shortly after this warning the Commission worked out a proposal to reserve a major share of the Community's maritime trade for European-built vessels.[87]

In a paper later submitted to the EC Commission in December 1975, the Commissioner for Industry said that in the absence of Japanese restraint, the EC was "determined to adopt unilateral measures to safeguard the Common Market shipbuilding industry".[88] An action programme was set out in the Commission's communication to the Council in May 1976, which recommended that the Community negotiate capacity reductions with Japan. If efforts to reach an OECD agreement failed, the Commission recommended that the EC should seek a bilateral agreement with Japan, and if this was not possible that the EC should take unilateral action including financial assistance to shipbuilding and shipping companies, or maritime and trade policy measures.[89]

During Working Party meetings in the fall of 1976 the EC delegation made repeated warnings that European countries could adopt protectionist measures in shipbuilding.[90] These threats did seem on the surface to have had some impact on

Table 6.1
Destination of EC Ship Exports*
(Per cent)

	OECD	Other W.Europe	Japan	North America
1970	49.3	43.7	0.1	0.5
71	57.3	52.3	0.1	0.5
72	60.2	49.1	1.1	8.5
73	52.9	33.1	0.1	19.5
74	34.9	27.9	0.1	6.0
75	37.4	36.0	0.1	1.3
76	25.1	21.6	0.1	3.0
77	21.6	15.3	0.1	2.4
78	23.9	13.8	0.1	4.1
79	16.7	12.8	0.1	1.8
80	17.9	13.6	0.1	2.9
81	17.9	13.4	0.4	4.0
82	20.9	15.5	0.2	5.1
83	32.6	16.1	0.1	9.1
84	25.8	7.4	0.7	17.1
85	27.9	11.6	0.5	14.9
86	32.2	17.0	1.2	13.6
87	29.2	21.4	0.4	6.8
88	34.1	17.2	1.0	15.7
89	30.3	25.0	1.4	3.4

*Only includes countries that were EC members during the year
listed. Excludes intra-EC trade. Figures based on value. SITC(rev.2)
7932

Source: OECD, *Statistics of Foreign Trade*, various issues.

Japan, since they were followed by the issuing of Japanese
government guidelines to shipbuilding companies for a
reduction of manhours worked in shipbuilding.

Despite continued threats of unilateral action and attempts
to pursue negotiations outside the OECD framework, Japan

Table 6.2
Destination of EFTA Ship Exports*
(Per cent)

	OECD	Western Europe	Japan	North America
1970	57.1	49.0	0.05	1.2
71	75.4	64.7	0.36	2.2
72	64.5	52.6	0.06	2.3
73	61.7	50.3	0.14	6.4
74	59.0	51.5	0.08	2.2
75	54.5	43.3	0.05	6.6
76	47.3	36.2	0.04	0.3
77	49.3	43.3	0.04	0.3
78	35.0	28.5	1.62	0.8
79	40.8	34.6	0.03	2.0
80	27.0	21.6	0.06	1.4
81	31.8	29.3	1.30	0.7
82	44.1	40.0	0.07	2.8
83	28.7	25.3	0.04	3.1
84	41.1	36.0	0.06	4.7
85	24.4	20.0	0.09	3.7
86	21.3	17.9	0.10	3.3
87	24.1	21.4	0.38	1.4
88	51.1	32.7	0.47	6.9
89	50.3	42.3	0.81	6.3

*Figures based on value. SITC(rev.2) 7932.

Source: OECD, *Statistics of Foreign Trade*, various years.

steadfastly resisted European pressure for a market sharing agreement. Japan's offer to increase ship export prices in February 1977 turned out to be a relatively minor concession when it was learned that the increase would be roughly 5 per cent, while Japan was accused of undercutting European bids for new orders by as much as 40 per cent.[91] Although Japan did end up with a share of new orders closer to that of Western Europe until 1980, this probably had more to do with the appreciation of the yen than with the government-imposed

241

Table 6.3
Destination of Japanese Ship Exports*
(Per cent)

	OECD	EC	Other W.Europe	North America
1970	41.8	22.6	37.9	0.4
71	28.7	34.9	24.6	0.6
72	31.7	1.4	29.6	0.7
73	33.0	11.2	21.2	0.3
74	25.6	12.9	12.5	0.2
75	18.0	7.3	9.7	0.1
76	26.6	8.9	16.6	0.2
77	34.8	12.1	21.6	0.4
78	36.2	12.0	19.5	3.1
79	37.0	11.4	22.4	0.3
80	26.1	9.2	8.7	8.1
81	33.6	22.8	8.1	0.2
82	23.6	15.6	5.9	0.6
83	29.8	22.2	3.7	2.2
84	19.9	16.0	2.8	0.1
85	22.9	10.4	3.0	8.4
86	9.5	7.1	0.1	0.4
87	20.7	11.4	0.1	8.3
88	6.2	1.8	1.4	2.7
89	8.4	1.6	1.5	1.6

*Figures based on value. SITC(rev.2) 7932.

Source: OECD, *Statistics of Foreign Trade*, various years.

price increase, which in any case was suspended at the end of 1978.[92] The 35 per cent capacity reduction announced by Japan in November 1978 did not seem to result primarily from European pressure, which had by this time greatly diminished, but rather reflected the Japanese government's realisation that demand for ships was not likely to recover significantly in the near future.[93] Japan held to its own production target set in the mid-1970s of 50 per cent of the world market by 1980, a level which it effectively maintained through the first half of the decade despite protests from European governments and ship-builders.

The ability of Japan to resist European pressure for a market sharing agreement was illustrated in late 1978 when the Japanese delegate told members of the Working Party that his government would not renew its 5 per cent price increase on ships built for export after the programme expired at the end of the year. The delegate told the Working Party that Japan was no longer prepared to damage its competitiveness while European governments were increasingly subsidising their shipbuilding industries. Despite strong opposition from European governments and the EC Commission, the Japanese went through with their plan to abandon the price control programme.[94] Thus, it seems clear that Japan was capable of maintaining and even increasing its dominance of the world shipbuilding market in the long term and that concessions made to the Europeans were intended to relieve some of the political pressure put on them, particularly when the Europeans displayed a willingness to resort to issue linkage strategies. Once this pressure was reduced, however, Japan was able to return to its planned market objectives.

In 1988, the EC Commission threatened to introduce a levy on ships loading or unloading at Community ports which were purchased in Japan at "abnormal" prices.[95] However, the threat was not followed up after Japan failed to commit itself to raise its prices, largely because of the practical difficulties involved in implementing such a levy. In retrospect, it appears that the Commission's threat was not a very serious one, and perhaps sensing this, Japan continued to resist European demands for a pricing accord.

(d) Influence of Institutions

The OECD seemed a logical forum for negotiations on ship-building, since member countries accounted for most of the world's production and trade of ships. Those countries produced over 90 per cent of the world's ships prior to 1975, and even after this share declined, they continued to produce an annual average of some three-quarters of the world total in the first half of the 1980s, and accounted for an even greater percentage of world ship exports. However, unlike the cases of

243

export credits and agriculture, where the OECD brought together the major extenders of export credits and exporters of agricultural products, and where the permanent forum of the Organisation helped keep proposals in the forefront until consensus could be built around them, after more than a decade of European demands, no agreement could be reached on market sharing.

While the OECD Secretariat played a key role in facilitating the conclusion of the three shipbuilding agreements, it was much less influential in the subsequent pattern of member country compliance with OECD agreements. Also, the more the shipbuilding issue became politicised, and the more polarised the two main parties became, the more difficult it became for the Secretariat to facilitate or participate in transgovernmental coalitions or to foster attitude change among delegates. Certainly on the question of a market sharing agreement there was not much scope for transgovernmental coalition-building or attitude change, as positions were pretty firmly entrenched.

In some areas of OECD activity in the shipbuilding field there was more opportunity for members of the Secretariat to play an influential role. For example, as concern increased among Working Party members over the growing production capacity in non-OECD countries, the Secretariat produced a report suggesting more contacts outside the OECD context among representatives of the shipbuilding industry from OECD and competitor countries to facilitate the exchange of information about investment and production plans.[96] It took some time for this proposal to gain acceptance, but in early 1985 an informal meeting did take place in Hong Kong which included representatives of Japanese and Korean shipbuilding companies, bankers from Western Europe, and OECD officials.[97] This meeting helped pave the way for the participation of Korea in the OECD Liaison Group the following year.

Proposals were also put forward by the Secretariat in 1980 and in 1984 for the elimination of all direct state aids to the shipbuilding industry, beginning with a 20 per cent reduction in such aids in 1982. While these proposals did not receive sufficient support to be implemented, they did serve as reminders to member states of their commitments under the General Arrangement.[98]

At least one part of the shipbuilding regime which was

developed in the OECD appeared to have clearly influenced the behaviour of member states. The Understanding on Export Credits for Ships was widely cited by member governments when demands were made by shipbuilders for more generous official support of export credits, and as was mentioned earlier, the record of compliance with the agreement was very good. In the case of the General Guidelines, there was also a high degree of compliance, in that there were significant capacity reductions made in most participating countries. However, compliance was probably more coincidental than it was the direct result of that agreement. Overcapacity was growing, and it appeared that there would be no improvement in the demand situation anytime soon, so more and more governments acknowledged that there was no alternative to allowing ship-yards to cut back or to close down. The weakest link in the shipbuilding regime was the General Arrangement, which failed to prevent most governments from increasing the subsi-disation of shipbuilding as the crisis situation grew.

The drift to increased neo-protectionism that characterised the overall trade regime during the 1970s was paralleled in the shipbuilding sector, which faced the same kinds of domestic pressures for government assistance that other sectors faced. But as in the overall trade regime, there was no wholesale abandoning of the principles and rules developed in the OECD to regulate state behaviour in shipbuilding. Despite domestic pressures, governments generally made an effort to comply with the letter, if not always with the spirit, of their commit-ments. When governments felt the need to take action inconsist-ent with these agreements, the general pattern was to find loopholes or to bend the rules, rather than to simply ignore them. For example, when the credit terms set out in the Under-standing on Export Credits for Ships were sometimes exceeded, this was almost always done within the context of a country's foreign aid programme, which was technically not prohibited by the agreement.

In the case of the General Arrangement, an attempt was normally made to justify new measures of government assist-ance by referring to them as "emergency" or "exceptional" measures, which were permitted under the agreement, indicat-ing that the intention was return to regime-sanctioned behaviour as soon as possible. Certainly, the interpretation of what constituted an emergency and how long "temporary" was rested with the participating governments, but the very fact that they even attempted to play within the rules indicates their desire to salvage the shipbuilding regime which had been developed over the years. Also, whenever it became clear that the rules established in more prosperous times had become unacceptable given the changing domestic political and economic climate, efforts were always made to revise the rules, as in the case of credit terms and target dates for the ending of government subsidies, rather than simply allowing them to fall into irrelevance.

Spain was one country which did decide to withdraw from the Understanding in March 1979 when it could not get enough support for an easing of export credit terms for ships. But other members of the Working Party moved quickly to revise the agreement in an attempt to maintain Spain's adherence to it. Japan was even willing to accept a discriminatory interest rate limit which permitted European countries to offer interest rates that were 0.5 per cent below the limit set for Japan. This incident illustrates, first of all, the seriousness with which OECD members took their legally "non-binding" commitments. If these agreements had no effect then one must ask why Spain bothered to withdraw formally from the Understanding. The Spanish government obviously felt an urgent need to offer more favourable credit terms, but was not willing simply to go ahead and offer these until after the notification period for withdrawal set out in the agreement had expired.

Secondly, the reaction of those members who had been opposed to an easing of the credit terms indicated their unwillingness to jeopardise the regime by continuing to insist on a maintenance of the status quo. There was a real fear that Spain's defection would lead to an unravelling of the whole shipbuilding regime, and even the largest shipbuilding countries were willing to make concessions to ensure that this did not happen.[99] Hence, although the shipbuilding regime was weakened by continued subsidisation of the industry, it did play at least some role in constraining the behaviour of states which adhere to it and in influencing the bargaining process within the OECD.

(e) Unit-level Variables

Domestic Group Opposition   It does not appear that Japan's success in resisting European pressure in the Working Party for a market sharing agreement was the result of constraints imposed by major domestic groups or interests in Europe on the bargaining position of the EC. The attempts made by European governments to impose restraint on Japanese production were the direct result of the high level of industry lobbying and labour unrest in the shipbuilding sector, especially during the 1970s. There were frequent worker protests over labour cutbacks in shipbuilding, and because unemployment in general was high in Europe at the time, these cutbacks were a particularly sensitive public issue.[100] The Association of West European Shipbuilders was a very active and vocal lobby both in the national capitals of European countries and at the headquarters of the Commission of the EC, and was a major supporter of EC proposals in the Working Party.[101]

Shipbuilding had become a politicised issue in Japan as well, where labour unrest was also experienced and the Shipbuilders' Association of Japan was an equally effective interest group.[102] This may have helped Japan to resist European pressure to a certain extent, since it could point to its own domestic sociopolitical problems related to the shipbuilding crisis, a factor with which European governments had a certain amount of sympathy because of their similar domestic situation.[103]

Governmental Cohesion   Of the unit-level variables examined here, the most important in influencing the outcome of the OECD negotiations and subsequent pattern of compliance was the lack of cohesion among member countries of the European Community. This disunity was partly over how to proceed in negotiations with Japan (for example, how much time to give the Japanese to take action), but most importantly over the punitive and protective trade measures to be taken in case of Japanese intransigence.

Japan could afford not to take seriously European threats of unilateral action because the EC was openly divided on such measures. This division was due in part to differences over such principles as the appropriate degree of government intervention

247

in the marketplace and the dangers of protectionism.[104] But there was also a more generalised concern among European governments about the costs of subsidising fundamentally uncompetitive industries and fuelling inflation by forcing European shipowners to purchase more expensive European-built ships. These differences prevented the EC Commission from gaining approval for a common policy on defensive measures or on government assistance to the shipbuilding sector.[105] Government aid was given in an unco-ordinated fashion by individual European governments, but this did not seriously interfere with Japan's plans to take 50 per cent of the world market by 1980.

Preference Intensity   Because the EC did not mobilise its capabilities in order to prevail over Japan on the question of the even sharing of new orders, it could be concluded that the EC did not have the "will" to exert itself. Doing so, however, would be to commit the same error as those who conclude that a direct causal link automatically exists between power resources and outcome whenever the stronger prevail over the weaker. As the preceding section demonstrated, the failure of the strong to prevail over the weak is not always due to a lack of will, but can often be attributed to other unit-level factors, which is why it is preferable to examine a number of such factors in each case.

It is difficult to speak of the commitment of the EC on shipbuilding, because in a larger sense than on other trade issues, there was no single European "will" on the shipbuilding issue. Some member countries were committed enough to EC demands to support the trade measures that would most forcefully support the Community's objectives, while others were clearly lacking in that commitment. In those countries with less commitment, competing domestic economic interests were responsible for their restraint, in particular concerns over harming their shipping interests and fueling inflation.

A consequence of the disunity in the EC was that all of the characteristics of a weak commitment were apparent, including a notable lack of attempts to link its demands on shipbuilding to unrelated trade issues, or to adopt restrictive measures on the import of Japanese ships. Furthermore, the shipbuilding issue was never propelled to the top of the decision-making hierarchy, as were at various times the issues of export credits, agriculture and steel. Shipbuilding was not raised in OECD Council Ministerial meetings during the 1970s and 1980s, and certainly was never a prominent issue at economic summit meetings.

In comparing the list of determinants of preference intensity proposed in Chapter Two, there does not appear to be any striking difference between the EC and Japan. In neither country were broader foreign policy interests or questions of ideology seriously involved. As was pointed out earlier, governments on both sides experienced public protest and lobbying by industry. It was only on the question of competing interests that a discernable difference appeared, and these interests were only strong in certain European countries. Hence, the essential factor explaining the failure of the EC to prevail over Japan was that of disunity, rather than lack of commitment.

(f) Changes in Interest Definition

There were three principal cases where changes in interest definition helped explain outcomes of OECD negotiations. The Japanese had been relatively reserved on European proposals for an agreement on export credits for ships during the 1960s. Only after Japan's share of world orders declined in the late 1960s (and after the British government began to give British shipbuilders credit terms more favourable than the Japanese government), did Japan have an interest in such an agreement. As a result, in 1968 and 1969, Japan campaigned more actively for international co-operation to reduce competition in government support of shipbuilding.[106]

The second case involved Japan's blocking of European attempts to bring non-OECD countries, South Korea in particular, into shipbuilding discussions. It was not until Japanese shipbuilders began to express concern over competition from South Korea in the early 1980s that Japan agreed to hold talks with South Korean shipbuilders and that the South Koreans finally began participating in OECD shipbuilding talks through the Liaison Group.[107] In the third case, the grudging acceptance of reductions in government assistance to shipbuilding by EC member countries in the early 1970s shifted in the 1980s as a result of changing conditions in the world shipbuilding market. The shipbuilding crisis changed the position of the Community to one of resisting further OECD commitments to reduce subsidies, and of supporting the elimination of deadlines in the General Arrangement.

7. *Conclusion*

The negotiation of the three shipbuilding agreements was characterised by a remarkably high degree of consensus among the member countries of the Working Party. This did not mean that discussions on shipbuilding in the OECD were always harmonious, however. On the most contentious issues, namely market sharing and "unfair" pricing, the expectations of the structural theories were not borne out. The European Community, which was the party with the greatest power capabilities both in general trade relations and in the ship trade issue area, failed to obtain a firm agreement from Japan to share new orders evenly with it, and failed to secure a commitment on the pricing of ships from either Japan or Korea. In other words, although Japan was more dependent on the European ship market than vice versa, this dependence did not necessarily translate into greater Japanese *vulnerability* because constraints within the European Community prevented it from effectively manipulating its relatively lower dependence.

The most puzzling aspect of this case, at least from a neorealist point of view, is why the EC did not prevail over these much weaker states. Once again, in this case study it was found that while institutional factors facilitated the development of the three agreements, they did not decisively alter the outcome of the negotiations, and were not sufficient to bring about a resolution to the EC-Japanese dispute on market sharing or pricing.

The part of the shipbuilding regime dealing with export credits did appear largely to be responsible for the restraint of participating countries, since compliance seemed to result from a high degree of consensus that the rules and norms set out in the Understanding were desirable. Self-help did not appear to play as strong a role as it did in other OECD export credit agreements, and only one or two cases of matching occurred each year.[108] On the other hand, compliance (and the

250

infrequency of efforts to alter the terms of the Understanding) may have been facilitated by the availability of other forms of assistance to shipbuilders, both through direct and indirect aid in the case of the EC, and by the ample advantage already afforded by lower costs in Japan.

The General Arrangement did not impose much of a constraint, partly because of the looseness of its wording, but also due to the acceptance that in a crisis situation the need for subsidies outweighed international commitments to reduce them. Also, because European countries were the chief violators of the principle of reduced subsidisation, and Japan was unable to force those countries to comply, structural explanations may have some value in this instance. However, there was not a total disregard for the subsidies regime, and some effort was made to conform at least to the letter of the agreement, if not always with the spirit. Finally, in the case of the General Guidelines, compliance was largely coincidental, since the crisis turned out to be longer than most countries expected, and there was no alternative but to cut production capacity.

The outcome of bargaining did not seem to have been influenced much by differences in domestic unity or commitment, but the third unit-level variable, coherence, provides the most convincing explanation for the outcome of the issue which was the subject of the most intensive bargaining. The European Community was constrained in the 1970s and early 1980s by a lack of unity over proposed measures to be taken against Japan, and when Japan sensed this disunity it continued to pursue its objectives unhindered. Finally, changes in the EC's interest played a significant role in explaining the desire of the EC to remove target dates in the General Arrangement for eliminating subsidies, although changes in interest did not explain the main anomaly (from a structural realist point of view) in this case study, which was the failure of the EC to impose a market sharing or pricing arrangement on Japan.

Notes

1 Also, the demand for supertankers, which had grown after the closing of the Suez Canal in 1967, dropped significantly with the re-opening of the Canal in 1974.
2 *Financial Times* 10 November 1986.

251

3 Notable exceptions included Spain and Turkey, which imposed highly restrictive import quotas, and Japan which, along with Spain, imposed customs duties during the 1960s.

4 *Financial Times* 10 November 1986.

5 From 1975 to 1980 Western Europe experienced a 77 per cent decline in ship production while Japan experienced a 63 per cent decline. IMF, *Trade Policy Developments in Industrial Countries*, by S.J. Anjaria, Z. Iqbal, L.L. Perez, and W.S. Tseng, (Washington, D.C.: IMF, 1981), pp. 11–12; IMF, *Trade Policy Issues and Developments*, by Shailendra J. Anjaria, Naheed Kirmani, and Arne B. Peterson, (Washington, D.C.: IMF, 1985), pp. 47–49.

6 For a more detailed examination of American policy, see Clinton H. Whitehurst, Jr., *The U.S. Shipbuilding Industry: Past, Present, and Future* (Annapolis, Md.: Naval Institute Press, 1986), especially chapters 4 and 5.

7 *OECD Observer*, no.17 (August 1965), pp. 13–16; OECD, *The Situation in the Shipbuilding Industry* (Paris: OECD, 1965).

8 The Working Party was chaired by the representative of a country that was not an active participant in the meetings, such as Portugal, Canada, Switzerland and Austria.

9 The United States became a member of the Working Party in July 1989.

10 The participants included Belgium, Canada, Denmark, Finland, France, Germany, Italy, Japan, the Netherlands, Norway, Spain, Sweden, the United Kingdom. Australia acceded to the Understanding in 1971.

11 *OECD Observer*, no. 71, August 1974, p. 39.

12 The agreement reached in the Working Party on 26 October 1979 was confirmed by the OECD Council on 30 January 1980.

13 Participants in the revised Understanding were Australia, Canada, the European Economic Community, Finland, Japan, Norway and Sweden.

14 Prior notification was to be sent by Telex to other participants one month before implementation of such decisions.

15 These obstacles were listed as follows: direct building subsidies; customs tariffs or any other import barriers; discriminatory tax policies; discriminatory official regulations or internal practices; specific aid for investment in and restructuring of the domestic shipbuilding industry. *OECD Observer*, no.41 (August 1969), pp. 11–13.

16 The European countries included Belgium, Denmark, Finland, France, Germany, the Netherlands, Norway, Spain, Sweden, the United Kingdom. Italy acceded to the Arrangement in July 1974.

17 Participants included Belgium, Denmark, Finland, France, Germany, Ireland, Italy, Japan, Norway, the Netherlands, Spain, Sweden, the United Kingdom.

18 This change was made because policies did not change as frequently as every six months. Instead, prior notification was to be

given of policy changes as they occurred. Interview with OECD official.

19 *Financial Times, The Times* 1 April 1976.
20 IMF, *Trade Policy Developments*, p. 12.
21 *The Guardian* 20 January 1977.
22 *Japan Times* 20 October 1972; *The Times* 7 August 1976; *Daily Telegraph* 19 October 1976, 27 September 1977, 3 March 1979; *Financial Times* 23 March 1978.
23 *Financial Times* 26 October 1972, 20 April 1978; *The Times* 13 November 1979.
24 *Daily Telegraph* 27 September 1977; *Financial Times* 26 October 1977, 9 November 1978.
25 *Financial Times* 26 October 1972, 30 April 1975, 10 January 1977, 28 September 1977, 13 December 1978, 5 July 1985; *Daily Telegraph* 23 December 1976, 5 December 1978, 26 July 1983, 20 August 1984; *Japan Times* 21 April 1978, *New York Times* 22 January 1979; IMF, 1981, p. 12; *Bulletin of the European Communities*, 10–1973, p. 50. An IMF report points out that while only two Working Party members were extending direct internal subsidies in 1975, by 1981 nearly all were doing so. IMF, *Trade Policy Developments*, p. 12.
26 For an extensive description of aid to shipbuilding in 14 OECD member countries, see OECD, *Measures of Assistance to Shipbuilding* (Paris: OECD, 1987).
27 *New York Times* 22 January 1979; *Financial Times* 13 December 1978, 16 July 1984, 21 August 1986; *Daily Telegraph* 26 July 1983.
28 *Financial Times* 28 September 1977, 21 January, 9 March 1982; *Daily Telegraph* 6 June 1978, 8 January 1982; *Japan Times* 8 November 1977, 21 April 1978; *The Times* 19 April 1978. Japan did not offer direct aid to shipbuilders, although it did support export credits within the OECD guidelines, as did all other Working Party participants.
29 *Bulletin of the European Communities* 10–1973, pp. 34–35, 50–51, 5–1975, p. 33, 7–1975, p. 31.
30 *Bulletin of the European Communities* 3–1978, p. 40.
31 *Bulletin of the European Communities* 4–1981, p. 21; *The Guardian* 30 April 1981.
32 *Financial Times* 15 February 1984, 23 November 1984; *The Guardian* 16 February 1984.
33 *Bulletin of the European Communities* 10–1986, p. 9; *Financial Times* 15 February, 23 November 1984, 6 February 1985, 20 November 1986; *The Guardian* 16 February 1984.
34 *Bulletin of the European Communities* 12–1986, pp. 65–66, 10–1986, pp. 9–11; *Financial Times* 23 December 1986; IMF, *Issues and Developments in International Trade Policy*, by Margaret Kelly, Naheed Kirmani, Miranda Xafa, Clemens Boonekamp, and Peter Winglee (Washington, D.C.: IMF, 1988), pp. 80–81.
35 *Bulletin of the European Communities* 12–1986, p. 65; *Financial Times* 31 October 1986; *The Guardian* 6 January 1984; Interview with UK government official.

36 *Financial Times* 23 December 1988; Interview with UK government official.
37 *The Economist* 30 October 1976.
38 *Financial Times* 19 November 1976; *Japan Times* 26 November 1976.
39 *Japan Times* 11 November 1978; *Financial Times* 9 November 1978.
40 *Financial Times* 18 July 1978.
41 *Financial Times* 8 December 1976.
42 The United Kingdom and Italy were opposed to EC reduction targets, while Germany and Denmark preferred to let market forces rather than government policy reduce capacity. *Bulletin of the European Communities* 4–1978, p. 35; *Financial Times* 24 April, 27 January 1978; *The Times* 24 April, 10 July 1978.
43 *Financial Times* 29 July 1978, 24 January 1985; *The Times* 10 July 1978; *International Herald Tribune* 21 September 1983.
44 *Financial Times* 11 September 1980, 23 November 1984, 5 July 1985.
45 Figures based on compensated gross tons. *Financial Times* 17 October 1987; *International Herald Tribune* 23 May 1988; IMF, *Issues and Developments*, pp. 80–81.
46 *Financial Times* 4, 16 and 18 March 1981.
47 *The Economist* 21 March 1981; *Japan Times* 30 October 1976; *Financial Times* 21 March 1977; *International Herald Tribune* 23 December 1976, 10 February 1977; *New York Times* 9 February 1977; *Bulletin of the European Communities*, 1976–12, p. 73; Interview with Swiss government official.
48 *The Times* 22 June 1971, 4 December 1971.
49 *Financial Times* 17 April 1978.
50 *Financial Times* 13 July, 7 November 1978; *Daily Telegraph* 13 July, 9 November 1978; *The Times* 9 November 1978.
51 *Daily Telegraph* 9 March 1979; *Financial Times* 9 March, 10 October 1979; *International Herald Tribune* 27–28 October 1979; *The Times* 5 February 1980. Spain resumed its adherence to the Understanding when it took up membership in the EC in 1986.
52 Interview with OECD official.
53 *The Times* 30 November 1971, 23 October 1972.
54 *Financial Times* 30 April 1975.
54 *The Times* 2 October 1980.
55 Interview with OECD official.
56 *Financial Times* 8 November 1972; *The Guardian* 9 December 1975; *The Times* 17 December 1975.
58 *Financial Times* 3 December 1975.
59 *Bulletin of the European Communities* 1976–5, p. 28.
60 *Bulletin of the European Communities*, 1976–12, pp. 58–59; *International Herald Tribune* 28 May 1976.
61 Interview with OECD official.
62 *Financial Times* 8, 10 November 1972; *The Times* 10 November 1972.
63 *The Guardian* 9 December 1975; *The Times* 17 December 1975.
64 *Bulletin of the European Communities* 1976–10, p. 50; *The Guardian, Financial Times* 28 October 1976.

65 *Bulletin of the European Communities* 1976–12; *Financial Times* 29 October 1976.
66 *Bulletin of the European Communities* 1976–12, p. 73; *Financial Times* 7, 8, 14 December 1976.
67 *Bulletin of the European Communities* 1977–1, p.149; *International Herald Tribune* 23 December 1976, 14 January 1977; *Financial Times* 5, 10 January 1977; *The Guardian* 4 January 1977.
68 *New York Times* 9 February 1977; *Financial Times* 10 February 1977; *International Herald Tribune* 10 February 1977.
69 *Financial Times, The Times* 25 February 1977.
70 *Bulletin of the European Communities* 1977–3, p. 63; *Financial Times, The Times* 24 March 1977.
71 *The Times* 5 May 1977.
72 *Bulletin of the European Communities* 5–1977, p. 40, 6–1977, pp. 32, 75; *The Times* 29 June 1977.
73 *Bulletin of the European Communities* 11–1977, p. 64; *Financial Times* 7, 9, 10 November 1977; *Japan Times* 8 November 1977; *International Herald Tribune* 10 November 1977.
74 *Financial Times* 11, 17, 19, 20 April 1978; *The Times* 19, 20, 27 April 1978.
75 *Financial Times* 7, 9, 10 November 1978; *Daily Telegraph* 8, 9, 10 November 1978; *The Times* 9, 10 November 1978.
76 *Bulletin of the European Communities* 10–1980, p. 71; *The Times* 1, 2 October 1980; *Financial Times* 1 October 1980.
77 *Financial Times* 4, 18 March, 27 November 1981; *International Herald Tribune* 19 March 1981.
78 *Financial Times* 1 April, 25 June 1982, 3 March 1983; *The Observer* 12 September 1982; *The Times* 2 April 1982.
79 *Bulletin of the European Communities* 12–1983, p. 22; *Japan Times* 1 December 1983; *Financial Times* 20 December 1983.
80 *Japan Times* 5 April 1984; *Financial Times* 25 October, 5 December 1984; *The Guardian* 7 November 1984.
81 IMF, *Issues and Developments*, pp. 80–81; Interview with UK government official.
82 *Bulletin of the European Communities* 3–1988, p. 30.
83 *Financial Times* 24 March, 19 April 1988, 4 April 1989; *International Herald Tribune* 12 April 1988. After the April 1988 agreement, the deputy director of the EC's Directorate-General for External Affairs, Jos Loeff, admitted that the Community was not seeking any expansion of European shipbuilding, but simply wanted to keep the sector a reasonable part of the economy. *The Times* 14 April 1988.
84 *Financial Times* 13 January 1977.
85 *The Observer* 13 February 1977; *The Guardian* 11 February 1977; *Financial Times* 18 March 1977; *The Times* 25 February 1977.
86 *New York Times* 9 February 1977; *Japan Times* 9 February 1977.
87 *International Herald Tribune* 10 November, 19 October 1972; *Financial Times* 8 November 1972, 3 August 1978.
88 *The Guardian* 9 December 1975; *The Times* 17 December 1975.

89 *Bulletin of the European Communities*, 1976–5, p. 28; *International Herald Tribune* 28 May 1976.
90 *Financial Times* 20 October, 14 December 1976; *Bulletin of the European Communities*, 1976–10, p. 50; *Japan Times* 4 December 1976.
91 *Financial Times* 25 February 1977.
92 *Financial Times* 13 July 1978; *Daily Telegraph* 13 July 1978; *Bulletin of the European Communities*, 1978–4, p. 74.
93 *Bulletin of the European Communities*, 1977–11, p. 64.
94 *Financial Times* 9 November 1978.
95 IMF, *Issues and Developments*, p. 81; *Financial Times* 24 March, 19 April 1988; *International Herald Tribune* 12 April 1988.
96 *Financial Times* 20 April 1978.
97 *Financial Times* 20 March 1985. This meeting was organised by the chairman of the International Maritime Industries Forum, who picked up on the suggestion of the OECD Secretariat. Interview with OECD official.
98 *The Times* 2 October 1980.
99 *Financial Times* 9 March 1979; *Daily Telegraph* 9 March 1979; *International Herald Tribune* 27–28 October 1979.
100 For a more lengthy discussion of labour and industry demands on governments during the shipbuilding crisis, see Bo Stråth, *The Politics of De-industrialisation: The Contraction of the West European Shipbuilding Industry* (London, New York: Croom Helm, 1987).
101 *Financial Times* 30 April 1975, 20, 26 October 1976, 5, 10 January, 7 November 1977; *The Guardian* 9 December 1975, 4 January, 7 November 1977; *The Times* 17 December 1975, 10 July 1978; *Daily Telegraph* 7 November 1977; *New York Times* 22 January 1979.
102 *The Guardian* 9 December 1975; *The Times* 17 December 1975; *Daily Telegraph* 10 February, 7 November 1978; *New York Times* 22 January 1979; *Financial Times* 6 June 1979.
103 *Daily Telegraph* 10 February 1977; *International Herald Tribune* 10 November 1977.
104 The greatest opposition came from Germany and Denmark, although Germany later began introducing subsidies.
105 *Financial Times* 14 December 1976, 12, 13 January 1977; *International Herald Tribune* 14 January 1977; *Japan Times* 23 December 1976, 13 January 1977; *The Times* 7 February 1977.
106 *The Times* 5 March 1965, 5 June, 1 December 1969.
107 *Bulletin of the European Communities*, 1977–6, p. 32; *Japan Times* 8 November 1977; *Financial Times* 17, 20 April, 10 November 1978, 3 March 1983, 25 October 1984; *The Times* 10 November 1978, 2 April 1982; *The Guardian* 7 November, 5 December 1984.
108 Interview with OECD official.

Chapter Seven

CONCLUSION

This study has revealed that contrary to some portrayals of the OECD as a place where like-minded parties collaborate harmoniously to produce fairly inconsequential statements, trade negotiations conducted in the OECD were often arduous and protracted, with the interests and perspectives of participating countries at times clashing strongly. The agreements which frequently resulted from these negotiations were of considerable significance to participants, while failures to reach agreement were the source of profound disappointment for some parties. Moreover, OECD talks were used as an instrument of foreign policy by certain member countries attempting to alter the behaviour of other countries.[1] Hence, it is entirely appropriate to ask who gained the most from these trade negotiations, and why. Because of the effort that went into crafting OECD agreements, and given the importance of the sectors examined, it is also desirable to ask what impact these agreements had on the trade-related policies and practices of OECD member countries, and why. This latter question is particularly important to the study of international relations because of the relative dearth of systematic evaluations of the impact of international regimes on state behaviour.

Explaining the Outcome of OECD Trade Negotiations

At first glance it appears that during the 1970s and 1980s, the United States prevailed in the negotiations on export credits and agricultural trade, while the European Community was successful in the steel trade negotiations and the outcome of the shipbuilding negotiations was closer to Japanese objectives.

A closer look at the negotiations reveals, however, that in some cases such simple conclusions are misleading. This is evident when one attempts to find explanations for the outcome of these negotiations.

The effort to explain the outcome of OECD trade negotiations began by examining a number of models derived from the established theoretical international relations literature. The most general finding of this study was that systemic models were inadequate in explaining or predicting the outcome of these negotiations. Moreover, the analysis of the four case studies indicated that unit-level variables were essential in explaining the outcome of bargaining in the OECD on trade matters.

The least reliable independent variable examined was the distribution of overall tangible capabilities. The United States did gain satisfaction in two of the three negotiations in which it participated, but there was evidence of an attempted linkage with military-security issues in only one case, that of export credits, and that attempt was a conspicuous failure. In the two areas where the US obtained its objectives, it did so only with great difficulty and after very long periods of time. However, there was no appreciable increase in the overall power capabilities of the US over these time periods that could account for its eventual success in the negotiations. In the fourth case, overall capabilities were seen to be less relevant due to the primarily economic nature of relations between the two principal parties, the EC and Japan, and the lack of significant security ties between them.

The international trade structure model was similarly unsatisfactory as an explanation for the outcome of the OECD negotiations. The United States was clearly dissatisfied with the outcome of the steel trade negotiations, and it was not able to impose its preferences on the other major participants, even during the periods of the 1980s when it was preponderant in international trade power. In fact, even in those cases where the US was generally satisfied, there is no indication that that outcome had anything to do with superior American trade power resources. On the issue of shipbuilding, where the EC was the dominant participant in terms of trade bargaining power, this advantage failed to bring about an OECD agreement which satisfied the Community. Only in the case of export credits did the implied threat of issue linkage appear to have

258

much of an influence on negotiations, when Japan was holding up an agreement in 1986. The US and EC complained about their growing trade deficits with Japan in the export credit talks, which did appear to have some effect on Japan and cleared the way for the 1987 agreement.

Perhaps the most surprising finding of this study was that the distribution of power resources within the specific trade sector under negotiation did not fare much better than the other two structural models in predicting or explaining outcomes. The United States possessed the greatest trade power resources in the steel sector, and the European Community predominated in ship trade capabilities, yet in each case the "hegemonic" power failed to attain its main objectives in the OECD talks. On the issues of export credits and agriculture, where the EC appeared to be the strongest party, the agreements reached were closer to American objectives.

In all four cases, such institutional factors as the nature of the intergovernmental organisation, the role of the Secretariat, and transgovernmental and transnational relations were found to have had a rather modest influence on negotiations. While they facilitated negotiations by clarifying issues, there is no evidence that these institutional factors fundamentally increased the power of weaker states or altered the outcome of any of the negotiations. One of the main objectives of the OECD is to make countries more aware of one another's situations and to prevent misunderstandings. While this kind of activity is widespread in the Organisation, the result is not always the reconciliation of opposing views. A greater awareness of other countries' problems and conditions quite often only means that differences and incompatibilities become clearer, and does not necessarily result in radical changes in the bargaining positions of states.

While concern for preserving the broader international trade regime was often expressed in OECD negotiations, this concern was not always strong enough to convince member countries to alter their bargaining positions. The liberalisation norm of the trade regime did not seem to have motivated delegations to reduce subsidies in any of the sectors examined here, and where agreement was reached to reduce government support, it was by and large inspired by the desire to relieve pressure on government budgets. The multilateralism norm seemed to be respected in export credit and agricultural trade negotiations, primarily because there was no effective alternative, such as bilateral negotiations or unilateral action. The EC maintained its support for the multilateral approach to the shipbuilding negotiations for a surprisingly long time, considering that these negotiations did not give the Community much satisfaction. Eventually, the EC circumvented the multilateral path, and in the late 1980s pursued bilateral negotiations with Japan and South Korea. However, when these negotiations failed to provide results acceptable to the EC, it turned its efforts back to the OECD forum. The norm of multilateralism had the weakest impact in the area of steel trade, a large part of which came to be controlled by bilateral agreements. These bilateral agreements also violated the non-discrimination norm of the trade regime.

Of the three unit-level variables examined in this study, domestic group opposition was the least influential. The degree of societal solidarity with government bargaining positions in OECD negotiations tended to be fairly high and evenly distributed. Indeed, it was usually found that these bargaining positions found their origins in the demands of domestic groups.[2] Instead of domestic groups in different countries forming transnational alliances and constraining the exercise of power by their governments, conflicts between states often arose directly from the incompatible interests of respective national groups. This finding may indicate that in international trade relations, domestic opposition will generally be less likely to constrain negotiators, because bargaining positions (and trade policy making in general) tend to be influenced by domestic groups to a greater extent than in other issue areas.[3]

Breakdowns in governmental cohesion did not generally explain departures from the outcomes predicted by structural models. In most cases states with superiority in either issue-specific or more general power resources were not constrained in the use of those resources by divisions among government departments or among key decision makers. The main exception was the case of shipbuilding, where the lack of cohesion among EC governments was seen to be the crucial factor preventing the EC from using access to its shipping market as an instrument of pressure against Japan.

The third unit-level variable tested in this study was the

intensity of a country's preferences. In the case of steel, the failure of the United States to bring about an agreement on the export of steelmaking equipment to developing countries was seen to be the consequence of a relatively weak commitment of the US government to that goal. Despite the overwhelming steel trade power resources at the disposal of the United States, it was unwilling to mobilise these resources any more than it had to in order to protect what the US government perceived to be a fundamentally uncompetitive industry. This was in sharp contrast with the cases of agriculture and export credits, where the US did act aggressively to back its demands, even though it was in a much weaker position in terms of power resources. In the latter two cases, the EC commitment to its position was equally strong, however, creating a stalemate in negotiations that lasted for several years. There did not appear to be any significant difference in level of preference intensity between the EC and Japan in the shipbuilding case, so this variable did not seem to be a major determinant of the outcome of negotiations.

The final factor to be considered in this analysis was the change in interest definition by participants. In the steel and shipbuilding negotiations there were no significant changes in interest definition or in bargaining positions on the major points of conflict. Agreement was reached on an automatic interest rate adjustment mechanism for export credits in 1983 largely as a result of falling world interest rates and the French government's preoccupation with its rapidly growing trade deficit. The 1987 agreement on tied aid credits was made possible by a change in the French government, which resulted in France placing a higher priority on reducing both its budget deficit and government involvement in the economy. It was also due to a number of changes in the situation inside the European Community, such as mounting budget constraints, the addition of new members and demands for increased spending in areas other than agriculture, as well as the pressure placed on the CAP by falling world agricultural prices, that the principle of reducing agricultural support came to be accepted at the 1987 Ministerial Council.

Explaining the Impact of OECD Agreements

The impact of OECD trade agreements on the policies and practices of member countries was somewhat mixed. The export credits agreements met with the greatest degree of compliance of all the agreements examined in this study. It is still too early to gauge the long-range impact of the agricultural trade agreement reached in the OECD in 1987, but the immediate progress was disappointing to many. Most of the points in the Steel Consensus and the Initial Commitments were respected, with the major exception of the prohibition on quantitative restrictions, which was violated when the European Community and the United States pursued VRAs with supplier countries. Finally, there was a high degree of compliance with two of the three shipbuilding agreements, the most important exception being the General Arrangement, which European countries infringed by introducing new state aids to the shipbuilding industry.

The overall capabilities and international trade structure models were not much more helpful in explaining the impact of OECD trade agreements than they were in explaining the outcome of bargaining. In none of the cases were linkages made with non-trade issues or with other trade sectors in an effort to enforce OECD agreements.

The issue structure model did, however, appear to have a certain measure of explanatory power. The possession of superior issue-specific power capabilities permitted the United States and the EC to disregard OECD norms on the use of quantitative restrictions on steel imports, since they did not have to fear retaliatory action from other countries in the steel trade sector. Also, the strength of the EC in the agricultural trade area enabled the Community to move slowly in substantially reducing agricultural support, despite American trade actions designed to put pressure on the Community. The superior resources of the EC in ship trade enabled countries of the Community to violate the General Arrangement by increasing their subsidisation of shipbuilding, without any fear of Japan taking punitive ship trade measures. In export credits, issue-specific resources helped to ensure compliance with the Consensus through the procedure of matching, but the distribution of those resources was not important since most participants had a relatively even ability to match orders.

Institutional factors did not appear to have influenced the pattern of compliance with agreements in the steel or agricultural trade areas, and within the shipbuilding sector their influence was limited to the Understanding on Export Credits for Ships. However, international institutions were crucial in explaining the compliance of states with all of the export credit agreements. The transparency provided by the exchange of information procedures set out in these agreements, along with the provision for matching offers which exceeded the guidelines, helped to ensure that violations were visible and that their effects were neutralised. In certain other cases where countries complied with regime rules and norms developed in the OECD, this compliance appeared to be largely the result of self-interest, and the policies and practices would probably have been carried out even in the absence of a regime. Examples of this were the reduction of production capacity in the steel and shipbuilding industries when it became apparent that structural changes in the world market had made such reductions inevitable.

Opposition from domestic groups did not prevent governments from complying with the export credit agreements, but in the other sectors, breaches of OECD commitments did seem to be affected to a large extent by domestic groups. Concern over the effects of downturns in demand for ships on the level of employment in certain regions led European governments to increase their subsidies for the shipbuilding industry, and intense lobbying by the steel industry in both the US and the EC resulted in the negotiation of quantitative import restrictions in the form of VRAs. Strong pressure from the farm lobby in Europe and in the United States was also largely responsible for hindering government efforts to substantially reduce agricultural subsidies after the 1987 agreement.

The degree of coherence in the policy-making process does not help to explain the impact of the agreements on export credits or steel trade, although divisions within the EC do appear to have influenced the pattern of state compliance with shipbuilding and agricultural trade agreements. In the absence of a unified Community policy on shipbuilding, member countries were free to contravene the General Arrangement by introducing a host of new state aids for the industry when the shipbuilding crisis began in the mid-1970s. Also, despite the 1987 Ministerial Declaration on agriculture, divisions remained within the Community on how far and how quickly agricultural support should be reduced, preventing any fundamental reforms in support policies.

Changes in interest definition did not appreciably affect the impact of OECD agreements on export credits, steel or shipbuilding. However, changing attitudes towards agricultural support helped explain the growth of efforts in the Community to restrict this support, although these attitudes tended to vary depending on changes in international agricultural prices. These price fluctuations could raise or lower the cost of EC support programmes, correspondingly raising and lowering the sense of urgency in reforming the CAP.

Evaluating the Independent Variables

In judging the explanatory power of various factors, it is helpful to determine whether the presence of certain independent variables is a *necessary* condition for the occurrence of the dependent variable, and whether it is *sufficient* to explain such an occurrence.[4] The four cases presented in this study, however, did not clearly establish the necessity or sufficiency of many of the independent variables examined, for various reasons. While certain variables appeared sufficient in some cases, the apparent connection was not supported in other cases. Often, there was no significant difference among countries in the levels of certain independent variables, so that conclusions about the influence of those variables could not always be drawn. Also, in some cases there were significant differences between countries in a number of variables, so conclusions could not be drawn definitively about which single variable was decisive.

Despite these difficulties, a certain number of patterns emerged from the cases examined here. First, none of the variables proved to be necessary to produce any given outcome. Different outcomes arose when there was no variance or change in independent variables, and similar outcomes were preceded by very different sets of conditions. Secondly, preponderance in capabilities, whether aggregate or disaggregated, did not prove sufficient to determine the outcome of bargaining. Thirdly, certain domestic variables did appear sufficient to explain bargaining outcomes in some of the cases. The lack of Community cohesion was a sufficient explanation of Japan's successful resistance of EC demands in shipbuilding, and the relatively weak American commitment to its objectives in steel trade negotiations was a sufficient explanation for its failure to prevail.

A major focus of this study was on bargaining outcomes defined in terms of certain parties prevailing over others. However, it may help to break the term "prevail" into two main elements. A party may prevail in negotiations by convincing other parties to accept most of its demands, either through appeals to reason or through coercion. This outcome can be termed "compellence", since the party has successfully compelled others to accept its views and (often) to change their behaviour. A party may also prevail in negotiations by successfully *resisting* the attempts of other parties to get it to change its views and/or behaviour. It is possible that the reasons for success in compellence are different from the determinants of successful resistance. Since this study did not reveal any cases where states were clearly compelled to accept an agreement to which they were opposed (with the possible exception of Japan's acceptance of the revision to the export credits Consensus in 1987), it was unable to substantiate this point.

The findings of this study did indicate that structural factors are not necessary or sufficient to explain successful resistance, and that superior capabilities are not sufficient to produce successful compellence. The EC and Japan were successful in resisting American demands in the steel trade negotiations, and Japan successfully resisted Community demands in shipbuilding negotiations. It may appear at first that the United States successfully compelled other parties to accept the agreements on export credits and agricultural trade (indeed, some American officials are still convinced of this), but it appears that the EC effectively resisted American demands until its interests changed independently of US pressure. However, it seems intuitively plausible that superiority in capabilities is at least a *necessary* condition for successful compellence, although such superiority would not be sufficient to bring about that result, as the steel trade case demonstrated. This would account for the fact that the distribution of capabilities did not seem to determine who prevailed in any of the negotiations examined here. However, further studies, particularly those where compellence appears to have occurred, would be necessary to confirm this hypothesis.

A pattern which emerged from this study with respect to compellence and deterrence was that it was far easier to resist the demands of other countries than it was to compel other countries to accept one's own demands.[5] This distinction helped to explain variations in the importance of some of the domestic factors. For example, on the export credits issue, where member countries of the EC were divided on interest rate increases, it was relatively easy to accept the status quo and reject US demands to increase them without reducing the cohesion of the Community in OECD negotiations. However, in the case of shipbuilding, where an active response was required in the face of Japanese resistance to EC demands, the divisions became much more important and prevented the Community from adopting the measures that would have been necessary to force Japan to comply.

This distinction may also help to resolve the divergent views about the effect of internal divisions on the outcome of bargaining. In the view of Keohane and Nye, such divisions may weaken the bargaining power of an otherwise strong state, while Robert Putnam has suggested that a lack of internal cohesion may actually strengthen a country's bargaining position.[6] Disunity among governmental subunits may be to one's advantage in *resisting* the demands of others to do something, as it helped the EC to resist American pressure to make concessions on export credits, but the same lack of cohesion may be a disadvantage when one is trying to *compel* another to change its behaviour, as in the case of the EC in shipbuilding negotiations.

Another distinction is helpful in evaluating the necessary and sufficient conditions for explaining the *impact* of agreements on state behaviour. The two types of possible reactions to agreements are compliance and non-compliance, and it seems possible that the determinants of each could be different. For example, superiority in issue-specific resources appeared to be a sufficient condition for non-compliance, since when the hegemonic power in an issue area failed to comply, it did not have to fear retaliatory action by other parties. This is illustrated in the cases of the European failure to comply with the agricultural trade agreement of 1987, its disregard for the General Arrangement in shipbuilding, and the violation of the principle of no quantitative restrictions on steel imports by the US and the EC.

The findings of this study do seem to lend support to the hypothesis that superiority in issue capabilities is a *necessary* condition of non-compliance, since the only major cases of non-compliance were committed by the preponderant powers in the respective issue areas. While issue-specific capabilities were relevant to the high degree of compliance with the export credit agreements, the *distribution* of those capabilities was not, since most participants were able to match the relatively small number of derogations that arose. This study also found that international institutions were not necessary conditions for compliance, although they may be *sufficient* to explain compliance, as the generally good record of compliance with the OECD arrangements on export credits indicated.

Although the influence of regimes was found to be relatively limited in most of the negotiations examined here, this could be due in part to the fact that the OECD's contribution to regime building is largely in the area of establishing principles and norms, or what has been called "meta-regimes".[7] Because interpretations of such principles and norms can vary quite a bit, establishing whether or not there was compliance is often problematic. Nevertheless, it is noteworthy that countries did make an effort to offer an interpretation of these principles which would make them appear to be acting consistently with meta-regimes. In the case of export credit practices, where precise rules and procedures were developed, compliance was much stronger. This seems to indicate that in general, meta-regimes will be limited in their short-term impact on policies and practices, even though they may have significant long-term effects, while regimes will have a more immediate and palpable influence on state behaviour.

The four case studies did not reveal any particular combination of two or three variables that proved to be necessary and sufficient conditions of compellence, resistance, compliance or non-compliance. It may have been expected that a party with overwhelmingly superior issue-specific resources and a strong commitment to its bargaining objectives would prevail in negotiations and enforce compliance with agreements it supported.

The case of shipbuilding seems to refute this hypothesis, however.

Capabilities and Leadership in International Negotiations

One of the principal conclusions of this study is that there is nothing inevitable about the outcome of conflicts in negotiations between strong and weak countries, whether strength is measured in aggregate or disaggregated terms. Control over resources does not necessarily bestow control over outcomes.[8] In Chapter Two, it was noted that neo-realists and neo-Marxists often explain failures of the stronger party to prevail as a tactical manoeuvre designed to maintain the allegiance of weaker parties.[9] However, it was seen that in some of the cases the United States failed to prevail even when it had strong incentives to do so, and when the perceived need to preserve alliance ties was weakening. Hence, alternatives to these structural explanations for anomalies must be sought.

This study does not suggest, on the other hand, that structure is irrelevant in international negotiations. The distribution of capabilities in most cases determined who the key actors were, who set the agenda and who was most likely to be able to block an agreement. This study focused on the behaviour of the US, the EC and Japan because these were the most active parties in OECD negotiations, in addition to being the most powerful participants. The United States generally set the agenda of the negotiations in which it was a participant, issuing demands to which other member countries were obliged to respond. In the shipbuilding case, this leadership role was assumed by the EC, which dominated Japan in trade and issue-specific power resources. In the absence of the initiatives by these leading powers, it is doubtful whether any agreement would have been reached in the issue areas examined.

The distribution of capabilities also tended to determine which parties held veto power in OECD negotiations. The only two participants who demonstrated the ability to block agreements in relative isolation were the United States and the European Community. Japan was able to delay the reaching of an agreement on export credits in 1986, but in the face of a unified US-EC front, its opposition was not tenable for long. Although the unanimity rule in OECD decision making theoretically means that even the smallest member country can veto a proposed agreement, in practice, such occurrences are extremely rare. Some of the case studies presented here demonstrate how a coalition of strong parties can often pressure obstructionist states to accept an emerging consensus.[10]

These observations raise an important point about leadership in international relations. It has been argued by some that the presence of a hegemon is necessary in establishing and maintaining international regimes, but there has been little detailed investigation into exactly how a hegemon accomplishes this task. The assumption of many neo-realists and neo-Marxists is that the hegemon simply imposes its preferences on lesser powers by virtue of its preponderant capabilities. More sophisticated versions of this view hold that the hegemon does not rely solely on coercion to get its way (through the use of threats and promises), but often controls the behaviour of lesser powers indirectly by imposing its ideology or system of beliefs on these countries, so that they will end up wanting the same things that the hegemon wants.[11]

This study indicates that such assumptions should not be carried too far, however. One would expect the impact of this ideological hegemony to be particularly evident in negotiations on principles and norms of international behaviour; the kind of negotiations which are typically conducted in the OECD. Yet as the cases examined here demonstrate, although it is true that the US seeks to gain acceptance for its own values and perspectives, it is not always successful in doing so, and must often make major concessions or even abandon its objectives.

While this study has demonstrated that the "hegemon" did not have an easy task of imposing its will in the 1970s and 1980s, closer examinations of the establishment of regimes during the 1940s and 1950s suggests that the degree to which the United States was able simply to impose regimes of its own design may have been exaggerated. For example, the United States often faced strong opposition from the United Kingdom in negotiations for the establishment of the Bretton Woods system, and was obliged to make a number of concessions to gain the acceptance of European countries, despite the overwhelming superiority of the US in the monetary field.[12]

Much ink has been spent recently over the effect of a decline of US hegemony on the survival of international regimes. If the role of the United States is seen as that of a leader rather than a hegemon, then many of the fears expressed recently may be allayed. As a leader in international negotiations, the United States has certainly shaped the agenda, ensuring that some form of agreement is reached, but leadership does not mean that the US necessarily obtains all or even most of what it demands in those negotiations. Nonetheless, by setting the agenda, a leader is at least able to ensure that negotiations are conducted on areas of primary concern to it, and that agreements are in the general direction preferred by it, even if not to the extent that it would like.

It is usually the most powerful party that plays such a leadership role, although the predominance need not be great for leadership to be exercised. The relative decline in general American predominance during the 1970s and 1980s did not prevent the US from continuing to act as a leader in international negotiations in the trade area, whether in the OECD or in the GATT.[13] Nor did this decline result in the erosion of the regimes established in the OECD context. In fact, in the export credits field, regimes were expanded in scope and strengthened during the 1980s, and a new principle of agricultural trade was agreed upon, which may have laid the groundwork for the eventual establishment of an agricultural trade regime.[14]

It seems likely that the United States will continue to play the role of leader in international trade relations for the foreseeable future, given the size of its market and its growing dependence on exports which can be expected to increase the intensity of its preferences in trade negotiations. This leadership role might be challenged to some extent by the EC, but given the more decentralised structure of decision-making in the Community, the EC is less likely to put forward any major initiatives affecting the trade regime and will probably tend to use its capabilities to block those initiatives put forward by the United States. Hence, US leadership will probably not be replaced by European leadership anytime soon. Even if the United States maintains its ability to act as the leader in multilateral trade negotiations, the growing ability of the European Community to block American initiatives may weaken the desire of the US to pursue the multilateral course, and the US could turn increasingly towards bilateral and unilateral solutions. But as the United States has had at least mixed success with the multilateral approach, future US trade policy will probably feature a blend of multilateralism, bilateralism and unilateralism, rather than a wholesale abandoning of international regimes.

Domestic Politics and International Trade Negotiations

This study does not reveal any clearcut patterns upon which a simple alternative model of international negotiations can be based that could match the elegance or parsimony of neo-realist or neo-liberal paradigms.[15] None of the domestic factors evaluated, or any particular combinations of such factors, appeared to be consistently necessary or sufficient conditions for explaining outcomes. Nor could the study establish any particular conditions under which specific domestic variables will be influential. This study tested a few domestic variables only. It may well be that there are other domestic variables which prove to be more important determinants in other cases or under different conditions. Further testing of these other factors and those examined here will be needed for us to have a greater understanding of the role played by variables operating at this level of analysis.

One general observation that seems clear from this study is that the most important variable in explaining outcomes in each case was a unit-level variable. In export credit and agricultural trade negotiations, it was changes in interest definition caused primarily by developments within the EC that permitted agreements in those sectors to be reached. In the steel negotiations, the relatively limited commitment of the US government appeared to be decisive, and in the shipbuilding negotiations the lack of cohesion within the EC permitted Japan to prevail.[16] To a larger degree than in any other foreign economic sector, trade policy is a part of domestic policy, and trade conflicts are the result of domestic politics.[17] As was demonstrated in the case studies presented here, the trade distorting measures adopted by governments, and the demands placed on trading partners, were the direct result of demands and pressure from domestic groups. However, it may be that no more specific generalisation can be made than that in international trade negotiations, at least, domestic factors will be extremely important in determining both the outcome of negotiations and the

271

impact of negotiated agreements, the most important factors depending on the particular case.[18]

One possible way of preserving a structural theoretical approach may be to view the domestic variables presented here as national attributes comprising intangible elements of power. In fact, some analyses of the determinants of power (and in some cases, of capabilities) have included intangible or qualitative elements.[19] Joining the tangible and intangible elements of power should yield an extremely strong model of international relations. However, the problem of measurement would remain, even if intangible variables are shifted to structural theories. Unlike tangible elements of power (such as size of population, GDP, military forces, and industrial capacity), the intangible factors presented here are far more volatile, and even if some way is found to measure them, there is often no way of predicting when they will appear or disappear. Opposition from domestic groups can arise any time, divisions within governments often develop unexpectedly, and the political and economic conditions which determine preference intensity and changes in interest definition can shift quickly.

From Theory to Case Studies and Back Again

This study began by developing models derived from certain theories of international relations in an effort to help explain the outcome of OECD trade negotiations and the impact of OECD trade agreements. What can this exercise now tell us about these theories? First, while it is acknowledged that single cases or small-n samples cannot confirm or disconfirm a theory, as was pointed out in Chapter Two, the findings of some case studies may have special value because the cases appear to fit all of the conditions specified in a particular theoretical formulation. Trade negotiations in the OECD during the 1970s and 1980s seem to constitute a particularly good case for testing propositions suggested by some neo-liberals that the influence of certain variables on the outcomes of international bargaining may be enhanced under conditions of complex interdependence.

These case studies supported the arguments of neo-liberals that the structural factors emphasised by neo-realists were inadequate to explain outcomes under these conditions, but the alternative models proposed by neo-liberals were also found to be insufficient. The most powerful actors did not always prevail, and international institutions did not always significantly influence either the outcome of negotiations or compliance with agreements. Both neo-realists and neo-liberals appeared to provide part of the picture, but without the addition of domestic variables, the picture was incomplete, even unrecognisable. One point which this study seems to indicate, then, is that it is essential to consider both system-level *and* unit-level variables when attempting to explain outcomes in international relations, at least those outcomes occurring under conditions of complex interdependence.

Rather than considering domestic factors only when systemic explanations are found to be wanting, as both neo-realists and neo-liberals tend to do, domestic variables and systemic variables should be examined *simultaneously* when testing hypotheses about causal relationships. The danger in testing parsimonious theories is that concentrating on a very few variables increases the chances that intervening variables will be confused for independent variables. Hence, the search for parsimony can contribute to the more general problem of inadequate empirical research. Researchers eager to seek confirmation of certain theoretical models, particularly their own, may be tempted to lower their critical standards and accept correlations which appear, on the basis of a superficial examination of events, to uphold the expectations of these models as evidence of a causal link between variables. They may also find themselves only selecting cases which support their models, ignoring inconvenient data, or misinterpreting facts.

These problems can be overcome by the methodology of structured, focused comparison, in which several variables are examined in each of a number of cases. This approach combines the strengths of historical research and model-building, by providing an ordered and systematic research strategy which carefully examines the details of cases to verify the causal links suggested by a particular theory. Examining a number of cases can indicate whether any findings are discrete, and examining a number of independent variables reduces the chances of reaching conclusions that are spurious.

There is certainly an appeal in simple explanations and depictions of the world, but in trying to simplify reality we always

273

run a serious risk of distorting it. Systemic theories run a similar risk. In this study, for example, it was seen how correlations between the application of pressure by the strongest party and its success in negotiations could be used as evidence of the usefulness of coercive strategies, even though closer examination of events revealed that other factors were in fact responsible for the outcome. A parallel to this situation in the security field can be seen in some interpretations of US-Soviet relations, in which changes in Soviet behaviour were attributed to the build-up of American military capabilities and to hardline US policies, simply because Soviet reforms followed these US policies and actions. Ignoring the significant developments which have taken place *within* the Soviet Union is a grave error, and could lead the United States to make dangerous miscalculations about the utility of coercion, encouraging it to adopt this strategy more frequently, even where such an approach would be ineffective or counterproductive.

Acknowledging the importance of domestic variables, particularly the ones examined in this study, complicates the task of theory development. As was noted earlier, attempts have been made elsewhere to introduce one or two relatively stable domestic variables (such as domestic structures) in an effort to preserve the parsimony of theories, but this may not advance our understanding of international relations if more important domestic variables are ignored simply because they are difficult to measure or anticipate.[20] This study has argued that domestic factors must be examined whenever hypotheses are being tested, even those that confine themselves to systemic variables. It has not presented any new *models* of domestic influences on international outcomes, or of domestic-systemic linkages, although it has made some suggestions along the way which model-builders may wish to consider. Hopefully, what this study *has* done is to demonstrate that the careful scrutiny of the generalisations contained in models through detailed case studies is as important a task in the development of international theory as the building of those models themselves.

The Future of the OECD in the International Trading System

What kind of role is the OECD likely to play in the field of international trade relations in the future? It will probably continue to be an important forum for the establishment of principles and norms of international trade, laying the groundwork for the subsequent development of more precise rules and procedures either within the Organisation itself or in other forums. In particular, the OECD can be expected to continue its work in harmonising national policies affecting international trade, an activity which will probably have growing relevance as domestic policies and practices become the focus of future trade disputes. In addition, the OECD's "horizontal" approach to economic problems will be increasingly valuable to member governments as trade issues become ever more complex and intertwined with various other types of issues.

Should the Uruguay Round negotiations fail to satisfy the major participants, one could expect that a number of areas of particular interest to OECD countries might be introduced in the framework of the Organisation.[21] Even if the GATT continues to be the principle forum for international trade negotiations, the OECD can still supplement the work of the GATT by working out agreements among a limited number of countries who wish to go beyond what is achievable in the GATT context, or who want to develop guidelines on issues primarily of interest to OECD countries. OECD-negotiated agreements can also provide a test of freer trade in new areas, and may encourage additional states to adhere once the workability and advantages of such agreements are demonstrated. These agreements may then be transferred to the GATT once they have received broad enough support.[22]

On issues where OECD countries are in conflict among themselves, such as agriculture, the work of the OECD will probably continue in an effort to strengthen norms and principles, and perhaps eventually to develop a limited number of rules and procedures. Also, should the international trading system fragment into regional trading blocs, the OECD could have an important role to play in managing conflicts among bloc leaders, all of which are represented in the OECD. A particularly valuable task for the OECD could be to work towards breaking down any new protectionist barriers that might eventually be erected around these blocs.

As a number of newly industrialising countries (NICs) reach a level of development close to that of OECD countries, there will probably be efforts made to admit them the Organisation.

This should increase the relevance of the OECD since the export-led growth of these countries can be expected to contribute to trade frictions as they compete more and more effectively with the current OECD members. Such a development would also likely strengthen the role of the OECD as a forum for inter-bloc co-operation, since these countries will likely emerge as key members of certain trade blocs.

By the end of the 1980s the OECD was already beginning to increase its contacts with non-member countries, and in the early 1990s institutionalised some of these contacts. In 1990, Mexico became a member of the Steel Committee and South Korea took up membership in the Council Working Party on Shipbuilding. In 1989 the Council of the OECD agreed to set up within the Secretariat a Centre for Co-operation with European Economies in Transition (CCEET), in order to assist countries of Central and Eastern Europe make the transition to market economies and to help them integrate into the multilateral trade system.[23] The OECD also established in 1989 a framework for dialogue with several market-oriented countries in East and South-East Asia, known within the Organisation as the Dynamic Asian Economies (DAEs). This dialogue included a series of informal workshops on various economic issues, including trade policies. The OECD has also increased its involvement a number of trade-related issue areas that are the source of growing concern to member countries, such as structural adjustment, industrial subsidies, competition policies and environmental policies.

The future role of the OECD in international trade relations looks quite promising. The Organisation's flexibility in dealing with new areas of interest and with newly emerging actors in the world trading system seems to ensure that it will be a key forum for the study, discussion and ultimately the negotiation of many of the central trade issues that emerge during the rest of this century and into the next century. A better understanding of the nature and impact of those negotiations seems more necessary than ever.

Notes

1 For a discussion of this point in other areas dealt with by the OECD, see Michael Henderson, "The OECD as an Instrument of National Policy", *International Journal* 36 (Autumn 1981), pp. 793–814.

2 This finding tended to hold true for the United States as well as for other countries, contrary to the conclusion reached by Keohane and Nye that the politicisation of issues by domestic groups tends to fragment government policy in the US. *Power and Interdependence* (Boston, Toronto: Little, Brown, 1977), p. 206.

3 One study of trade policy making argues that domestic constraints may in fact be more important than international constraints when governments must make a decision on whether or not to adopt overtly protectionist measures. H. Richard Friman, "Rocks, Hard Places, and the New Protectionism: Textile Trade Policy Choices in the United States and Japan", *International Organization* 42 (Autumn 1988), pp. 691, 700–701.

4 For a further discussion of this distinction, see Vinod K. Aggarwal, *Liberal Protectionism* (Berkeley: University of California Press, 1985), pp. 187–188.

5 This finding is somewhat similar to Thomas C. Schelling's observation that it is easier to *deter* than it is to *compel. Arms and Influence* (New Haven: Yale University Press, 1966), pp. 69–78, 100.

6 Keohane and Nye, *Power and Interdependence*, pp. 207–208; Robert D. Putnam, "Diplomacy and Domestic Politics: The Logic of Two-level Games", *International Organization* 42 (Summer 1988).

7 Aggarwal, *Liberal Protectionism*, p. 18.

8 Jeffrey Hart, "Three Approaches to the Measurement of Power in International Relations", *International Organization* 30 (Spring 1976), pp. 299–305. See also, Robert L. Rothstein, "Epitaph for a Monument to a Failed Protest? A North-South Retrospective", *International Organization* 42 (Autumn 1988), pp. 732–740; and Oran R. Young, "The Politics of International Regime Formation: Managing Natural Resources and the Environment", *International Organization* 43 (Summer 1989), p. 354.

9 A possible objection to generalising the findings of this study is that the OECD trade negotiations took place within a particular security context. It is not surprising to some that the trade issues under negotiation were not linked to military-security issues, or that there was not a greater use of trade power capabilities or even issue-specific capabilities. In the face of a common security threat, these trading partners may have made a conscious effort to maintain friendly relations and a stable trading system, and the superior overall capabilities of the US may not have been fully mobilised in order to serve this security objective. In negotiations among countries that do not share such concerns, the processes and outcomes of bargaining may be quite different indeed, and if relations between East and West continue to improve, this pattern of restraint may even change among OECD member countries. However, the

degree of harmony among Western allies in the extended Cold War period should not be exaggerated. Often bitter conflicts arose among these allies on various trade and other economic issues from the 1950s through to the 1980s. Furthermore, it has been found that the linking of issues was constrained by domestic politics even on such "high politics" issues as East-West energy trade or the Soviet invasion of Afghanistan. See, Bruce W. Jentleson, *Pipeline Politics: The Complex Political Economy of East-West Energy Trade* (Ithaca and London: Cornell University Press, 1986).

10 There are always exceptions to this pattern, however, when a relatively weak state has an extremely strong commitment to an issue or position of major importance to it which appears to be threatened by a proposed agreement. An example of this is seen in Switzerland's successful blocking of an OECD agreement on banking secrecy in 1985, which was supported by the vast majority of other member countries. *International Herald Tribune* 2 October 1986.

11 Robert W. Cox, "Gramsci, Hegemony and International Relations: An Essay in Method", *Millennium: Journal of International Studies* 12 (Summer 1983), pp. 162–175; Robert W. Cox, "Social Forces, States and World Orders: Beyond International Relations Theory", *Millennium: Journal of International Studies* 10 (Summer 1981), pp. 126–155. Stephen D. Krasner also argues, for example, that "international organisations are a useful instrument for a hegemonic state because they can help to veil domination". *Structural Conflict: The Third World Against Global Liberalism* (Berkeley: University of California Press, 1985), p. 62. See also the discussions of this point in Joseph S. Nye, Jr., "The Changing Nature of World Power", *Political Science Quarterly* 105. no. 2 (1990); and G. John Ikenberry and Charles A. Kupchan, "Socialisation and Hegemonic Power", *International Organization* 44 (Summer 1990).

12 See Alan S. Milward, *The Reconstruction of Western Europe 1945–51* (London: Methuen and Co., 1984); Charles P. Kindleberger, *Power and Money: The Economics of International Politics and the Politics of International Economics* (London: Macmillan, 1970), pp. 108–111; John Gerard Ruggie, "International Regimes, Transactions, and Change: Embedded Liberalism in the Postwar Economic Order", in *International Regimes*, ed. Stephen D. Krasner (Ithaca and London: Cornell University Press, 1982), fn.88; and Ikenberry and Kupchan, "Socialisation and Hegemonic Power", pp. 300, 302.

13 If hegemony is considered a prerequisite for regime building and maintenance within the regime issue area only, then the argument that US hegemony is eroding will not always be accurate. The measurement of trade capabilities presented in Chapter Two suggests that while there was an erosion of US dominance in trade bargaining capabilities after the early 1970s, this dominance was restored by the mid-1980s.

14 Indeed, it could be argued that the more a state finds itself becoming interdependent in the world, the more it will attempt to control the behaviour of its partners in order to reduce its vulnerability to

external influence. Hence, the United States, which was becoming increasingly dependent on the international economy during the 1970s and 1980s, displayed greater vigour in attempting to assert itself in international trade relations over this period. Even though the material conditions for asserting itself in trade negotiations were less favourable (due to its rising dependence on export markets), the motivation of the US to prevail may have been generally greater than that of the EC and Japan for whom high levels of interdependence had long been a fact of life.

15 In a number of studies attempts have been made to isolate one or two key domestic variables in an effort to provide a parsimonious theory while at the same time avoiding the limitations of purely systemic theory. However, to date none of these has had much success in identifying domestic variables that are necessary and sufficient to produce certain outcomes or that have even proved to *favour* certain outcomes in a large number of cases. See Peter J. Katzenstein, "Conclusion: Domestic Structures and Strategies of Foreign Economic Policy", *International Organization* 31 (Autumn 1977); Peter J. Katzenstein, "International Relations and Domestic Structure: Foreign Economic Policies of Advanced Industrial States", *International Organization* 30 (Winter 1976); G. John Ikenberry, "The Irony of State Strength: Comparative Responses to the Oil Shocks in the 1970s", *International Organization* 40 (Winter 1986); Stephen D. Krasner, *Defending the National Interest: Raw Materials Investments and U.S. Foreign Policy* (Princeton, N.J.: Princeton University Press, 1978).

16 In these last two cases, the unit-level explanations were determinant despite the overwhelmingly asymmetrical distribution of ship trade resources between the EC and Japan, and the similar situation of asymmetry in steel trade capabilities between the US on the one hand and Japan and the EC on the other. These examples seem incompatible with the suggestion made elsewhere that domestic variables will only tend to be influential when there is a relatively symmetrical distribution of power (Aggarwal, *Liberal Protectionism*, pp. 189–191). Even where there is such a wide disparity in capabilities, therefore, domestic variables must continue to be evaluated. As this study did not examine trade relations between developed and developing countries, where such asymmetries are greater, it was not able to determine the extent to which this assertion holds true for negotiations outside the OECD area.

17 Stephen D. Cohen and Ronald I. Meltzer, *United States International Economic Policy in Action: Diversity in Decision Making* (New York: Praeger, 1982), pp. 5–6, 191–194; and John S. Odell, "Understanding International Trade Policies: An Emerging Synthesis", *World Politics* 43 (October 1990), p. 162.

18 This conclusion is shared by Gilbert R. Winham in his examination of the Tokyo Round negotiations. *International Trade and the Tokyo Round Negotiations* (Princeton, N.J.: Princeton University Press, 1986), pp. 390–391. Other studies that have reached a similar con-

clusion include Charles P. Kindleberger, "Group Behaviour and International Trade", *Journal of Political Economy* 59 (1951), pp. 30–46, and Andrew Shonfield, ed., *International Economic Relations of the Western World 1959–1971. Volume I, Politics and Trade* (London: Oxford University Press, 1976), p. 44, both cited in Winham.

19 This is the approach recommended by David A. Baldwin: "Emphasis on skill and will in conversion processes makes it all too easy for the power analyst to avoid facing up to his mistakes. In estimating the *capabilities* of states, the probability of successful conversion should be included in the estimate. In estimating *probable* power, the likelihood of sufficient commitment should also be included." (emphasis in the original) "Power Analysis and World Politics: New Trends versus Old Tendencies", *World Politics* 31 (January 1979), p. 170. Hans Morgenthau considers "national character" a possible element of power, and devotes a chapter to the "quality of diplomacy". *Politics Among Nations: The Struggle for Power and Peace*, 5th ed. (New York: Alfred A. Knopf, 1978); Kenneth N. Waltz includes "political stability and competence" in his list of capabilities. *Theory of International Politics* (Reading, Mass.: Addison-Wesley, 1979), p. 131. Ray S. Cline's formula for measuring power includes "strategic purpose" and "will to pursue national strategy". *World Power Assessment: A Calculus of Strategic Drift* (Boulder, Col.: Westview Press, 1975), p. 11.

20 Robert Putnam argues that a more adequate account of the domestic determinants of international relations must stress *politics*, including parties, interest groups, legislators, public opinion, and elections, not simply executive officials and institutional arrangements. "Diplomacy and Domestic Politics", p. 432.

21 A suggestion along these lines has been made recently by Gary Hufbauer, "Beyond GATT", *Foreign Policy* 77 (Winter 1989–90).

22 C. Michael Aho and Jonathan David Aronson, *Trade Talks: America Better Listen!* (New York: Council on Foreign Relations, 1986), pp. 124–125.

23 By 1990 some Eastern European governments had expressed their desire to become members of the Organisation. *Financial Times* 4 June 1990.

BIBLIOGRAPHY

I. Documents

AUSTRALIA. BUREAU OF AGRICULTURAL ECONOMICS. *Agricultural Policies in the European Community: Their Origins, Nature and Effects on Production and Trade*. Canberra: Australian Government Publishing Service, 1985.

AUSTRALIA. *Year Book Australia*. Various issues.

CANADA. *Canada Yearbook*. Various issues.

CANADA. *Government Assistance to Export Financing*. By A. Raynauld, J.-M. Dufour, and D. Racette. Ottawa: Supply and Services Canada, 1983.

CANADA. DEPARTMENT OF EXTERNAL AFFAIRS. *A Review of Canadian Trade Policy: A Background Document to Canadian Trade Policy for the 1980s*. Ottawa: Supply and Services Canada, 1983.

EUROPEAN COMMUNITIES. COMMISSION. *Agricultural Situation in the Community*. Various issues.

EUROPEAN COMMUNITIES. COMMISSION. *Agriculture: Statistical Yearbook*. Various issues.

EUROPEAN COMMUNITIES. COMMISSION. *Bulletin of the European Communities*. Various issues.

EXPORT-IMPORT BANK OF THE UNITED STATES. *Report to the U.S. Congress on Export Credit Competition and the Export-Import Bank of the United States*. Various issues.

FOOD AND AGRICULTURAL ORGANISATION. *Commodity Review and Outlook*. Various issues.

FOOD AND AGRICULTURAL ORGANISATION. *FAO Production Yearbook*. Various issues.

FOOD AND AGRICULTURAL ORGANISATION. *FAO Trade Yearbook*. Various issues.

GATT. *Basic Instruments and Selected Documents*, 9th Supplement. Geneva: GATT, 1961.

GATT. *Basic Instruments and Selected Documents*, 28th supplement. Geneva: GATT, 1982.

GATT. *Basic Instruments and Selected Documents*, 29th Supplement. Geneva: GATT, 1983.

IBRD. *The Benefits and Costs of Official Export Credit Programs of Industrialised Countries: An Analysis.* By Heywood Fleisig and Catharine Hill. Washington: IBRD, 1984.

IBRD. *World Development Report.* Various issues.

IMF. *The Common Agricultural Policy of the European Community: Principles and Consequences.* By Julius Rosenblatt, Thomas Mayer, Kasper Bartholdy, Dimitrios Demekas, Sanjeev Gupta, and Leslie Lipschitz. Washington, D.C.: IMF, 1988.

IMF. *Direction of Trade Statistics.* Various issues.

IMF. *Developments in International Trade Policy.* By Shailendra J. Anjaria, Zubair Iqbal, Naheed Kirmani, and Lorenzo L. Perez. Washington, D.C.: IMF, 1982.

IMF. *IMF Survey.* Various issues.

IMF. *International Financial Statistics.* Various issues.

IMF. *International Financial Statistics: Supplement on Trade Statistics.* Washington, D.C.: IMF, 1988.

IMF. *Issues and Developments in International Trade Policy.* By Margaret Kelly, Naheed Kirmani, Miranda Xafa, Clemens Boonekamp, and Peter Winglee. Washington, D.C.: IMF, 1988.

IMF. *Trade Policy Developments in Industrial Countries.* By S.J. Anjaria, Z. Iqbal, L.L. Perez, and W.S. Tseng. Washington, D.C.: IMF, 1981.

IMF. *Trade Policy Issues and Developments.* By Shailendra J. Anjaria, Naheed Kirmani, and Arne B. Peterson. Washington, D.C.: IMF, 1985.

JAPAN. *Statistical Yearbook of the Ministry of Agriculture, Forestry and Fisheries.* Various issues.

NEW ZEALAND. *New Zealand Official Yearbook.* Various issues.

OECD. *Agricultural Policies, Markets and Trade: Monitoring and Outlook.* Various issues.

OECD. *Agricultural Trade with Developing Countries.* Paris: OECD, June 1984.

OECD. *Arrangement on Guidelines for Officially Supported Export Credits.* Paris: OECD, 1988.

OECD. *Activities of OECD.* Various issues.

OECD. *Costs and Benefits of Protection.* Paris: OECD, 1985.

OECD. *The Export Credit Financing Systems in OECD Member Countries.* Paris: OECD, October 1976.

OECD. *The Export Credit Financing Systems in OECD Member Countries.* Paris: OECD, 1982.

OECD. *The Export Credit Financing Systems in OECD Member Countries.* 3rd ed. Paris: OECD, 1987.

OECD. *Government Finance Statistics Yearbook.* Various issues.

OECD. *The Instability of Agricultural Commodity Markets.* Paris: OECD, 1980.

OECD. *The Iron and Steel Industry.* Various issues.

OECD. *Issues and Challenges for OECD Agriculture in the 1980s.* Paris: OECD, April 1984.

OECD. *Main Economic Indicators.* Various issues.

OECD. *Measures of Assistance to Shipbuilding, 1980.* Paris: OECD, 1979.

OECD. *Measures of Assistance to Shipbuilding, 1983.* Paris: OECD, 1984.

OECD. *Measures of Assistance to Shipbuilding.* Paris: OECD, 1987.

OECD. *National Accounts.* Various issues.

OECD. *National Policies and Agricultural Trade.* Paris: OECD, 1987.

OECD. *National Policies and Agricultural Trade. Country Study: Australia.* Paris: OECD, 1987.

OECD. *National Policies and Agricultural Trade. Country Study: Austria.* Paris: OECD, 1987.

OECD. *National Policies and Agricultural Trade. Country Study: Canada.* Paris: OECD, 1987.

OECD. *National Policies and Agricultural Trade – European Economic Community.* Paris: OECD, 1987.

OECD. *National Policies and Agricultural Trade. Country Study: Finland.* Paris: OECD, 1989.

OECD. *National Policies and Agricultural Trade. Country Study: Japan.* Paris: OECD, 1987.

OECD. *National Policies and Agricultural Trade. Country Study: New Zealand.* Paris: OECD, 1987.

OECD. *National Policies and Agricultural Trade. Country Study: Norway.* Paris: OECD, 1990.

OECD. *National Policies and Agricultural Trade. Country Study: Sweden.* Paris: OECD, 1987.

OECD. *National Policies and Agricultural Trade. Country Study: Switzerland.* Paris: OECD, 1990.

OECD. *National Policies and Agricultural Trade. Country Study: United States.* Paris: OECD, 1987.

OECD. *OECD Economic Outlook: Historical Statistics.* Various issues.

OECD. *OECD Observer.* Various issues.

OECD. *Policy Perspectives for International Trade and Economic Relations.* Report by the High Level Group on Trade and Related Problems to the Secretary-General of the OECD. Paris: OECD, 1972.

OECD. *Press Release.* Various issues.

OECD. *Problems of Agricultural Trade.* Paris: OECD, 1982.

OECD. *Review of Agricultural Policies in OECD Member Countries 1980–1982.* Paris: OECD, October 1983.

OECD. *The Situation in the Shipbuilding Industry.* Paris: OECD, 1965.

OECD. *Statistics of Foreign Trade.* Various issues.

OECD. *Steel in the 80s: Paris Symposium.* Paris: OECD, 1980.

OECD. *The Steel Market and Outlook.* various issues.

OECD. *World Steel Trade Developments 1960–1983.* Paris: OECD, 1985.

UNITED NATIONS. *Commodity Trade Statistics.* Various issues.

UNITED NATIONS. *Industrial Statistics Yearbook.* Various issues.

UNITED NATIONS. *International Trade Statistics Yearbook.* Various issues.

UNITED NATIONS. *World Trade Annual.* Various issues.

UNITED NATIONS CONFERENCE ON TRADE AND DEVELOPMENT. *UNCTAD Commodity Yearbook.* Various issues.

UNITED NATIONS. DEPARTMENT OF ECONOMIC AND SOCIAL

AFFAIRS. *Export Credits and Development Financing: Part One – Current Practices and Problems.* New York: UN, 1966.

UNITED STATES. CONGRESS. HOUSE. COMMITTEE ON AGRICULTURE. *Agricultural Provision Proposals to Omnibus Trade Legislation: Hearing.* 99th Cong., 2nd sess., April 15, 1986.

UNITED STATES. CONGRESS. HOUSE. COMMITTEE ON AGRICULTURE. *Agricultural Trade Act of 1978: Hearings before the Subcommittee on Departmental Investigations, Oversight, and Research.* 95th Cong., 2nd sess., February 28, March 1, May 31, 1978.

UNITED STATES. CONGRESS. HOUSE. COMMITTEE ON AGRICULTURE. *Export of U.S. Agricultural Commodities: Hearing before the Subcommittee on Oilseeds and Rice and the Subcommittee on Livestock and Grains.* 95th Cong., 1st sess., October 12, 1977.

UNITED STATES. CONGRESS. HOUSE. COMMITTEE ON AGRICULTURE. *General Agricultural Export and Trade Situation: Hearing.* 97th Cong., 2nd sess., March 9, 1982.

UNITED STATES. CONGRESS. HOUSE. COMMITTEE ON AGRICULTURE. *Review of Agricultural Exports and Trade: Hearing.* 98th Cong., 1st sess., October 18, 1983.

UNITED STATES. CONGRESS. HOUSE. COMMITTEE ON AGRICULTURE. *Trade and International Economic Policy Reform Act of 1987: (Title VI: Agricultural Trade): Hearing.* 100th Cong., 1st sess., March 31, 1987.

UNITED STATES. CONGRESS. HOUSE. COMMITTEE ON AGRICULTURE AND COMMITTEE ON FOREIGN AFFAIRS. *Review of Agricultural Trade Issues: Joint Hearing.* 98th Cong., 1st sess., April 7, 1983.

UNITED STATES. CONGRESS. HOUSE. COMMITTEE ON BANKING, CURRENCY AND URBAN AFFAIRS. *Oversight Hearings on the Export-Import Bank: Staff Report of the Subcommittee on International Trade, Investment and Monetary Policy.* August 1976

UNITED STATES. CONGRESS. HOUSE. COMMITTEE ON BANKING, CURRENCY AND URBAN AFFAIRS. *Oversight Hearings on the Export-Import Bank: Hearings before the Subcommittee on International Trade, Investment and Monetary Policy.* 94th Cong., 2nd sess., May 10 and 11, 1976.

UNITED STATES. CONGRESS. HOUSE. COMMITTEE ON BANKING, CURRENCY AND URBAN AFFAIRS. *Oversight Hearing on the Export-Import Bank: Hearings before the Subcommittee on International Trade, Investment and Monetary Policy.* 96th Cong., 1st sess., May 21, 1979.

UNITED STATES. CONGRESS. HOUSE. COMMITTEE ON BANKING, CURRENCY AND URBAN AFFAIRS. *Oversight Hearings on the Export-Import Bank: Hearings before the Subcommittee on International Trade, Investment and Monetary Policy.* 96th Cong., 2nd sess., June 12 and 19, 1980.

UNITED STATES. CONGRESS. HOUSE. COMMITTEE ON BANKING, FINANCE AND URBAN AFFAIRS. *Oversight Hearing on the Export-Import Bank: Hearings before the Subcommittee on International*

Trade, Investment and Monetary Policy. 100th Cong., 1st sess., May 21, 1987.

UNITED STATES. CONGRESS. HOUSE. COMMITTEE ON BANK-ING, FINANCE AND URBAN AFFAIRS. *To Amend and Extend the Export-Import Bank Act of 1945: Hearings before the Subcommittee on International Trade, Investment and Monetary Policy.* 95th Cong., 2nd sess., March 13, 15, 16, and 17, 1978.

UNITED STATES. CONGRESS. HOUSE. COMMITTEE ON BANK-ING, FINANCE AND URBAN AFFAIRS. *To Extend and Amend the Export-Import Bank Act of 1945: Hearings before the Subcommittee on International Trade, Investment and Monetary Policy.* 95th Cong., 1st sess., March 25 and 28, 1977.

UNITED STATES. CONGRESS. HOUSE. COMMITTEE ON FOREIGN AFFAIRS. *Export Controls on Oil and Gas Equipment: Hearings and Markup.* 97th Cong., November 12, 1981; May 25, August 4 and 10, 1982.

UNITED STATES. CONGRESS. HOUSE. COMMITTEE ON FOREIGN AFFAIRS. *Export Credit Subsidies: Hearing before the Subcommittee on International Economic Policy and Trade.* 97th Cong., 1st sess., November 18, 1981.

UNITED STATES. CONGRESS. HOUSE. COMMITTEE ON FOREIGN AFFAIRS. *Hearings and Markup before the Subcommittee on International Economic Policy and Trade: Omnibus Trade Legislation, Vol.I.* 99th Cong., 1st sess., October 2, 1985.

UNITED STATES. CONGRESS. HOUSE. COMMITTEE ON FOREIGN AFFAIRS. *Omnibus Trade Legislation (Volume I): Hearings and Markup before the Subcommittee on International Economic Policy and Trade.* 99th Cong., 1st sess., October 2 and 22, November 5, 1985.

UNITED STATES. CONGRESS. HOUSE. COMMITTEE ON FOREIGN AFFAIRS. *Omnibus Trade Legislation (Volume III): Hearing before the Subcommittee on International Economic Policy and Trade.* 99th Cong., 2nd sess., March 12, 18, April 17, 22, 1986.

UNITED STATES. CONGRESS. HOUSE. COMMITTEE ON FOREIGN AFFAIRS. *Review of the Mixed Credits Program: Hearings before the Subcommittee on International Economic Policy and Trade.* 98th Cong., 2nd sess., January 26, March 5, 1984.

UNITED STATES. CONGRESS. HOUSE. COMMITTEE ON FOREIGN AFFAIRS. *United States-European Community Trade Relations: Problems and Prospects for Resolution: Hearing before the Subcommittee on Europe and the Middle East.* 99th Cong., 2nd sess., July 24, 1986.

UNITED STATES. CONGRESS. HOUSE. COMMITTEE ON WAYS AND MEANS. *Administration's Comprehensive Program for the Steel Industry: Hearings before the Subcommittee on Trade.* 95th Cong., 2nd sess., January 25 and 26, 1978.

UNITED STATES. CONGRESS. HOUSE. COMMITTEE ON WAYS AND MEANS. *American and Foreign Practices in the Financing of Large Commercial Aircraft Sales. Hearing before the Subcommittee on Trade.* July 14, 1978.

UNITED STATES. CONGRESS. HOUSE. COMMITTEE ON WAYS

AND MEANS. *Certain Tariff and Trade Bills: Hearings before the Subcommittee on Trade.* 97th Cong., 1st sess., May 5 and June 15, 1981.

UNITED STATES. CONGRESS. HOUSE. COMMITTEE ON WAYS AND MEANS. *Problems of the U.S. Steel Industry: Hearings before the Subcommittee on Trade.* 98th Cong., 2nd sess., April 26, May 2, 8, June 20 and August 3, 1984.

UNITED STATES. CONGRESS. HOUSE. COMMITTEE ON WAYS AND MEANS. *U.S. Trade Policy-- Phase I: Administration and Other Public Agencies: Hearings before the Subcommittee on Trade.* 97th Cong., 1st sess., 2 November 1981.

UNITED STATES. CONGRESS. HOUSE. COMMITTEE ON WAYS AND MEANS. *World Steel Trade--Current Trends and Structural Problems. Hearing before the Subcommittee on Trade.* September 20, 1977.

UNITED STATES. CONGRESS. SENATE. COMMITTEE ON AGRICULTURE, NUTRITION AND FORESTRY. *Preparing for the GATT: A Review of Agricultural Trade Issues: Hearings before the Subcommittee on Foreign Agricultural Policy.* 99th Cong., 2nd sess, June 3 and 17, July 22 and 29, August 5, 1986.

UNITED STATES. CONGRESS. SENATE. COMMITTEE ON AGRICULTURE, NUTRITION AND FORESTRY. *Review of the MTN: Hearing.* 96th Cong., 1st sess., May 7, 1979.

UNITED STATES. CONGRESS. SENATE. COMMITTEE ON AGRICULTURE, NUTRITION AND FORESTRY. *International Agricultural Trade Negotiations in the mid-1980's: Hearing.* 99th Cong., 2nd sess., April 2, 1986.

UNITED STATES. CONGRESS. SENATE. COMMITTEE ON APPROPRIATIONS. *Agriculture, Rural Development, and Related Agencies Appropriations for Fiscal Year 1983: Hearings before a Subcommittee--Part 2.* 97th Cong., 2nd sess., March 25,26,30, April 1,13, 1982.

UNITED STATES. CONGRESS. SENATE. COMMITTEE ON BANKING, HOUSING AND URBAN AFFAIRS. *Competitive Export Financing: Hearing before the Subcommittee on International Finance.* 96th Cong., 2nd sess., May 22, 1980.

UNITED STATES. CONGRESS. SENATE. COMMITTEE ON BANKING, HOUSING AND URBAN AFFAIRS. *Competitive Export Financing Act of 1981: Hearing before the Subcommittee on International Finance and Monetary Policy.* 97th Cong., 1st sess., July 20, 1981.

UNITED STATES. CONGRESS. SENATE. COMMITTEE ON BANKING, HOUSING AND URBAN AFFAIRS. *Economic Conditions in Specialty Steel Industry: Hearing.* 97th Cong., 2nd sess., January 5, 1982.

UNITED STATES. CONGRESS. SENATE. COMMITTEE ON BANKING, HOUSING AND URBAN AFFAIRS. *Oversight Activities of the Export-Import Bank: Hearing.* 99th Cong., 1st sess., February 5, 1985.

UNITED STATES. CONGRESS. SENATE. COMMITTEE ON BANKING, HOUSING AND URBAN AFFAIRS. *Subsidized Export Financing: Hearing before the Subcommittee on International Finance and Monetary Policy.* 97th Cong., 2nd sess., July 22, 1982.

UNITED STATES. CONGRESS. SENATE. COMMITTEE ON BANK-

ING, HOUSING AND URBAN AFFAIRS. *Trade and Technology in the Steel Industry. Hearing before the Subcommittee on International Finance.* November 19, 1979.

UNITED STATES. CONGRESS. SENATE. COMMITTEE ON FINANCE. *Import Relief for the Specialty Steel Industry: Hearing before the Subcommittee on International Trade.* 97th Cong., 2nd sess., September 29, 1982.

UNITED STATES. CONGRESS. SENATE. COMMITTEE ON FINANCE. *Problems in International Agricultural Trade: Hearing before the Subcommittee on International Trade.* 95th Cong., 1st sess., July 13, 1977.

UNITED STATES. CONGRESS. SENATE. COMMITTEE ON FINANCE. *US- European Communities Steel Pipe and Tubes Agreement. Hearing before the Subcommittee on International Trade.* September 19, 1983.

UNITED STATES. CONGRESS. SENATE. COMMITTEE ON FOREIGN RELATIONS. *A NATO Strategy for the 1990s: Hearing before the Subcommittee on European Affairs-- Part 5.* 99th Cong., 1st sess., October 3, 1985.

UNITED STATES. CONGRESS. SENATE. COMMITTEE ON FOREIGN RELATIONS. *International Trade Distortions Harming U.S. Agricultural Exports: Hearing.* 98th Cong., 2nd sess., 26 June 1984.

UNITED STATES. CONGRESS. SENATE. COMMITTEE ON FOREIGN RELATIONS. *The Steel Industry. Hearing before the Committee on Foreign Relations.* July 6, 1984.

UNITED STATES. DEPARTMENT OF AGRICULTURE. *Agricultural Statistics.* Various issues.

UNITED STATES. DEPARTMENT OF AGRICULTURE. *World Agriculture: Situation and Outlook Report.* Various issues.

UNITED STATES. DEPARTMENT OF STATE. "Agricultural Trade with the European Community". By Robert D. Hormats. *Department of State Bulletin* 82 (no.2060), March 1982, pp.43–45.

UNITED STATES. DEPARTMENT OF STATE. *United States Contributions to International Organizations: Report to the Congress.* Various issues.

UNITED STATES. FEDERAL TRADE COMMISSION. BUREAU OF ECONOMICS. *The United States Steel Industry and its International Rivals: Trends and Factors Determining International Competitiveness: A Staff Report.* By Richard M. Duke, et al. Washington, D.C.: GPO, 1977.

UNITED STATES. PRESIDENT (Ford, 1974–1976). "Import Relief Determination Under Section 202(b) of the Trade Act: Memorandum for the Special Representative for Trade Negotiations, March 16, 1976". *Federal Register*, Vol. 41, March 18, 1976, p. 11269.

II. *Newspapers, Magazines and Newsletters*

Aviation Week and Space Technology
The Banker
Business Week
Daily Telegraph
The Economist
Euromoney
Far Eastern Economic Review
Financial Post (Toronto)
Financial Times
The Guardian
Globe and Mail (Toronto)
International Herald Tribune
International Trade and Finance
International Trade Reporter
Japan Times
Journal of Commerce
Keesing's Contemporary Archives
Le Monde
New York Times
The Observer
Sunday Times
The Times (London)
Wall Street Journal

III. *Books*

AGGARWAL, Vinod K. *Liberal Protectionism: The International Politics of Organized Textile Trade.* Berkeley, Los Angeles, London: University of California Press, 1985.

AHO, C. Michael and Jonathan David ARONSON. *Trade Talks: America Better Listen!* New York: Council on Foreign Relations, 1986.

AUBREY, Henry G. *Atlantic Economic Cooperation: The Case of OECD.* New York: Praeger, 1967.

AXELROD, Robert. *The Evolution of Cooperation.* New York: Basic Books, 1984.

BARON, David P. *The Export-Import Bank: An Economic Analysis.* New York, London: Academic Press, 1983.

CAMPS, Miriam. *"First World" Relationships: The Role of the OECD.* Paris, New York: Atlantic Institute for International Affairs, Council on Foreign Relations, 1975.

CLINE, Ray S. *World Power Assessment: A Calculus of Strategic Drift.* Boulder, Col.: Westview Press, 1975.

COHEN, Stephen D. and Ronald I. MELTZER. *United States International Economic Policy in Action: Diversity in Decision Making.* New York: Praeger, 1982.

COX, Robert W., Harold K. JACOBSON, Gerard and Victoria

CURZON, Joseph S. NYE, Lawrence SHEINMAN, James P. SEWELL, and Susan STRANGE. *The Anatomy of Influence: Decision Making in International Organization*. New Haven: Yale University Press, 1973.

CRANDALL, Robert W. *The U.S. Steel Industry in Recurrent Crisis: Policy Options in a Competitive World*. Washington: Brookings Institution, 1981.

CURRY FOUNDATION, ed. *Confrontation or Negotiation: United States Policy and European Agriculture*. Millwood, N.Y.: Associated Faculty Press, 1985.

DAM, Kenneth W. *The GATT: Law and the International Economic Organization*. Chicago and London: University of Chicago Press, 1970.

DESTLER, I.M. *Making Foreign Economic Policy*. Washington, D.C.: Brookings Institution, 1980.

EMERY, James J., Norman A. GRAHAM, et al. *The U.S. Export-Import Bank: Policy Dilemmas and Choices*. Boulder, Col.: Westview, 1984.

ESMAN, Milton J., and Daniel S. CHEEVER. *Common Aid Effort: The Development Assistance Activities of the Organisation for Economic Development and Cooperation*. Columbus: Ohio State University, 1967.

FEINBERG, Richard E. *Subsidizing Success: The Export-Import Bank in the U.S. Economy*. New York: Cambridge University Press, 1982.

GARDNER, Bruce L., ed. *U.S. Agricultural Policy: The 1985 Farm Legislation*. Washington, D.C.: American Enterprise Institute, 1985.

GEORGE, Alexander L., David K. HALL, and William R. SIMONS. *The Limits of Coercive Diplomacy: Laos, Cuba, Vietnam*. Boston: Little, Brown and Co., 1971.

GILPIN, Robert. *War and Change in World Politics*. Cambridge: Cambridge University Press, 1981.

GOLDBERG, Walter H. *Ailing Steel: The Transoceanic Quarrel*. Aldershot: Gower, 1986.

HARRIS, A.W. *U.S. Trade Problems in Steel: Japan, West Germany, and Italy*. New York: Praeger, 1983.

HARTLAND-THUNBERG, Penelope, and Morris H. CRAWFORD. *Government Support for Exports: A Second-Best Alternative*. Lexington, Mass.: Lexington Books, 1982.

HATHAWAY, Dale E. *Agriculture and the GATT: Issues in a New Trade Round*. Washington: Institute for International Economics, 1987.

HAYWARD, Keith. *International Collaboration in Civil Aerospace*. New York: St. Martin's, 1986.

HILLMAN, Jordan Jay. *The Export-Import Bank at Work: Promotional Financing in the Public Sector*. Westport, Conn., London: Quorum Books, 1982.

HIRSCHMAN, Albert. *National Power and the Structure of Foreign Trade*. Berkeley: University of California Press, 1945.

HODIN, Michael W. *A National Policy for Organized Free Trade: The Case of U.S. Foreign Trade Policy for Steel, 1976–1978*. New York: Garland, 1987.

HOGAN, William. *World Steel in the 1980s: A Case of Survival*. Lexington, Mass.: Lexington Books, 1983.

HOWELL, Thomas R., William A. NOELLERT, Jesse G. KREIER, and Alan Wm. WOLFF. *Steel and the State: Government Intervention and Steel's Structural Crisis*. Boulder and London: Westview Press, 1988.

HUDSON, Ray, and David SADLER. *The International Steel Industry: Restructuring, State Policies and Localities*. London and New York: Routledge, 1989.

HUFBAUER, Gary Clyde, and Joanna Shelton ERB. *Subsidies in International Trade*. Washington: Institute for International Economics, 1984.

HUFBAUER, Gary Clyde, and Howard F. ROSEN. *Trade Policy for Troubled Industries*. Washington: Institute for International Economics, 1986.

IKLÉ, Fred Charles. *How Nations Negotiate*. New York: Harper and Row, 1964.

INSTITUTE FOR INTERNATIONAL ECONOMICS, AND INSTITUTE FOR RESEARCH ON PUBLIC POLICY. *Reforming World Agricultural Trade: A Policy Statement by Twenty-nine Professionals from Seventeen Countries*. Washington, D.C.: Institute for International Economics, 1988.

JENTLESON, Bruce W. *Pipeline Politics: The Complex Political Economy of East-West Energy Trade*. Ithaca, N.Y. and London: Cornell University Press, 1986.

JOHNSON, D. Gale, Kenzo HEMMI, and Pierre LARDINOIS. *Agricultural Policy and Trade: Adjusting Domestic Programs in an International Framework*. New York and London: New York University Press, 1985. Trilateral commission Report no.29.

JONES, Kent. *Impasse and Crisis in Steel Trade Policy*. London: Trade Policy Research Centre, 1983.

JONES, Kent. *Politics vs. Economics in World Steel Trade*. London: Allen and Unwin, 1986.

JOSLING, Timothy. *Problems and Prospects for U.S. Agriculture in World Markets*. Washington, D.C.: National Planning Association, 1981.

KEOHANE, Robert O. *After Hegemony: Cooperation and Discord in the World Political Economy*. Princeton, N.J.: Princeton University Press, 1984.

KEOHANE, Robert O., and Joseph S. NYE. *Power and Interdependence: World Politics in Transition*. Boston, Toronto: Little, Brown, 1977.

KEOHANE, Robert O., and Joseph S NYE, Jr., eds. *Transnational Relations and World Politics*. Cambridge, Mass.: Harvard University Press, 1972.

KINDLEBERGER, Charles P. *Power and Money: The Economics of International Politics and the Politics of International Economics*. London: Macmillan, 1970.

KNORR, Klaus. *The Power of Nations: The Political Economy of International Relations*. New York: Basic Books, 1975.

KRASNER, Stephen D. *Defending the National Interest: Raw Materials Investments and U.S. Foreign Policy*. Princeton, N.J.: Princeton University Press, 1978.

KRASNER, Stephen D., ed. *International Regimes*. Ithaca and London: Cornell University Press, 1983.

KRASNER, Stephen D. *Structural Conflict: The Third World Against Global Liberalism*. Berkeley: University of California Press, 1985.

LALL, Arthur. *Modern International Negotiation*. New York and London: Columbia University Press, 1966.

LEVINE, Michael K. *Inside International Trade Policy Formulation: A History of the 1982 US-EC Steel Arrangements*. New York: Praeger, 1985.

LOUBERGÉ, Henri, et Pierre MAURER. *Financement et assurance des crédits à l'exportation: Aspects théoriques et pratiques en vigeur dans les pays européens*. Genève: Librairie Droz, 1985.

MILWARD, Alan S. *The Reconstruction of Western Europe 1945–51*. London: Methuen and Co., 1984.

MORGENTHAU, Hans J. *Politics Among Nations: the Struggle for Power and Peace*, 5th ed. New York: Alfred A. Knopf, 1978.

NATIONAL CENTER FOR FOOD AND AGRICULTURAL POLICY. *Mutual Disarmament in World Agriculture: A Declaration on Agricultural Trade*. By Twenty-Six Agricultural Trade Policy Experts from Eight Countries and Two International Organisations. Washington, D.C.: Resources for the Future, 1988.

OLSON, Mancur, Jr. *The Logic of Collective Action: Public Goods and the Theory of Groups*. Cambridge, Mass.: Harvard University Press, 1965.

PAARLBERG, Robert L. *Fixing Farm Trade: Policy Options for the United States*. Cambridge, Mass.: Ballinger, 1988.

PEARCE, Joan. *Subsidised Export Credit*. London: Royal Institute of International Affairs, 1980.

PETIT, Michel. *Determinants of Agricultural Policies in the United States and the European Community*. Washington, D.C.: International Food Policy Research Institute, 1985.

PETIT, Michel, et al. *Agricultural Policy Formation in the European Community: The Birth of Milk Quotas and CAP Reform*. Amsterdam: Elsevier, 1987.

PREEG, Ernest H. *Traders and Diplomats: An Analysis of the Kennedy Round under the General Agreement on Tariffs and Trade*. Washington: Brookings Institution, 1970.

PRUITT, Dean G. *Negotiation Behavior*. New York: Academic Press, 1981.

PUTNAM, Robert D., and Nicholas BAYNE. *Hanging Together: Cooperation and Conflict in the Seven-Power Summits*. Revised and Enlarged Edition. Cambridge, Mass.: Harvard University Press, 1987.

RAPP, David. *How the U.S. Got into Agriculture*. Washington, D.C.:Congressional Quarterly Inc., 1988.

RODRIGUEZ, Rita M., ed. *The Export-Import Bank at Fifty: The International Environment and the Institution's Role*. Lexington, Mass: D.C. Heath, 1987.

ROTHSTEIN, Robert L. *Global Bargaining: UNCTAD and the Quest for a New International Economic Order*. Princeton, N.J.: Princeton University Press, 1979.

RUBIN, Seymour J. *The Conscience of the Rich Nations: The Development*

Assistance Committee and the Common Aid Effort. New York: Harper and Row, 1966.

SCHELLING, Thomas C. *Arms and Influence.* New Haven: Yale University Press, 1966.

SCHELLING, Thomas C. *The Strategy of Conflict.* Cambridge, Mass.: Harvard University Press, 1960.

SCHEUERMAN, William. *The Steel Crisis: The Economics and Politics of a Declining Industry.* New York: Praeger, 1986.

SNYDER, Glenn H., and Paul DIESING. *Conflict among Nations: Bargaining, Decision Making, and System Structure in International Crises.* Princeton, N.J.: Princeton University Press, 1977.

SPERO, Joan Edelman. *The Politics of International Economic Relations,* 3rd ed. London: George Allen and Unwin, 1985.

STRÅTH, Bo. *The Politics of De-industrialisation: The Contraction of the West European Shipbuilding Industry.* London, New York: Croom Helm, 1987.

TODD, Daniel. *The World Shipbuilding Industry.* London: Croom Helm, 1985.

WALTON, R.E., and R.B. McKERSIE. *A Behavioral Theory of Labor Negotiations* New York: McGraw-Hill, 1965.

WALTZ, Kenneth. *Theory of International Politics.* Reading, Mass.: Addison-Wesley, 1979.

WARLEY, T.K. *Agriculture in an Interdependent World: U.S. and Canadian Perspectives* Montreal: C.D. Howe Research Institute, Washington, D.C.: National Planning Association, 1977.

WHITEHURST, Clinton H., Jr. *The U.S. Shipbuilding Industry: Past, Present, and Future.* Annapolis, Md.: Naval Institute Press, 1986.

WINHAM, Gilbert R. *International Trade and The Tokyo Round Negotiation.* Princeton, N.J.: Princeton University Press, 1986.

WOOLCOCK, Stephen, Jeffrey HART, and Hans VAN DER VEN. *Interdependence in the Post-multilateral Era.* Cambridge, Mass.: Center for International Affairs and University Press of America, 1985.

ZARTMAN, I. William, and Maureen R. BERMAN. *The Practical Negotiator.* New Haven and London: Yale University Press, 1982.

IV. *Articles*

ALGER, Chadwick F. "Personal Contacts in Intergovernmental Organizations". In *International Behavior,* pp.523–547. Ed. Herbert C. Kelman (New York: Holt, Rinehart and Winston, 1965).

AVERY, Graham. "Agricultural Policy: European Options and American Comparisons". *European Affairs,* no.1 (Spring 1987): 62–74.

BALDWIN, David A. "Power Analysis and World Politics: New Trends versus Old Tendencies". *World Politics* 31 (January 1979): 161–194.

BALLANCE, Robert. "Industry-specific Strategies in a Protectionist World". *Intereconomics* 20 (November/December 1985): 275–283.

BLANDFORD, David, William H. MEYERS, and Nancy E.

SCHWARTZ. "The Macroeconomy and the Limits to US Farm Policy". *Food Policy* 13 (May 1988): 134–139.

BROWN, Susan E. "Review of "The Consequences of U.S. and European Support Policies" and "Impacts of EC Policies on U.S. Export Performance". In *Confrontation or Negotiation: United States Policy and European Agriculture*. Ed. The Curry Foundation. Millwood, N.Y.: Associated Faculty Press, 1985.

BUTLER, Nicholas. "The Ploughshares War between Europe and America". *Foreign Affairs* 62 (Fall 1983): 105–122.

BYATT, I.C.R. "Byatt Report on Subsidies to British Export Credits". *Journal of World Trade Law* 7 (June 1984): 163–178.

COHEN, Benjamin J. "The Political Economy of International Trade". *International Organization* 44 (Spring 1990): 261–281.

COX, Robert W. "Gramsci, Hegemony and International Relations: An Essay in Method". *Millennium: Journal of International Studies* 12 (Summer 1983): 162–175.

COX, Robert W. "Social Forces, States and World Orders: Beyond International Relations Theory". In *Millennium: Journal of International Studies* 10 (Summer 1981): 126–155.

CRANDALL, Robert. "The EC-US Steel Trade Crisis". In *Europe, America and the World Economy*, pp.17–49. Ed. Louis Tsoukalis. Oxford: Basil Blackwell, 1986.

DUFF, John M., Jr. "The Outlook for Official Export Credits". *Law and Policy in International Business* 13, no.4 (1981): 891–959.

ECKSTEIN, Harry. "Case Study and Theory in Political Science". In *Handbook of Political Science*, Vol. VII, pp.79–138. Ed. F.I. Greenstein and N.W. Polsby. Reading, Mass.: Addison-Wesley, 1975.

FINLAYSON, Jock A., and Mark W. ZACHER. "The GATT and the Regulation of Trade Barriers: Regime Dynamics and Functions". In *International Regimes*, pp.273–314. Ed. Stephen D. Krasner. Ithaca and London: Cornell University Press, 1982.

FISHER, Roger. "Negotiating Power: Getting and Using Influence". *American Behavioral Scientist* 27 (November/December 1983): 149–166.

FRIMAN, H. Richard. "Rocks, Hard Places, and the New Protectionism: Textile Trade Policy Choices in the United States and Japan". *International Organization* 42 (Autumn 1988): 689–723.

GEORGE, Alexander L. "Case Studies and Theory Development: The Method of Structured, Focused Comparison". In *Diplomacy: New Approaches in History, Theory, and Policy*, pp.43–68. Ed. Paul Gordon Lauren. New York: Free Press, 1979.

GREENWALD, Joseph A. "Dealing with the Agricultural Trade Crisis in the Uruguay Round Negotiations". *The World Economy* 10 (June 1987): 227–228.

GRIECO, Joseph M. "Anarchy and the Limits of Cooperation: A Realist Critique of the Newest Liberal Institutionalism". *International Organization* 42 (Summer 1988): 485–507.

HARSANYI, John. "Measurement of Social Power, Opportunity Costs and the Theory of Two-Person Bargaining Games". *Behavioral Science* 7, no.1 (1962): 67–80.

293

HART, Jeffrey. "Three Approaches to the Measurement of Power in International Relations". *International Organization* 30 (Spring 1976): 289–305.

HENDERSON, Michael. "The OECD as an Instrument of National Policy". *International Journal* 36 (Autumn 1981): 793–814.

HENDRICKS, Gisela. "Germany and the CAP: National Interests and the European Community". *International Affairs* 65 (Winter 1988/89): 75–87.

HOEKMAN, Bernard M. "Determining the Need for Issue Linkages in Multilateral Trade Negotiations". *International Organization* 43 (Autumn 1989): 693–714.

HUFBAUER, Gary. "Beyond GATT". *Foreign Policy* 77 (Winter 1989–90): 64–76.

IKENBERRY, G. John. "The Irony of State Strength: Comparative Responses to the Oil Shocks in the 1970s". *International Organization* 40 (Winter 1986): 105–137.

IKENBERRY, G. John and Charles A. KUPCHAN. "Socialisation and Hegemonic Power". *International Organization* 44 (Summer 1990): 283–315.

JONES, Kent. "Trade in Steel: Another Turn in the Protectionist Spiral". *The World Economy* 8 (December 1985): 393–408.

JOSLING, Tim. "Agricultural Policies and World Trade: The US and the European Community at Bay". In *Europe, America and the World Economy*, pp.50–82. Ed. Louis Tsoukalis. Oxford: Basil Blackwell, 1986.

JOSLING, Tim. "Agricultural Trade among Friends: The Parlous State of U.S. Trade Relationships with the Industrialised West". In *Confrontation or Negotiation: United States Policy and European Agriculture*, pp.179–198. Ed. The Curry Foundation. Millwood, N.Y.: Associated Faculty Press, 1985.

KATZENSTEIN, Peter J. "Conclusion: Domestic Structures and Strategies of Foreign Economic Policy". *International Organization* 31 (Autumn 1977): 879–920.

KATZENSTEIN, Peter J. "International Relations and Domestic Structure: Foreign Economic Policies of Advanced Industrial States". *International Organization* 30 (Winter 1976): 1–46.

KATZENSTEIN, Peter J. "Introduction: Domestic and International Forces and Strategies of Foreign Economic Policy". *International Organization* 31 (Autumn 1977): 587–606.

KAWAHITO, Kiyoshi. "Japanese Steel in the American Market: Conflict and Causes". *The World Economy* 4 (September 1981): 229–250.

KEELEY, James F. "Toward a Foucauldian Analysis of Regimes". *International Organization* 44 (Winter 1990): 83–105.

KEOHANE, Robert O. "The Demand for International Regimes". In *International Regimes*, pp.141–171. Ed. Stephen D. Krasner. Ithaca and London: Cornell University Press, 1982.

KEOHANE, Robert O. "International Institutions: Two Approaches". *International Studies Quarterly* 32 (December 1988): 379–396.

KEOHANE, Robert O., and Joseph S. NYE. "Transgovernmental

Relations and International Organisations". *World Politics* 27 (October 1974): 39–62.

KEOHANE, Robert O., and Joseph S. NYE, Jr. *"Power and Interdependence* Revisited". *International Organization* 41 (Autumn 1987): 725–753.

KRASNER, Stephen D. "State Power and the Structure of International Trade". *World Politics* 28 (April 1976): 317–347.

KRASNER, Stephen D. "Structural Causes and Regime Consequences: Regimes as Intervening Variables". In *International Regimes*, pp.1–21. Ed. Stephen D. Krasner. Ithaca and London: Cornell University Press, 1982.

MAINDRAULT, Marc. "Les crédits à l'exportation". *Etudes Internationales* 8 (décembre 1977): 630–647.

MAOZ, Zeev. "Power, Capabilities, and Paradoxical Conflict Outcomes". *World Politics* 61 (January 1989): 239–266.

MAOZ, Zeev. "Resolve, Capabilities, and the Outcome of Interstate Disputes, 1816–1976". *Journal of Conflict Resolution* 27 (June 1983): 195–229.

MARCH, James G. "The Power of Power". In *Varieties of Political Theory*, pp.39–70. Ed. David Easton. Englewood Cliffs, N.J.: Prentice-Hall, 1966.

MARKS, Matthew J. "Remedies to "Unfair" Trade: American Action Against Steel Imports". *The World Economy* 1 (January 1978): 223–237.

MAYER, Leo V. "Agricultural Policy in a Changing Domestic and International Environment". In *United States Agricultural Policy 1985 and Beyond*, pp.133–153. Ed. Jimmye S. Hillman. University of Arizona, 1984. Mimeograph.

MELITZ, Jacques, and Patrick MESSERLIN. "Export Credit Subsidies". *Economic Policy* 4 (April 1987): 150–175.

MELTZER, Ronald I. "The Politics of Policy Reversal: The US Response to Granting Trade Preferences to Developing Countries and Linkages Between International Organizations and National Policy Making". *International Organization* 30 (Autumn 1976): 649–668.

MESSERLIN, Patrick A. "Export-credit Mercantilism à la Française". *The World Economy* 9 (December 1986): 385–408.

MEYERS, William H., R. THAMODARAN, and Michael HELMAR. "Impacts of EC Policies on U.S. Export Performance in the 1980s". In *Confrontation or Negotiation*, pp.136–172. Ed. The Curry Foundation. Millwood, N.Y.: Associated Faculty Press, 1985.

MOORE, John L., Jr. "Export Credit Arrangements". In *Emerging Standards of International Trade and Investment: Multinational Codes and Corporate Conduct*, pp.139–173. Ed. Seymour J. Rubin and Gary Clyde Hufbauer. Totowa, N.J.: Rowman and Allanheld, 1984.

MORAVCSIK, Andrew M. "Disciplining Trade Finance: The OECD Export Credit Arrangement". *International Organization* 43 (Winter 1989): 173–205.

MUELLER, Hans, and Hans VAN DER VEN. "Perils in the Brussels-Washington Steel Pact of 1982". *The World Economy* 5 (November 1982): 259–278.

NAU, Henry R. "The Diplomacy of World Food: Goals, Capabilities, Issues and Arenas". *International Organization* 32 (Summer 1978): 775–809.

NYE, Joseph S., Jr. "The Changing Nature of World Power". *Political Science Quarterly* 105, no. 2 (1990): 177–192

NYE, Joseph S., Jr. "Neorealism and Neoliberalism". *World Politics* 40 (January 1988): 235–251.

ODELL, John S. "Understanding International Trade Policies: An Emerging Synthesis". *World Politics* 43 (October 1990): 139–167.

PAARLBERG, Robert L. "United States Agricultural Objectives and Policy Options". In *Confrontation or Negotiation*, pp.227–253. Ed. The Curry Foundation. Millwood, N.Y.: Associated Faculty Press, 1985.

PATRICK, Hugh, and Hideo SATO. "The Political Economy of United States-Japan Trade in Steel". In *Policy and Trade Issues of the Japanese Economy: American and Japanese Perspectives*, pp.197–238. Ed. Koza Yamamura. Seattle and London: University of Washington Press, 1982.

PETIT, Michel. "The Politics and Economics of CAP Decision Making" In *Confrontation or Negotiation*, pp.57–83. Ed. The Curry Foundation. Millwood, N.Y.: Associated Faculty Press, 1985.

PUTNAM, Robert D. "Diplomacy and Domestic Politics: The Logic of Two-level Games". *International Organization* 42 (Summer 1988): 427–460.

RAY, John E. "The OECD "Consensus" on Export Credits". *The World Economy* 9 (September 1986): 295–309.

RAY, John E. "Recent Changes in The OECD 'Consensus' on Export Credits", Paris: 1988. Mimeograph.

RODRIGUEZ, Rita M. "Exim's Mission and Accomplishments: 1934–1984". In *The Export-Import Bank at Fifty: The International Environment and the Institution's Role*, pp.1–33. Ed. Rita M. Rodriguez. Lexington, Mass.: D.C. Heath, 1987.

ROTHSTEIN, Robert L. "Epitaph for a Monument to a Failed Protest? A North-South Retrospective". *International Organization* 42 (Autumn 1988): 725–748.

RUGGIE, John Gerard. "International Regimes, Transactions, and Change: Embedded Liberalism in the Postwar Economic Order". In *International Regimes*, pp.195–231. Ed. Stephen D. Krasner. Ithaca and London: Cornell University Press, 1982.

SATO, Hideo, and Michael W. HODIN. "The U.S.-Japanese Steel Issue of 1977". In *Coping with U.S.-Japanese Economic Conflicts*, pp.27–72. Ed. I.M. Destler and Hideo Sato. Lexington, Mass.: D.C. Heath, 1982.

SAYLOR, Thomas R. "The Usefulness of Existing and Alternative Trade Negotiating Mechanisms". In *Confrontation or Negotiation*, pp.195–210. Ed. The Curry Foundation. Millwood, N.Y.: Associated Faculty Press, 1985.

SCHUH, G. Edward. "International Agriculture and Trade Policies: Implications for the United States". In *U.S. Agricultural Policy: The*

1985 Farm Legislation, pp.56–78. Ed. Bruce L. Gardner. Washington, D.C.: American Enterprise Institute, 1985.

STEIN, Arthur. "Research Note: The Politics of Linkage". *World Politics* 33 (October 1980): 62–81.

STRANGE, Susan. "Cave! Hic Dragones: A Critique of Regime Analysis". In *International Regimes*, pp.337–354. Ed. Stephen D. Krasner. Ithaca and London: Cornell University Press, 1982.

SWINBANK, Alan. "The Common Agricultural Policy and the Politics of European Decision Making". *Journal of Common Market Studies* 27 (June 1989): 303–322.

TALBOT, Ross B. "The Foundations of the CAP and the Development of U.S.-EC Agricultural Trade Relations". In *Confrontation or Negotiation*, pp.15–53. Ed. The Curry Foundation. Millwood, N.Y.: Associated Faculty Press, 1985.

TANGERMANN, Stefan. "Special Features and Ongoing Reforms of the CAP". In *Confrontation or Negotiation*, pp.84–106. Ed. The Curry Foundation. Millwood, N.Y.: Associated Faculty Press, 1985.

TANGERMANN, Stefan. "The Repercussions of U.S. Agricultural Policies for the European Community". In *U.S. Agricultural Policy: The 1985 Farm Legislation*, pp.329–344. Ed. Bruce L. Gardner. Washington, D.C.: American Enterprise Institute, 1985.

TANGERMANN, Stefan, T.E. JOSLING, and Scott PEARSON. "Multilateral Negotiations on Farm-support Levels". *The World Economy* 10 (September 1987): 265–281.

WAGNER, R. Harrison. "Economic Interdependence, Bargaining Power, and Political Influence". *International Organization* 42 (Summer 1988): 461–483.

WALLEN, Axel. "The OECD Arrangement on Guidelines for Officially Supported Export Credit: Past and Future". In *The Export-Import Bank at Fifty: The International Environment and the Institution's Role*, pp.97–104. Ed. Rita M. Rodriguez. Lexington, Mass.: D.C. Heath, 1987.

WALTER, Ingo. "Protection of Industries in Trouble--the Case of Iron and Steel". *The World Economy* 2 (May 1979): 155–187.

WALTERS, Robert S. "The U.S. Steel Industry: National Policies and International Trade". In *The Emerging International Economic Order: Dynamic Processes, Constraints, and Opportunities*, pp.101–127. Ed. Harold K. Jacobson and Dusan Sidjanski. Beverly Hills, London, New Delhi: Sage, 1982.

WARNECKE, Steven J. "The American Steel Industry and International Competition". In *The International Politics of Surplus Capacity: Competition for Market Shares in the World Recession*, pp.137–149. Ed. Susan Strange and Roger Tooze. London: Allen and Unwin, 1981.

WELLONS, Philip A. "Banks and the Export Credit Wars: Mixed Credits in the Sicartsa Financing" In *The Export-Import Bank at Fifty: The International Environment and the Institution's Role*, pp.167–203. Ed. Rita M. Rodriguez. Lexington, Mass.: D.C. Heath, 1987.

WENDT, Alexander E. "The Agent-Structure Problem in International

Relations Theory". *International Organization* 41 (Summer 1987): 335–370.

WINHAM, Gilbert R. "The Mediation of Multilateral Negotiations". *Journal of World Trade Law* 13 (May:June 1979): 193–208.

WOLF, Peter. "International Organization and Attitude Change: A Re-examination of the Functionalist Approach". *International Organization* 27 (Summer 1973): 347–371.

WOOLCOCK, Stephen. "Iron and Steel". In *The International Politics of Surplus Capacity: Competition for Market Shares in the World Recession,* pp.67–79. Ed. Susan Strange and Roger Tooze. London: Allen and Unwin, 1981.

WOOLCOCK, Stephen. "The Steel Industry: A Codification of National Norms". In *Interdependence in the Post-Multilateral Era: Trends in U.S.-European Trade Relations,* pp.15–66. By Stephen Woolcock, Jeffrey Hart and Hans van der Ven. Boston, London: Center for International Affairs and University Press of America, 1985.

YOUNG, Oran R. "The Politics of International Regime Formation: Managing Natural Resources and the Environment". *International Organization* 43 (Summer 1989): 349–375.

INDEX

Agency for International
  Development (AID), 75–6, 111
Agriculture, Committee for, 115,
  116, 117, 119, 121–2
Allen, H. K., on export credits,
  73
American Farm Bureau
  Federation, 150
American Soybean Association,
  150
Amstutz, Daniel G., on CAP
  reform, 145–6
Andriessen, Frans, on farm
  policy, 133–4
Arrangement on Guidelines for
  Officially Supported Export
  Credits, *see* Consensus, the
  (export credits)
Association of West European
  Shipbuilders, 247
Australia, agricultural trade, 110,
  114, 132, 136, 138, 139, 155–6

Baker, James, on agricultural
  trade, 132
Balladur, Edouard, on export
  credits, 93–4
Barraclough, William, on steel
  trade, 192
Bergland, Bob, on agricultural
  trade, 152
Bergsten, C. Fred, on export
  credits, 71–2, 87, 88

Block, John, on agricultural
  trade, 135, 144, 153–4
Bohn, John A., on export credits,
  73–4, 76, 83
Brock, William, on export credits,
  75

Canada: agricultural trade, 110,
  112, 114, 127, 132, 155–6, trade
  balances, 136, 138, 139; export
  credits, 58, 64, 65, 72, 82;
  Export Development
  Corporation (EDC), 58
Carter, President Jimmy, on
  export credits, 83, 87
Centre for Co-operation with
  European Economies in
  Transition (CCEET), 276
Committee for Agriculture, 115,
  116, 117, 119, 121–2
Commodity Credit Corporation
  (CCC), 111
Consensus on Converging
  Export Credits Policies of July
  1976, *see* Gentlemen's
  Agreement (export credits)
Consensus, the (export credits),
  49–53, 59–68; compliance
  with, 72, 95; matrix rate
  negotiations, 90–3
Cornell, Robert, on export
  credits, 70–1, 88
Council Working Party Six on
  Shipbuilding, 221–2, 231, 232;

negotiations, 231, 244; steel
trade negotiations, 171, 197-9
Shipbuilding, Council Working
Party Six on, 221-2, 231, 232;
agreements, 222-5; market
sharing, 232-8
Solomon Task Force on Steel
Industry, 180
South Korea, ship trade, 217-18,
219, 236-8, 249
Soviet Union, see USSR
Spain, ship trade, 228, 230-1, 246
Special Committee for Iron and
Steel, 170-1
Steel Caucus in Congress, 203,
205
Steel Committee, 173-6, 194,
204-5, 206, 207; influence on
steel agreements, 196-201;
Initial Commitments, 174, 175,
176, 183-9, 192, 193, 203,
compliance with, 184-5, 186
Steel Consensus, 172-3, 174, 175,
176-83, 191-3, 203, 206
Steel Corporation (US), 182
Steel Symposium, 194, 198-9
Strauss, Robert, on steel trade,
192
Sweden, ship trade, 226, 228,
229, 230, 231, 235

Tokyo Round, 120, 152
Trade Committee, 116, 117;
Export Credits and Credit
Guarantees Group (ECG), 45,
53-6, 59, 81, Exchange of
Information System (EIS),
46-7, 56, 60
Trade Mandate study, see
Ministerial Trade Mandate
(MTM)
Trade and Related Problems,
High Level Group on, report,
see Rey report

United Kingdom: agricultural
trade, 132, 150, 156; export
credits, 44, 55, 58, 74; ship
trade, 230, 231

United States: Agency for
International Development
(AID), 75-6, 111; agreements,
impacts explained, 262-4;
agricultural trade, 8, 109,
110-11, 115, 158, 159,
bargaining positions and
outcomes, 130-4, domestic
group oppositoin, 150,
government cohesion, 150-1,
impact of OECD agreements,
127, 128, institutional influence,
147-9, interest definition, 156,
international structure, 135,
overall capabilities, 134-5,
preference intensity, 152-6,
trade balances, 136, 138-9,
140-6; American Farm Bureau
Federation, 150; American
Soybean Association, 150;
capabilities and leadership in
international negotiations,
268-71; Commodity Credit
Corporation (CCC), 111;
domestic politics and
international trade
negotiations, 271; export
credits, 7, 44, 46, 55, 58, 94,
bargaining positions and
outcomes, 60-8, derogation
from Consensus, 58-9, 72,
domestic group opposition,
84-5, governmental cohesion,
85-6, influence of institutions,
79-83, interest definition, 90,
91-3, international trade
structure and, 71, issue
structure, 71-9, overall
capabilities, 68-70, preference
intensity, 87-90; Export-
Import Bank, see Eximbank;
International Trade
Commission, 179; Labor-
Industry Coalition for
International Trade, 85;
National Association of
Manufacturers, 84; National
Centre for Food and
Agricultural Policy, 127;

For Product Safety Concerns and Information please contact our EU representative GPSR@taylorandfrancis.com
Taylor & Francis Verlag GmbH, Kaufingerstraße 24, 80331 München, Germany

www.ingramcontent.com/pod-product-compliance
Ingram Content Group UK Ltd.
Pitfield, Milton Keynes, MK11 3LW, UK
UKHW021833240425
457818UK00006B/185